A Child Grows Up

A

Child

A New Approach to Child Development

Grows

Up

By Candida Clifford Peterson

Alfred Publishing Co., New York

Library of Congress Catalog Card Number: 73-89779
ISBN: 0-88284-012-6

Printed in the United States of America

Alfred Publishing Co., Inc.
75 Channel Drive, Port Washington, N.Y., 11050

Contents

Preface   *ix*

Introduction: Perspective   *3*

Chapter 1: THE FIRST YEAR   *11*

Methods of developmental psychology. Observation and experimentation. **Parental attitudes:** Before birth. **State of the newborn. Longitudinal versus cross-sectional research. Individual differences in infancy.** Activity, mood, distractibility, smiling. **Prenatal development and behavior. Stranger fear.** Separation anxiety hypothesis. Incongruity hypothesis. **Piaget's theory.** Assimilation and accomodation.

BIRTH TO TEN MONTHS OLD (Diary)

Chapter 2: ONE YEAR OLD (Diary)   *24*

AGE ONE—1
Motor development. Overview of the first year. Walking. The invariant sequence. Maturation versus practice. **Speech.** Biological basis. Crying and Babbling. Distinctive features. **Concept development.** Generalization of word meanings. First concepts. Direction of cognitive growth. Concept versus complex.

Chapter 3: NEARLY FIFTEEN MONTHS OLD (Diary)   *36*

AGE ONE—2
Classical conditioning. Operant conditioning. Behavior modification.

Contents

Temper tantrums. **Freud's theory.** Structure of personality. Psychosexual stages. **Toilet training. Identification.** Psychoanalytic theory. Social learning theory. Cognitive developmental theory. **Linguistic invention.**

Chapter 4: FIFTEEN MONTHS OLD (Diary) *49*

AGE ONE—3
Conscience. Influence of "love-oriented" versus "power-assertive" rearing. **Language development.** Holophrastic speech. **The object concept. Perception of pictures. Depth perception.**

Chapter 5: THE THIRD HALF YEAR (Diary) *60*

AGE ONE—4
Selective attention. Schema discrepancy theory. **Sensation.** Vision. Hearing. Tough. Taste. Smell. **Perceptual learning.** Gibson's distinctive feature theory. **Teaching names for things. Pivot grammar. Piaget's theory.** Delight in the familiar.

Chapter 6: EIGHTEEN MONTHS OLD (Diary) *70*

AGE ONE—5
Telegraphic speech. Three hypotheses. **Theories to explain language development.** Imitation. Expansion. Innate capacity. **Thinking.** Motor, ikonic, and symbolic representation. **Relation of thought and speech.** The thinking of deaf child. **Social interaction with peers.** Infants. Monkeys. Progressive development.

Chapter 7: ALMOST TWO (Diary) *84*

AGE ONE—6
Negativism. Learning theory. Independence. **Attachment.** Imprinting. Psychoanalytic theory. Reinforcement theory. Determinants in monkeys. **Memory.** Developmental changes. Short- and long-term. Recall, recognition and relearning. Attention. Verbal coding and rehearsal. Motivation.

Chapter 8: TWO YEARS OLD (Diary) *96*

AGE TWO—1

Contents

Emotional development. Watson's approach. Differentiation of the emotions. **Anger**. Change with age. Causes of outbursts. **Language development**. Negation. **Cognitive growth**. Vygotsky's theory. Egocentric and inner speech.

Chapter 9: TWO AND A QUARTER (Diary) *112*

AGE TWO—2
Children's art. Three theories. **Nursery school**. **Peer influences on social development**. Peer reinforcement. Peer modeling. **Altruism**.

Chapter 10: TWO AND A HALF (Diary) *128*

AGE TWO—3
Aggression. Modeling. Reward. Sex differences. Frustration. Cooperation. **Games**. Stages. Rules. **Piaget's theory**. Egocentrism. Questions children ask. **Presleep Monolog**.

Chapter 11: THREE YEARS OLD (Diary) *143*

AGE THREE
Birth order and siblings. Advantages and disadvantages of the first-born. Explanations. Only children. **Children's play**. Exercise. Fantasy. Formal. Constructive. Theories. **How mothers speak to children**.

Chapter 12: FOUR YEARS OLD (Diary) *156*

AGE FOUR—1
Learning. Positive and negative transfer. Reversal and nonreversal shifts. Mediation theory. Learning Set. **Reasoning**. Gestalt theory. Insight in champanzees. The development of inference. **The role of the incentive in children's learning**.

Chapter 13: FOUR AND A HALF (Diary) *170*

AGE FOUR—2
Intelligence testing. Binet. WISC. Raven's Matrices. Group tests. **Creativity**. Tests. Verbal creativity. **Werner's theory of development**. Synaesthesia. **Children's poetry**.

Contents

Chapter 14: FIVE YEARS OLD (Diary)   *182*

AGE FIVE—1
Cognitive development. Transition in mental growth. **Conservation.** Liquid amount. Number. Mass. Weight. Volume. **Number ability. Relational concepts. Thoughts about thinking. Social contact in school. Conformity. Competition.**

Chapter 15: FIVE AND A HALF (Diary)   *199*

AGE FIVE—2
Punishment. Suppression. Severity. Parental practices. Children's views of punishment. **Self-confidence and self-assertion. Fear.** Developmental changes. Influence of experience. **Education.** Methods of teaching reading. **Part versus whole perception.**

Chapter 16: SIX YEARS OLD (Diary)   *215*

AGE SIX
Dependency. Instrumental and emotional. Age changes. Sex differences. **Sociometric measurement. Popularity.** Personality variables. Body build. **Television.** TV and aggression. TV and intellectual development. **Moral development.** Lying. Moral judgment.

Chapter 17: SEVEN YEARS OLD (Diary)   *234*

AGE SEVEN
Childrens humor. Relation of humor to age. Riddles. Classification ability. **Problem solving: Impulsivity and Reflectivity. Curiosity. Education.** Discovery methods of teaching. **Motor skills.** Erikson's theory. Scale of development of skills. Factors which influence proficiency.

Chapter 18: SUMMARY   *251*

References   *255*

Glossary   *267*

Index   *271*

Preface

One of the questions I ask each new undergraduate class to whom I lecture on developmental psychology is: "Do you have, or have you had recently, close contact with young children—a child of your own, a younger brother or sister, or children you may be working with on a part-time job?"

Almost invariably the answer is no. Answers to other questions usually reveal that the students *intend* to work closely with children, as a teacher, parent, counselor, pediatric nurse, and so forth, that this

Preface

is indeed their main reason for taking the course. But at least for the present, they propose to study children without the nuisance of having them underfoot.

Contrast these students—immersing themselves in theory, with no children to relate their study to—with the young parent and the inexperienced teacher and social worker who have no background in psychology. Their problem might be described as *too much child*. They are required to act and make crucial decisions in the face of what often seems inexplicable behavior. They generally manage somehow, for learning comes quickly in actual experience, but often, this managing comes at the cost of needless tears, worries, and frustrations. How helpful it would be to have a child psychologist on hand to explain to them the seemingly unexplainable and to have good scientific evidence in support of this explanation.

As young as the discipline of scientific child psychology is, it has included under it a considerable body of hitherto unexamined data and has produced much that is challenging and illuminating, albeit of a theoretical nature. Largely because of it, children are not now, as they often were in the past, considered merely young adults, with all that implies in the way of supposedly desirable behavior and the nature of their thought processes. Primarily as a result of research and experiment by child psychologists, children are no longer looked upon as unformed vessels of clay, awaiting the hand of an adult to mold and shape them and give them their true character. If all that child psychology were to teach us is that children are both like adults and markedly different, it would be enough, for it is the interplay of this sameness and difference that provides the key to an understanding of children and, through children, to an understanding of mankind in general.

As developmental psychologists continue to explore their field, to collect new data and test new theories, many other cherished beliefs may yield to scientific evidence. This is true of conservation of number. Experiments have demonstrated that to a typical preschool child, one row of five pennies may appear to have more pennies in it than another row of five, merely because the pennies are spaced farther apart in the first.

All this is by way of reaffirming that the study of developmental psychology may indeed be of help in practical affairs and that its findings can be useful immediately to those who have children in their care. The time may, and no doubt should, come when all such persons—parents and professionals alike—will find access to a child psychologist as easy and natural as it now is to a pediatrician. There may well come a time when on each mother's bookshelf, alongside the Bible and Dr. Spock, will be found an equally well-thumbed volume on developmental psychology. Pending that time, it behooves us to make developmental psychology as stimulating and meaningful as we can.

What better way than by having in every classroom a growing child to care for and observe? Then the various topics covered in the course—from the maturation of the nervous system to the effects of birth order on personality development, which must seem like hopelessly separate and isolated domains to the beginning student—would fall in place. With a living, breathing, "whole" child to unify the topics, they could become part of a well-ordered experience in which life and learning, practice and theory would be interrelated. Or should bringing a child into every developmental classroom prove impractical, we might let it be a requirement of the course that each student become a temporary foster parent. Day-to-day contact with an adopted child, would inevitably give rise to questions, the answers to most of which could be provided in lecture and textbook.

Clearly the incorporation of a parent's diary into this book is not a true substitute for a real child, in the classroom or in the student's home, although the diary does have certain advantages. It can embrace a longer period of development than a school semester and cover a wider range of ages, and it can, like any written work, be consulted and reviewed as often as desired. It can also help counter a tendency of developmental psychology, in the hands of all but the most expert of teachers, to become a sometimes dry, sometimes airy, exposition of isolated aspects of an anonymous human child. It can, in short, serve as a reminder that we study the perception, motor skills, socialization, emotion, intelligence, language, conscience, and personality of the child not for their sake alone but for a better understanding of the child himself and that these have meaning only as together they combine to form an integrated, functioning whole.

From the diary, where we see a child growing up, we turn to the body of the book for answers to questions the diary may provoke and for light—based on the best scientific evidence contemporary psychology has to offer—on the behavior it describes. We continue to study perception, motor skills, emotion, socialization, language,

Preface

intelligence, personality, and conscience. Only we now study them not as separate entities but as each may bear on a newly unfolding aspect of a child's life as revealed in the diary. We come to know this unique child, and in her we see the generality of children, for we see her—always with the help of professional psychologists—as encompassing all children, typical and likewise atypical. Her name is Candida.

Candida is also my name. Arthur Clifford, my father, kept the diary purely as a labor of love, with no other purpose in mind, nor for any other eyes than his. After I had decided to become a psychologist, he offered to let me read it. This was several years ago, and it was then that the seeds of this book were sowed.

A note to my fellow teachers: in your choice of a textbook, primary or supplementary, you are frequently asked to make an either-or decision—either choose a book which stresses research data and valid psychological theorizing or choose one that will awaken the students' interest in the *real* child lurking somewhere behind the *S*'s and *n*'s of experimental reports and the figures in behavioral age-norms. My earnest belief is that no such decision is necessary with this book and that both objectives may be attained, both desirable purposes served.

The diary, I feel, serves the second purpose of such a textbook. It portrays the day-to-day existence of a living, normal child through the eyes of a psychologically naive parent. The commentary that accompanies the diary serves the first purpose. In the commentary I tackle the psychological principles, theories, and data pertinent to my diarist-father's observations and through this medium introduce the student to the methods of experimentation in a way I feel makes sense: as a vehicle for clarifying casual observations.

With the diary and commentary side by side, the book also provides a unifying link between developmental psychology (with a capital *D* and *P*) and a parent's or layman's view of child development. Candida's mother kept independently a much briefer weight, height, and health record. To fill some of the gaps in the longer work, expecially the missing first 10 months, it is summarized here: *At birth Candida's weight was six pounds, 15 ounces, her length, or height, 20 inches; these were respectively 9 pounds and 21 inches at four weeks; then 11 pounds, 12 ounces and 23 inches at eight weeks; 13 pounds, four ounces and 24 inches at 11 weeks; 15 pounds, 4 ounces and 26 inches at 16 weeks; 18 pounds, 8 ounces and 27 inches at 28 weeks; 19 pounds, 14 ounces and 29 inches at 36 weeks; and 22 pounds, 10 ounces on her first birthday. No height is recorded for that day, but from other data I deduce she was almost exactly 30 inches tall. Meanwhile, her first and second teeth (bottom and front) appeared simultaneously at 24 weeks, her third at 29 weeks, fourth at 31, and fifth at 37 weeks. The sixth arrived unheralded, but the seventh and eighth appeared in the 47th and 49th weeks, respectively. Partially breast-fed for seven months, she sat up alone at 28 weeks and crept at 30. In her 34th week, the record states, she "pulled herself up alone and got back down again." Two weeks later she "walked around her crib and playpen, hanging on to sides." On February 22, less than four weeks before her first birthday, she "stood alone, raised to standing position, and got down again without touching anything"; and on March 22, three days after her birthday, she "took her first step alone." Meanwhile, at about nine months, she had uttered her first words: "da da," "ma ma," "ba ba," "ah da," "an ba." She was ill for the first time, of an ailment described as intestinal flu, on the last day of her first year, but recovered quickly. Her second, and only second-year, illness was a slight case of tonsillitis in late spring. She had chicken pox, an eye infection, and intestinal flu (twice) in her third year, tonsillitis in her fourth, tonsillitis and measles in her fifth, and tonsillitis rather frequently from then on until the tonsils were removed.*

ACKNOWLEDGMENTS

I wish to express my gratitude, first of all, to my father who could not have imagined when he wrote the diary that it would end up in book form, and to my husband, James Peterson, for his invaluable help with the manuscript and his constant encouragement. I could with absolute justice name at least 20 psychologists who, in person or through their work, were most helpful in my formative period. But three deserve special mention: Professors Tracy S. Kendler, Martin D.S. Braine, and Lila Ghent Braine.

Special thanks are due Dr. Thomas Cassell of Wayne State University for his very perceptive criticism and to Dr. Louise Beem of DuPage Community College, Dr. Carol Dweck of the University of Illinois, Dr. Claire Jacobs of Northeastern Illinois University, and Dr. Diane Papilia of the University of Wisconsin for reading the manuscript and giving helpful suggestions.

Finally, I wish to thank my editor, William Knowles, for his almost day-by-day encouragement and the individual who stood behind him as the book was being developed, Alfred Publishing Company's Morton Manus.

A Child Grows Up

Introduction: Perspective

This book is about a child growing up and a psychologist's, or rather many psychologists', views of how children grow up. The child is a girl. She was born in Detroit in the late 1940s to middle-class parents, older than average to be raising a first child. (Her mother was 37 and her father 39 when she was born.) The psychologists range from Piaget to Freud, from Watson to Werner, and from Vygotsky to Sears (for a complete listing see the references) and their theories span the wide-ranging field of contemporary child development.

Introduction: Perspective

As a branch of psychology, child development shares the larger discipline's concern with the scientific study of behavior. As a science, it strives both for publicly verifiable facts and descriptions (as opposed to anecdotal impressions or the unsubstantiated opinions of "Experts") and for logically sound, encompassing, and testable theories which blend the facts into systems which explain past events and predict future ones. A concern with child development, however, also adds a new dimension to the study of behavior. As well as studying the static aspects of behavior, such as how children of various ages act, developmental psychology studies the *process* of behavior change and includes questions such as what factors are responsible for change, whether the changes are sudden or gradual, whether they are permanent or temporary, whether they incorporate or erase what went before, and whether they induce benefits or liabilities.

Charles Spiker [1966, p. 40] defines development as "changes which normally occur with an increase in chronological age of the child." Ernest Nagel [1957] suggests limiting the term to changes that are relatively permanent (to exclude cyclic variations over time and to draw attention to the irreversability of changes like language acquisition—a child born deaf never being identical to one who became deaf after learning to talk) and to those which are cumulative, in the sense that each new change builds on what went before and helps to determine future changes (for example, a child's dropping out of school at the age of 14 reduces his chances of completing a college education and increases the likelihood of his pursuing a menial occupation as an adult). Nagel also notes that some researchers are inclined to reserve the term "development" for positive changes that lead the individual toward greater self-regulation and increased independence from environmental fluctuations.

The history of child development has centered on a number of heated debates, including the *nature-nurture* controversy and the issue of *continuity* versus *discontinuity* in developmental change. At the *nature* end of the former debate is the doctrine of *predeterminism*, which holds that the regulation of development was primarily internal and determined before birth, with experience, or nurture, merely setting wide limits on the realization of hereditary potential. French philosopher Jean-Jacques Rousseau (1712-78), an early proponent of this view, felt that the child developed best when allowed to do so naturally, with a minimum of interference from

4

adults, and he advised parents: "Leave childhood to ripen in your children. Beware of giving anything they need today if it can be deferred without danger to tomorrow" (Kessen [1965, p. 81]). Other predeterminists were G. Stanley Hall and his pupil Arnold Gesell, whose maturational outlook stimulated many studies of motor development.

The other pole of the nature-nurture dichotomy is occupied by the historical *tabula rasa,* or blank slate, doctrine which assigns the leading role in development to experience. The philosopher John Locke (1632-1704) coined the term to refer to the state of the infant's mind at birth, although he personally was not a complete believer in the blank slate, as seen in his description of children's innate love of power: "We see children (as soon almost as they are born, I am sure long before they can speak) cry, grow peevish, sullen, and out of humour, for nothing but to have their *wills:* they would have their desires submitted to by others; they contend for a ready compliance from all about them; especially from those that stand near, or beneath them in age or degree, as soon as they come to consider others with those distinctions" (Kessen [1965, p. 67]). A more encompassing tabula rasa position was taken up by John B. Watson who wrote: "The behaviorists believe that there is nothing from within to develop. If you start with a healthy body, the right number of fingers and toes, eyes, and the few elementary movements that are present at birth, you do not need anything else in the way of raw material to make a man, be that man a genius, a cultured gentleman, a rowdy or a thug" (Watson [1928, p. 41]).

In contemporary developmental psychology, this polarized debate has given way; currently, both nature and nurture are thought to play important parts in developmental change since, to quote Anne Anastasi: "The reacting organism is a product of its genes and its past environment, while present environment provides the immediate stimulus for current behavior." Anastasi herself views heredity and environment as interacting in development, as she puts it: "the nature and extent of the influence of each type of factor is dependent upon the occurrence of the other" [1958, p. 197].

The historical *continuity-discontinuity* debate can be illustrated by borrowing D.B. Harris's [1957] analogy of a pair of scientists viewing a flight of broad stairs from different angles. The one at the top looking down sees only the surfaces of the stairs, separated from one another by thin lines, and is impressed by their continuity. The other,

Introduction: Perspective

viewing the staircase from in front, focuses on the massive faces of the risers which appear to be separated from one another by great jumps and is impressed by the discontinuity. In its application to child development, the continuity position views developmental change as a steady progression of quantitative increments, and states, *Natura non facit saltum* (nature makes no leap). By contrast, the discontinuity view of development, as a series of qualitative changes or stages, is summed up in the phrase, "life is made up of interruptions."

Like the nature-nurture controversy, the *stage* debate has declined in importance in contemporary child psychology, where the either-or dichotomy it posed is seen to apply with more validity to individual preferences in data-gathering and theorizing than to the segmentation of reality. For example, the child's language development can be represented as a continuous process if the researcher is interested in the number of words in the vocabulary at successive ages (for example, McCarthy [1954]) while discontinuities appear to the researcher who attempts to determine the grammatical system underlying the speech of different-aged children. In addition, the recognition that transitional periods of quantitative change (for example, the practicing and perfection of the walking skill) generally precede and follow qualitative change (for example, from creeping to walking) and that a given change can occur at different times in the lives of different children has tended to blur the edges of the historically separate viewpoints.

William Kessen [1962] feels that the notion of *stage* is essential to a complete theory of development, although he distinguishes between the meaningful and trivial uses of the term. The latter include using *stage* as a paraphrase for age (for example, "He's at the toddler stage"), for observation ("He's at the teething stage"—meaning simply that he's teething), and as a shorthand description of the environment ("He's at the nursery school stage"—meaning that he attends nursery school). According to Kessen, the stage concept can be incorporated in theory-building in a meaningful way, to indicate either when to apply a given set of rules or when to insert a given parameter into a theoretical equation.

In addition to the stage concept, Kessen specifies two other essential requirements for a developmental theory. One is a means of specifying the relationship between stages and individual differences so that the appropriate stage-placement of a given child can be determined, and a child's behavior within a given stage can be predicted. The other is specification of the "rules of transition," which determine how an individual progresses from one stage to the next. There are three major theoretical approaches to child development; each places a different emphasis on the three theoretical prerequisites outlined by Kessen.

Learning theory takes as its model the *S-R*, or stimulus-response, association and applies principles derived from experimental research with animals and adults (as well as children) to the understanding of child development. Such principles, including those of *classical* and *operant* conditioning, *reinforcement*, *observational learning*, and *discrimination* and *mediation*, constitute Kessen's mechanisms of transition or means by which the individual child's life experiences, accumulated as he grows older, effect relatively permanent changes in his modes of thinking and reacting to his environment.

Psychoanalytic theory, based on the insights of Sigmund Freud and his followers during the course of their treatment of the mentally ill, applies a conflict model to the understanding of development. It views the growth of the child's personality, and to a lesser extent his intellect, as the result of a progressive and unconscious struggle between the child's biological wants and the demands imposed on him by other people. The struggle takes different forms at different times during the lifespan, giving rise to a series of five stages of psychosexual development. Thus psychoanalytic theory devotes attention to Kessen's *stage* factor. However, it also postulates that individual children will react differently in a given stage—for example, those for whom conflict in an early stage is intensified may experience greater conflict in successive stages, boys may react differently from girls, and children from one-parent families may differ from those with two parents, and so it also emphasizes Kessen's individual difference factor.

Cognitive-developmental (or *organismic*) is a name given to theories which view the child as an active maker of his own developmental destiny (in contrast to the more passive pictures of the child as a recipient of learning or as a victim of inevitable conflict). Two major theorists, Jean Piaget and Heinz Werner, have formulated such theories, both of which will be discussed later. Piaget postulates a sequence of periods through which the cognitive function progresses and thus meets Kessen's requirement for a stage theory. During

Introduction: Perspective

the first, or *sensorimotor,* period (birth to age 2), the child adapts to his environment at the level of simple activity, acquiring the abilities to look at what he is listening to or reaching for, to vary actions deliberately, to find hidden objects, to imitate, and to combine activities to reach a given goal. In the *preoperational* period (age 2 to 7) he strives to come to grips on an intellectual or symbolic level with the practical problems mastered in the earlier period. This is achieved during the *concrete operational* period (age 7 to 11), when concepts of real objects and events are organized into stable, logical systems. Finally, during the *formal operational* period of adolescence, thought is freed of the bonds of real experience and the here and now to deal with hypothetical issues, probability, and all possible solutions to a given problem. While the major thrust of Piaget's theory is the delineation of these stages, he also formulated the transition processes of *assimilation* and *accommodation* (discussed in the next chapter).

Heinz Werner defined development as changes obeying the *orthogenetic* rule, which states: "wherever development occurs, it proceeds from a state of relative globality and lack of differentiation to a state of increasing differentiation, articulation, and hierarchic integration" [1957, p. 126]. The concept of differentiation is illustrated in Bridges' postulate that the feelings of fear, anger, and disgust are almost indistinguishably blended in the infant *distress* emotion and that the general emotion is gradually broken down into the emotions to which we, as adults, give the names fear, anger, and so forth. Articulation and hierarchic integration occur when differentiated components are coordinated into whole structures, as when discrete sounds are united in the proper sequence to produce a spoken word or sentence.

Still another controversial issue in child development is whether the primary aim of the child psychologist should be to formulate and test theories of development through "pure," or "basic," research or whether it should be to conduct applied research into the socially significant concerns of child welfare. Leon J. Yarrow [1973] sees this issue as another false and potentially harmful dichotomy, since "it might be detrimental for human welfare and for science if either view became ascendant and were accepted as the only correct approach" [p. 5]. He notes that practical application has served as a valued stimulus to pure research, while adults' practical dealings with children have been improved through insight afforded by basic theorizing, and states: "The gradually accumulating knowledge about the young infant and his sensitivities which has penetrated into the popular consciousness has influenced our individual as well as society's feelings toward children. In many ways it has influenced what we do with children—our laws, institutions, and the kinds of services provided for them" [p. 2]. This interdependence of theory and popular vision should become clearer in succeeding chapters as the abstract issues dicussed in this introduction are seen to weave in and out of the life of a child growing up.

1
The
First
Year

Of the many methods of investigation available to the developmental psychologist, the baby diary is the oldest. A typical baby diary consists of a day-by-day record of significant events in the life of a child. About 1900 it came into vogue as a method of child study, partly through the work of Charles Darwin [1877], who published some observations he had made of his son Doddy's first two years of life. Another 19th-century diarist was Bronson Alcott, the father of the author of *Little Women*. On beginning a diary devoted to one of his

The First Year

infant daughters, Alcott wrote:

> The history of one human mind, commenced in infancy and faithfully narrated by the parent until the child should be able to assume the work himself, and carried onward through all the vicissitudes of life to its close, would be a treasure of inconceivably more value to the world than all the systems concerning the mind which philosophers have built to this day. It would be a history of human nature—a history which has never yet been written, a revelation of human character for which we look in vain amid the vices and crimes, the virtues and sacrifices, of those pages which now bear that name. (Shepard [1938])

In recent years there has been a trend in psychology away from the diary in favor of more systematic observational and experimental techniques. It is nevertheless true that no other method of psychological investigation matches the diary's ability to provide a description of the *whole* child, together with the *presence* that timely—but at the same time unstructured—record-keeping affords. The close correspondence of accuracy to freshness of record was shown in one recent study (Robbins [1963]) when parents' recollection of salient events, such as whether their infants were fed on schedule or demand, altered markedly over a span of as little as two years. Nor has the baby diary been entirely superseded by other methods of psychological research. Much contemporary theory concerning infants' understanding of objects, time, and space owes its existence to the careful diaries in which Jean Piaget recorded the growth and development of his three infant children.

The baby diary falls into one of the two principal approaches to child study, the method known as *observation*. The other method is called *experimentation*. Both methods involve observation of children's behavior, the difference being that in the first, the observer interferes as little as possible in the child's activity, which is allowed to take place in a natural setting such as home or playground. In experimentation, the psychologist deliberately manipulates factors thought to influence the child's behavior, and does so in a laboratory setting so that other influences can be eliminated or controlled.

Most of the other observational techniques in use besides the diary impose criteria for scoring and recording behavior and for determining the reliability of the observers. For example, in the time-sampling method, the investigator decides in advance on a specific behavior to be observed and on the amount of time to be devoted to each subject. In a typical time-sampling study of aggression (Walters, Pearce, and Dahms [1957]), each child in a nursery school was observed for a total of 40 one-minute intervals. Any aggression the child engaged in during the interval was recorded as a checkmark beside the appropriate category. A comparison of records kept by two independent observers determined rater reliability. Later, when the investigators counted the checkmarks and made other computations, they came up with results such as, the older nursery schoolers were more aggressive than the very young ones, and boys were more aggressive than girls.

To study aggression by the experimental method, the psychologist begins with a hypothesis which might be, for example, that frustration is a causative factor. He subjects one group of children, called the *experimental* group, to a frustrating experience such as seeing attractive toys just out of reach. He then compares their level of aggression to that of a *control* group who do not experience frustration. Meanwhile, by conducting the experiment in a laboratory, he can equalize or eliminate other likely causes of aggression such as hunger, fatigue, sex, and age of subjects, or interference by another child.

There are innumerable variations on this basic experimental procedure. The widely applied experimental method is the preferred technique approach in developmental psychology for uncovering cause-effect relationships. Where ethical or practical considerations preclude experimentation, observational techniques are in order. These range from the highly circumscribed time-sampling method, which lends itself well to gathering data about specific behavior in typical children to the open-ended diary which, though less precise and rigorous, compensates by its breadth of view and the vibrant picture it paints for us of the whole, living child.

In these pages you will become familiar with the work of numerous psychologists as their findings, experimental and observational, are examined side by side with those recorded in Candida's baby diary by her father. You may also acquire an appreciation of the richness of the diary method as a source of ideas for psychological research when the diarist's observations are interpreted in the light of current developmental psychology. Often a point he noted or wondered about has been the subject of psychological inquiry in the laboratory or a natural setting. Sometimes such a point becomes a keystone in a theory of child development such as that of Freud or

The First Year

Piaget. Most often, it is one of the numerous incidental details, unimportant in themselves, which in their totality make the life and study of a growing child so fascinating. We begin with one such detail, the diarist's recollection of how, just before his child was born, he speculated on its sex and "predicted a boy, just as I often predict against my wishes, so that the consolation of being right may partly balance disappointment."

The Diary

JANUARY 29: Candida at ten months and ten days. Someday I'll try to remember what she was at this time. Even now I have half forgotten her earlier personality. The morning when she was born, when I dozed in a chair in Peggy's hospital room: how my teeth chattered after the nurse told me to come up to the delivery room. The message was so noncommital; it could mean anything. Partly from lack of sleep and partly from an until then well guarded fear for Peggy, I felt a momentary panic that was only relieved when I met young Dr. Roberts (for the first time). "You have a baby girl." "A girl? Dr. Flaherty said it would be a girl." I had of course predicted a boy, just as I often predict against my wishes, so that the consolation of being right may partly balance my disappointment.

"Would you like to see her?" "Yes."

There they were out in the hall, Peggy and Candida. Peggy was sleeping heavily, her face very red (from the scopolamine as I learned later). Candida was in a canvas basket. Her skin was very tight over the bones of her face and forehead. Her eyes wer closed and she lay very still, but neither the doctor nor the nurses seemed to consider this extraordinary, so I guessed it was all right too.

They wheeled Peggy to the elevator and down to her room. I went with her. The night nurse, with whom I had become somewhat acquainted (she had brought me a glass of chocolate milk and told me about herself and her husband), tied boards on the side of the bed. "They toss around a bit when they come out of scope. I had one patient fall on the floor."

From time to time Peggy appeared to recover consciousness and each time I tried to make her understand that she was the mother of a beautiful daughter. But she merely agreed amiably. In the intervals between she babbled incoherently about the stop lights on Grand River Avenue. (Coming to the hospital was her first experience with Grand River's new

15

The First Year

block system of traffic signals.) She chattered too
about routine things at home. Tears came to my eyes but I
could not then, nor can I now, tell exactly why.

Peggy, I know, was never so happy as she was that week
in the hospital. She was born to be a mother and now at
last, after many years and many disappointments, she
was. Candida would be very happy in having such a mother.

Is Candy happy now? I don't know. She is not unhappy.
She laughs a great deal--more, I believe, than most
babies. She takes delight in any new article she gets
hold of, and says, "Hiss-s-s, Hiss-s-s" over it. She
enjoys imitating and being imitated. She hums when the
vacuum cleaner hums, barks softly when Blackie barks,
and she and I have a game we both get a big bang out of: a
grimace that she invented, drawing back her lips with
her mouth open as if she were ready to scream but is
holding it back. I copied it and she recognized it on me.
Now she does it expecting me to imitate her, and when I do
it she imitates me.

In moments like those I presume she's happy. But what
of most of the time, when she's eating, standing up and
sitting down in her play-pen as she does most of her
waking time, going out in her buggy, bathing, sleeping?
At night--right now for instance--she tosses a good
deal, kicks the rails of her crib, and whimpers. I
presume she's dreaming. Is she after something? Is she
already dissatisfied with things as they are and looking
forward to something better?

She gets along very well with people; she likes them
and smiles at them--unless she's either hungry or
sleepy.

In the oldest of all published baby diaries, that written by Dr. Jean
Héroard about the heir to the French Throne who was born in 1601,
we read of the same kind of wager as the diarist's in the first paragraph
of this diary passage. It was important to Henri IV, under the rules of
royal succession, that his unborn child be a boy. He divorced his first
wife for her failure to produce anything but daughters, and married
Marie de Medici in hopes that she would bear him a son. Henri IV
tried to hedge against being disappointed by wagering 1,000 écus
with the financier Zamet that the coming child would be a girl.

That the preference for male offspring—rooted in such institutions as feudal succession, the subservience of women, and the dowry—continues into the present is revealed in recent attitude studies, notably one by Dinitz, Dynes, and Clarke in 1954. These investigators interviewed college students and found that when they asked what sex the student would prefer if he or she could have only one child, 91 percent of the male students and 66 percent of the female wanted a boy. A generation later, a follow-up study by Peterson [1973] revealed essentially no change in the attitude of future mothers. However, there was a small but significant change on the part of future fathers. Whereas less than 1 in 10 in the earlier survey wanted their only child to be a girl, in the later survey the proportion wanting a girl was more than 1 in 6.

Of importance to developmental psychology is what effects such attitudes may have on the child after he is born. Are boys more welcome because they are more hoped for and therefore received with more affection? Apparently not, judging from a study of Swedish mothers who were interviewed before and after giving birth (Uddenberg, Almgren and Nilsson [1971]). These women adjusted quickly to a child of the sex opposite the one they hoped for, even to the point of believing they had wished for the one they got. Other research has shown middle-class mothers displaying more affection toward infant girls, talking to them more than to infant sons (Kagan [1971]) and imitating their vocalizations more (Moss [1967]).

On the other hand, is the pronounced male favoritism exhibited in parents' prenatal hopes a determinant of traits such as "pride of manhood" in little boys and "lady-like" decorum in little girls? Here the evidence strongly indicates that the top-heavy preference for male children in our culture affects aspects of a child's sex role development, particularly preference for the sex role. Boys from nursery school to the fourth grade were found by D.G. Brown [1958] to express a stronger preference for the masculine role than girls for the feminine role. This was manifested in an indirect way, by preference for male or female cosmetics (shaving articles versus rouge and face powder) and directly as well, by the expressed wish to become a mother or a father when grown.

All babies are different—or are they? The diarist says of Candida: "She laughs a great deal—more, I believe, than most babies." Everyone is aware of physical differences apparent from the time the baby is born, differences in size, shape of face, color of eyes, and so

The First Year

forth. But what about behavior? The kinds of behavior babies are capable of at birth and in the months immediately thereafter, consisting mainly of various hereditary reflexes such as sucking and startling are so simple relative to what the child will be capable of later on and are found so universally in human infants, that there seems little likelihood of one baby being much different from another. Yet most parents of more than one child will assert that each baby was different, that each from birth had its own unique personality, and objective research backs them up.

The research of Thomas, Chess, Birch, Hertzig, and Korn [1963] is a case in point. Using what is called the *longitudinal* method, they followed the same group of infants over a two-year period, making observations of their behavior at frequent, regular intervals. The complementary approach, known as the *cross-sectional* method, calls for taking a different sample of children at each of the ages studied, so that the one-year-olds in the study would be an entirely different group of children from the two-year-olds.

The researchers began with a group of 80 babies and their parents who supplied detailed descriptions of the way the babies acted and reacted to life's routines. Based on these interview protocols, the authors came up with a set of nine traits for rating infants, including activity level, distractibility, and quality of mood. Their first finding was that by using these traits, it was possible to discriminate between infants even in the earliest months of life. Some infants were more active than others, some were more cheerful, etc., which demonstrated that individual differences between babies do exist almost from birth.

The second finding emerged when the researchers looked at what happened to each individual infant as he or she grew older. They found strong evidence for the stability of the traits. A baby who was characterized as highly active at one week of age tended also to be high in activity at age two. Of special interest, in light of the diary entry, was the finding that the most stable of all traits was quality of mood, that there were indeed in this sample of 80 babies some who consistently laughed more than others, and some who cried more or complained more or were more unfriendly, and continued at this level over the two years of the study.

Other evidence concerning the existence and stability of individual differences in infants' cheerfulness comes from a longitudinal study of 180 babies begun at Harvard in 1964 by Jerome Kagan who

18

sought evidence of the persistence, or continuity, of infant personality traits. Giving special attention to the activity known as smiling, Kagan noted that in the first two weeks after birth all smiling can be described as the *reflex smile,* an apparent symptom of how the baby feels internally, which bears no real relation to external events. Later, between two and eight weeks, the *social smile* appears. Its name derives from the fact that it is most easily elicited by human faces and voices. This smiling reaches a peak at four months of age when, as Burton White noted [1971], it is "symptomatic of a chronically positive affect tone which makes them [infants] a delight for parents, photographers and researchers." After four months there is a decline in social smiling, which reaches a low ebb at 7 to 13 months. By about 27 months, which was the oldest age Kagan studied, social smiling had begun to increase again.

As well as noting this age function in smiling behavior, Kagan studied the stability of smiling in individual infants. He found modest but reliable evidence of stable individual differences. Babies who had been great smilers at four months smiled more than other babies at 13 and 27 months. Furthermore, the tendency to smile was the most stable of all the individual difference variables Kagan studied.

The fact that individual differences in mood quality and the tendency to smile appear so early in an infant's development suggests that they are not a simple reflection of differences in the cheerfulness or smilingness of the adults the infant comes in contact with. This was confirmed by Wayne and Marsena Dennis [1941] who found that two infants who had never been smiled or laughed at developed smiling and laughter at approximately the same age as normal infants.

Individual differences have been noted among babies even before they were born, notwithstanding the difficulty which the inaccessibility of the living fetus poses for investigation of prenatal behavior. Relying on reports from the mother, listening by stethoscope, and direct observation of nonviable fetuses removed surgically for medical reasons, researches have measured fetal activities which include heart beat, respiration, thumb-sucking, squirming, kicking, stretching, rhythmic activity, swallowing, and the knee jerk, grasp, and startle reflexes. As early as the second month after conception, movement can be induced in the fetus by direct electrical stimulation of its muscles. During the third and fourth months the

The First Year

nervous system comes to mediate behavior, and reflex responses to tactile stimulation are observed. By the fifth month of pregnancy, most mothers feel the baby moving around, and the fetal heart beat is audible. At this point each fetus's uniqueness becomes apparent.

Many women who are pregnant for a second or third time remark that the present baby kicks a lot more or a lot less than the previous one. Mechanical recordings of fetal activity reveal significant differences between fetuses. The most active fetuses tend to score higher than their less energetic counterparts on tests of infant motor development administered six months after birth (Richards and Nelson [1938]). Another dimension of individual difference is heart rate: some fetuses show wide fluctuations in rate from second to second, while others have a more stable pattern. Similar individual differences among adults have been found to correlate with differences in personality. Adults with highly variable heart rates tend to be more compulsive, indecisive, and introspective and to have greater conflicts over dependency. Some implications of this for the development of personality were drawn out by Lester Sontag [1966] when he followed a group of 12 fetuses into adulthood and found that those who had had the stablest prenatal heart rates also had the stablest heart rates as adults, and vice versa. He concluded that certain physiological components of personality appear before birth, due either to heredity or the uterine milieu, and may go on to influence the way an individual incorporates postnatal life experiences.

The drop in social smiling which Kagan found at 7 and 13 months is probably related to an aspect of the infant's social development which makes its appearance at about this time, the phenomenon of *stranger fear*. This, as its name implies, is a somewhat unaccountable fear of strangers that most babies are afflicted with between 7 and 10 months of age, unaccountable because, as Rene Spitz [1950] points out, very few infants can have had bad experiences with strangers. His explanation for it, based on the premise that fear of losing one's mother is the basic anxiety of early infancy, is that the baby first has his hopes raised by the stranger's general resemblance to her and then, perceiving that it is not she, thinks she is lost.

H.R. Schaffer [1966] derived a different explanation for the phenomenon from a longitudinal study of the growth of *stranger fear* among 36 Scottish infants. He never observed stranger fear in an infant until after it had learned to recognize his mother's face, so he inferred that a necessary precondition for the fear is the incongruity brought about by the stranger's face resembling the mother's familiar one, but at the same time being different. In addition, he noted that the babies typically showed no fear of an immobile stranger gazing at them from a distance, while showing intense fear when the stranger approached suddenly, spoke loudly, or tried to pick them up. He concluded that it is not strangeness or incongruity alone that frightens babies—since they typically show no fear or unfamiliar, inanimate objects—but strangeness which is thrust upon them too suddenly for them to be able to cope with it by any means other than fearful withdrawal.

The diary reveals no evidence of stranger fear in Candida at the age of 10 months: "She gets along very well with people; she likes them and smiles at them." This is doubly unusual in light of Schaffer's findings, which showed that stranger fear had emerged by the age of 10 months in 32 of his 36 infants and that it emerged earliest in children without brothers and sisters and in girls. However, he also noted that fear was not an inevitable response to all strangers: "inexplicable variations took place from month to month, in that the infant would sometimes show fear and sometimes not" [p. 101]. The possible absence of stranger fear now demands an explanation, which may, in turn, throw greater light on the reasons for its presence.

Candida at 10 months not only recognized faces but a facial grimace of hers which her father imitated. He says, "Now she does it expecting me to imitate her, and when I do she imitates me." The process of imitation which 10-month-old Candida is very much involved in—imitating dogs and vacuum cleaners, as well as the human face—has a central place in the theory of cognitive development advanced by Jean Piaget. (At the age of 15 the young Piaget began publishing scientific articles in the field of biology. His precocity afforded him what he describes in his autobiography (Boring [1952]) as "some amusing experiences." He had to decline invitations to meet foreign "colleagues," being too embarrassed to let on that he was only a schoolboy. When, after an offer of a position as curator of the Geneva Museum's mollusk collection forced him at last to confess it, a journal refused to publish another of his articles solely on the grounds of his age.) Piaget's early interest in biology persisted when, partly as a result of observations of his three children, he

21

turned his attention to the question of how thought originates and develops in the mind of the child. Thus the two central processes in his theory of the growth of the intellect, *assimilation* and *accommodation*, are drawn from biology. Assimilation occurs in biology when elements from outside are incorporated into the organism, as when food is eaten, digested, and converted to body tissue. Analogously, assimilation occurs for Piaget when a new item is incorporated into a behavior pattern, or *schema*. The young infant assimilates nipples, pacifiers, and thumb into the at-first purely reflex behavior of sucking—Piaget's *sucking schema*. The schema is the psychological counterpart for Piaget of the biological structure, and it consists of an integrated pattern of behavior elements. Just as a structure in biology can be as simple as a toe or as complex as a digestive system, schemas range from the simple sucking reflex of the newborn to the *schema of intuitive qualitative correspondence* (a method school-aged children use for deciding the numerical equality of groups of numbers). Later we see Candida assimilating new elements into a schema when, "she likes to throw practically anything she sees on the floor: her toys if they are not already there, my ties, my brush and comb, Peggy's combs, papers of all kinds." Here the schema is one of throwing onto the floor and toys, ties, combs, and papers have been assimilated to it. Presumably, if she were given a new toy she would assimilate it to this same schema by throwing *it* on the floor.

Accommodation, states Piaget, occurs when there is a snag in the assimilation process. Thus a breast-fed infant must accommodate his sucking pattern on his first encounter with a bottle in order to keep the inanimate nipple in his mouth. Similarly, if the new toy Candida was given was too heavy to be assimilated to the throw-on-the-floor pattern she might accommodate the latter to include rolling or pushing onto the floor. Piaget views intellectual development as being propelled forward by these two processes of assimilation and accommodation. In activities he would describe as intelligent, the two processes occur in equal proportion; they are in balance. In other activities, however, the balance may swing heavy on the side of assimilation or accommodation. Piaget called the former *play* and the latter *imitation*.

As one of the three primary activities in his theory of development, Piaget has studied the process of imitation intensively, partly by observation of his three children. He found that at five months of age there were two limitations on the ability to imitate, which applied to all three of his children. They could imitate only those actions they were already capable of performing spontaneously and likewise only those that involved a part of their own body which was visible to them.

So Lucienne, as recorded in her father's baby diary, could accurately imitate the opening and closing of his hand. But at seven months he wrote: "When she yawned several times in succession I seized the opportunity to yawn in front of her but she did not imitate me" [1962, p. 28]. She could see her hand, but she could not see her mouth. At around 10 months, Piaget's children were all able to imitate facial expressions without the help of a mirror. He describes a mutual imitation sequence with Jacqueline:

> Jacqueline invented a new schema, which consisted of pressing her lips together and making her lower lip stick out by putting her tongue against it. While she was doing it of her own accord, I did the same thing three times, and she watched my mouth as she went on doing it. The same evening she began to do it again. When I did it five minutes after she had stopped, she imitated me twice in succession. When on the following days I reproduced the same movement without her having made it beforehand, she did not react, and I concluded that it had been a case of pseudo-imitation. But a month later I repeated the experiment when Jacqueline had not done it more than twice, and as soon as I imitated her, she imitated me in return. The next day I did it without her having done it. She imitated me immediately, then smiled and touched her lips with her right forefinger, as if to verify the connection between what she saw happening to me and what she herself felt. (1962, p. 34.)

The time finally arrives when a child has developed the art of imitation to the point of imitating an absent model through memory. Jacqueline demonstrated this at one year and four months. She had watched in amazement while a boy of her age threw a temper tantrum, and on the following day threw one herself in a near-perfect imitation. Candida, who in her imitation of the facial grimace revealed at 10 months her ability to involve parts of her body she could not see, will at age 13 months be seen imitating through memory what Piaget calls *deferred imitation of words*.

2
One
Year
Old

APRIL 28: At 13 months Candy walks well, without holding on. She can't run or anything like that, but she can turn around in the middle of the room, stoop over and pick something off the floor, and only when she has to get somewhere in a very great hurry does she now drop to her hands and knees.

She is into everything, knows how to open cupboard doors, even if they don't have handles——and most of ours

don't. She enjoys pulling books off their shelves,
pulling or tearing off the dust jackets, and throwing
the books on the floor. In fact, she likes to throw
practically anything she sees on the floor: her toys if
they are not already there, my ties, my brush and comb,
Peggy's combs, papers of all kinds (though in recent
times she has been letting magazines alone; they were
her major interest for awhile). On the other hand, she
likes to pick things off the floor as long as there is
someone to hand them to.

She enjoys going after her ball and she carefully
carries it all the way back to be rolled or bounced away
again. Somehow she just can't see the idea of rolling or
bouncing herself: it must be carried. She will hunt her
ball if you ask her where it is; and ball or "ba" is one of
the words she knows and speaks. Others are "bottle" (very
distinctly), "bok" for box, "puk" for paper, "book,"
"nut," "ti" for tongue, "tik" for stick or toothpick,
"bah" or "bop" (with great emphasis on the final p) for
Blackie, and "da," "dot," or "dottle" for daddy.

Some words stand for several things. "Bottle" means
first of all her nursing bottle, then any bottle or
container that looks like a bottle. "Bottle" also means
"give me," probably because she wants every bottle she
sees. Hence, by transference, "bottle" is the name she
gives to any new thing that does not fall into one of her
other categories of names.

"Dot" means "take me" or "pick me up" or "yes, I
wanted you to pick me up." This might be because, about
the time that she began to take an active interest,
rather than mere passive acquiescence, in being picked
up, I used to ask her, "Want to come to Daddy?" Her answer
was to raise her arms and say "da."

Peggy gave her a pebble today and she immediately
called it a "nut," probably because it was about the size
and shape of a walnut. For awhile she was saying "bikie"
for Blackie but has since relapsed to the simpler "bop."
And after being once told worriedly, "Be careful of
Daddy's glasses," she combined the two words "daddy's"
and "glasses" into a single "doggle." This word, too,
has now dropped out of her vocabulary.

Another thing she lost for a time, and that I missed,
was her special grimace. But now and then——as a favor to
me, I suspect——she does it again fleetingly.

25

One Year Old

She likes to make a door swing and says "do." She must
have something to play with when she eats. And she is as
cheerful and sweet—tempered as ever, is fond of people,
especially other children. She is still very much an
infant, will not drink milk except from her bottle (and
only then lying down), must have a bottle during the
night, and takes two naps a day. But her personality is
developing so naturally and completely that I think
doing something about these things would only throw
unnecessary hazards in her path and for very little gain
otherwise.

MAY 24: Generally speaking, Candy divides her
physical world into three large categories: "bottles,"
"bocks," and "oddles." "Bottles" are containers of
almost any description, but especially of glass, and
articles that have a distinct hole or cavity in them,
like bottle caps and toothpaste tubes. (I imagine she
senses the cavity because they give so easily when
bitten.)"Bock," derived from box, and block, is anything
resembling those things, anything squarish or cubical,
and sometimes, by inference, just anything. "Bock" also
means "give it back." An "oddle"——her way of saying
handle——is anything long and anything easy to grasp and
put in the mouth.

Those are the three largest categories, but there
are several others, smaller and more precisely
identified. "Ball," for example, means just that: a
ball. A "nut" is a kind of small ball of irregular shape.
A "piece" is something very small, like a crumb or a hair,
something that has to be picked up with the fingernails.
And quickly got rid of, I might add, because when Candy
goes to the trouble of picking such a thing up she
strongly insists that you take it from her.

Most of the things she identifies are firm, solid
things. Among them are her "doll," correctly
pronounced, and "ti" for stick, "dah" for jar, and a
special word for the garden tractor which Peggy
understands but that I have as yet not heard too clearly.
For the genera of limp things, she has no term, but she
particularizes "tie," "puh" for paper, and "tok" for
sock.

"Boy" is any kid heard yelling or the sound of a
bicycle. "Dirl" is a girl, i.e., Candy herself. She calls

26

her mother "Mom" or "Mum." This, like "Dot," which she
calls me, now means "pick me up."

Candida's first year, though in no way exceptional, was really one
of stupendous achievement. From a condition of utter helplessness,
unable even to raise her head, she learned or developed the ability to
hold her head firmly erect, to turn over by herself, to sit up, to creep
over the floor, grasp tiny objects, rise to her feet, and walk—all in the
space of a single year. And now, "at 13 months Candy walks well,
without holding on."

There are certain achievements, and walking is one of them, that
are milestones in every child's—or for that matter, every
mother's—life. What is the proper time for a child to begin walking or
sitting up by himself or acquiring such dexterity with his fingers that
he can pick up a piece of lint? It varies. Mary Shirley, who in 1931
visited the homes of 25 infants at weekly intervals in their first year
and monthly in their second, found that among her subjects the
onset of walking without support varied from 50 to 76 weeks, or from
approximately one year to 18 months, with a median age of 15
months.

More recently (Hindley, Filliozat, Klackenberg, Nicolet-Meister,
and Sand [1966]), another such normative survey—so called because its aim was to discover an "age norm" for a particular
behavior—covered 1,000 children in five major European cities. The
ages at which these children began walking alone ranged from about
10 months to about 19 months. The norm, or mean age, for walking
alone was found to be 12½ months in Brussels and Stockholm and
13½ months in Paris, London, and Zurich. If a difference in norms of
from 12½ to 15 months were not enough, a survey of African children
in Uganda placed their average age for unassisted walking at nine
months (Geber and Dean [1964]).

Besides collecting normative data on walking and other motor
skills (creeping, sitting, finger dexterity, etc.) Shirley [1931] examined
the more analytic question of how walking develops. She was particularly interested in whether the sequence of skill mastery preceding
walking is as invariable as the time-honored precept, "you must
creep before you can walk" implies. Although none of the infants she
tested actually did walk before they crept, the time lag between first
creeping and first walking ranged from as short as five weeks to as
long as 21 weeks. She found several minor inversions of the typical

sequence, for example, an occasional baby who was able to pull himself to standing before creeping, but she concluded that babies, as a rule, "follow a general pattern in which postural control precedes effort at locomotion, effort precedes success at locomotion, and some form of locomotion precedes walking. With rare exception, all babies go through each stage, but there are minor differences in the sequence of stages from baby to baby."

The general uniformity of this sequence has caused many psychologists to question whether it is entirely correct to say, "The baby learns to walk," whether it would not be better to say, "The baby walks because it is time to walk." The argument applies not only to walking but to a host of other behaviors which we normally think of as acquired skills but which, proponents of this "nature" view assert, have no more need to be "learned" than do other parts of the developing process such as crying when in pain or growing taller. According to this line of reasoning, virtually every new skill the infant manifests is all part of his genetic inheritance, and *maturation* rather than *learning* is the label to apply to it.

The question was studied extensively by Wayne Dennis [1940, 1941, 1960] in at least three separate cultures, with the aim of determining to what extent a motor skill such as walking is acquired through practice and to what extent it is due to maturation of innate capacities. Among the Hopi Indians he compared two groups of infants, those who in accordance with tradition were strapped to cradle boards with their movements severely restricted during a large portion of their prewalking lives, and those who from early infancy on were free to move as they wished. Dennis found no significant difference between the two groups as to the time it took them to start walking. For both, it was around 14 months. Although this evidence suggested a maturational interpretation—that no prior preparation is necessary for walking and that when the time is ripe, the child walks—Dennis noted that the cradled infants did have some opportunity to exercise skills during brief intervals each day when they were off their boards.

A second study [1941] involved twin girls who were raised by Dennis and his wife under more severely restricting conditions than the traditional Hopi. The babies were kept on their backs in cribs and were never propped up by adults into sitting or standing postures. The Dennises found that sitting and standing did not develop spontaneously in either baby by the age when they normally occur. However, with a minimum of practice thereafter, both twins were able to sit and stand. Restriction was discontinued after this demonstration, and walking occurred at a normal age in one of the twins. (The other's walking was retarded, but this finding was confounded by the fact that she also had experienced some brain damage at birth.)

In a third study, Dennis [1960] visited orphanages where infants were kept on their backs to lighten the workload. These babies were later found to be considerably retarded in walking, convincing Dennis that experience and the opportunity to practice the locomotor skills that lead to walking is essential. So too is neuromuscular maturity. When both come together, the child walks.

At around the time the infant takes his first unaided steps, he achieves another developmental milestone and speaks his first meaningful word. The parallel between the sequence of motor developments, on one hand, and steps in the growth of vocalization ability, on the other, was drawn by Eric Lenneberg [1969] as support for the view that in the development of language, too, there is a large component of biological maturation.

The diary notes a parallel between motor skill and speech. At the same time Candy was demonstrating her ability to retrieve and carry a ball, she was naming it *ba*. She spoke other words as well, among them, *bottle*, *bok* (box), *puk* (paper), *book*, *nut*, *ti* (tongue), *tik* (stick), *ba* or *bop* (Blackie) and *da*, *dot*, or *dottle* (Daddy).

Like walking, her meaningful speech was preceded by a steadily emerging sequence of vocal abilities, beginning at birth with a purely physiological action known as the birth cry. So it is with all babies. What is at first a cry without meaning becomes in ensuing weeks more socially motivated. The sounds diversify and may even attach themselves to particular needs. Mothers attuned to these different shadings of tone and measure are often able to interpret them and respond to the need—hunger, fatigue, and so on.

Most of the sounds a baby makes while crying are vowel sounds. The typical baby begins to produce consonants at around the age of three months, beginning with the gutturals *(g, k)* formed at the base of the tongue. Such sounds are what is commonly known as "cooing" or "gooing" and, like a kitten's purr, are welcomed as an expression of internal well-being.

At four to six months, other consonants are acquired and combined with vowels to produce the type of speech known as babbling. Unlike crying and cooing, expressive in different ways of a baby's

One Year Old

mood, babbling seems to be sheer vocal exercise, done for the pleasure of doing it. Because the sounds resemble words, parents often mistake babbling for a baby's first speech, as Candida's mother no doubt did in identifying, at nine months, her "first words" as *da da*, *ma ma*, *ba ba*, *ah da*, and *ah ba*. The difference is that in speech the baby goes beyond vocal play and tries to give sounds a meaning by relating them to objects and events.

The speech-like quality of babbling gave rise to the belief, once widely held, that the infant begins to babble as an attempt to imitate his parents' speech. This view was denied by the observation that deaf babies, even those who were born deaf and could thus have found no language models to imitate, babble as much as normal infants initially. As babbling continues, hearing infants begin to outstrip their deaf counterparts, both in the frequency and variety of sounds they produce. As additional proof against the idea that they take their cues from adult speech, however, an inventory of the sounds made by these hearing babies toward the end of the babbling period is found to include virtually all of the sounds of all human languages. Babies who have never heard anything but English, babble French and German gutterals, Russian consonant clusters, and numerous other sounds they themselves will have difficulty with if they undertake the study of foreign languages as adults.

Although a baby's versatility in making sounds exceeds that of his parents as long as he limits himself to babbling, the reverse is true when he attempts to produce sounds deliberately. The dividing line between babbling and true speech is often difficult to draw, as babies may continue to babble even after they begin to use words meaningfully. Most parents, however, notice occasions when the child seems to be trying to convey a meaning by the sounds he utters. And these sounds, which the baby uses deliberately to express ideas, consist of only a small subset of those in his parents' language, perhaps only the consonant *p* and the vowel *a* to begin with. Even Candida, with the modest repertoire of words listed above, makes use of only seven consonants (b,p,t,d,k,l,n).

This limitation on purposeful sounds often forces the child to make the sounds he can produce do double, or even triple, duty. Candida lets *ba* do the work of both *ball* and *Blackie*. The diary notes: "Oddly enough, she isn't disturbed over a single word meaning several different things: her own limited control over consonants often makes this necessary."

Thus *phonological development*, or the growth of a child's ability to pronounce speech, consists of steady refinements from use of a single sound (where an adult would use many) to an eventual perfect correspondence in phonetic structure between the child's words and those of his language community. This development is orderly in all children. For example, all children speak *t* before being able to speak *k* (McNeill [1970]), a fact which accounts for the baby-talk translation of *come here* into *tum here*. The same kind of translation occurs in other languages when parents attempt to simplify their speech in imitation of their children: the *k* to *t* transformation is found in Syrian, Marathi, Comanche, and Spanish baby talk (Ferguson, [1964]).

Roman Jakobson [1941] has proposed the "distinctive feature" concept to explain the regular order of mastery of sounds as a child acquires deliberate speech. Jakobson postulated that all children acquire distinctive features one at a time in the same order, and this explains the gradual progress towards one-to-one correspondence with adult sounds. Before a particular feature is acquired, the child treats sounds with and without the feature as identical. The class of equivalent sounds is then divided and redivided as each new feature is registered.

A typical distinctive feature is the element of "voice." The presence of vibration of the vocal cord turns voiceless *f* into what is otherwise the same consonant: *v*. Another example is voiced *b* versus its unvoiced twin *p*. In the diary we see that Candida's speech at 13 months has incorporated this particular distinctive feature except for her use of *dot* or *dottle* for *daddy*, where the unvoiced *t* incorrectly replaces the voiced *d*.

She has, however, still to master another distinctive feature, that of separating velar consonants, which are formed at the base of the tongue (for example, *k* and hard *g)* from nonvelar consonants. Thus in her word for *paper– puk–* she clings to velar *k* when nonvelar *p* is called for; and in *bop,* her word for *Blackie,* the reverse is true.

The child's first words are of interest to psychologists for their meanings as well as their phonetic characteristics. As in the case of phonetic development, the child's first word meanings are often very different from the meanings adults give to the same words. We see this in Candida when "*Bottle* means first of all her nursing bottle, then any bottle or container that looks like a bottle. *Bottle* also means *give me*, probably because she wants every bottle she sees. Hence, by transference, *bottle* is the name she gives to any new thing that does not fall into one of her other categories of names."

Piaget [1962] noted a similar course of extensions in meaning when 13-month-old Jacqueline was taught the name *bow-wow* for the landlord's dog. On successive days she applied the word to a pattern on the rug which resembled a schematic drawing of a dog, a horse (viewed from her balcony), a baby in a pram (also seen from the balcony), some hens, horses, prams, cyclists, and the landlord himself. Three months later she reserved it for dogs only. Another baby diary reports that a child who learned *mooi* for *moon* applied it to cakes, faces, a postmark and the letter *o* (Chamberlain and Chamberlain [1904]), and still another tells of a boy who learned *quack* for a duck swimming in a pond and later applied it to water, a coin with an eagle on it, and then to coins in general (Vygotsky [1962]).

Psychologists who have investigated the phenomenon have identified several factors which determine how children extend their early vocabulary to new situations. William Stern (cited in Lewis [1936]) emphasized the objective physical similarity between the original object the name was learned for and the new objects the child generalized it to. Candida's first extension of "bottle" can be explained on this basis since her nursing bottle physically resembles other bottles in shape, function, material, and so on. Lewis himself felt that the emotional context in which the child initially learned a word played a major role in determining what new objects or situations the word would be applied to. As an example, Candida learned "bottle" while experiencing a desire for her nursing bottle and used the word again whenever she felt the same emotion, expanding its meaning to something like *give me*. Piaget stressed the child's idiosyncratic point of view and proposed subjective, as opposed to Stern's objective, similarity as yet another basis for extension. Although he felt there was little objective resemblance between a horse and a pram, they were subjectively alike to Jacqueline because she glimpsed both of them from her balcony. Another instance is Candida's use of her name for her father as a request to be picked up: "*Dot* means *take me* or *pick me up* or *yes, I wanted you to pick me up*." Piaget similarly observed Laurent saying *Daddy* to Jacqueline as she bent over him with outstretched arms. According to Piaget, the baby's subjective perspective unifies all the people who pick him up, despite obvious objective differences between them. Furthermore, these infants' use of one name for a person (daddy) and an activity (picking up) is in keeping with Piaget's description of the sen-

32

sorimotor period as one in which the child knows his world through his actions, while things and actions are not as clearly differentiated as they are for an adult. This fusion of object and activity is also found for other items in Candida's vocabulary, for example, *ghi* to name both a drink and a way of drinking, and *door* for both the object and its operation.

When a child calls objectively different things (for example, bottle caps and toothpaste tubes) by a common name such as *bottle*, he is forming a concept. In fact, concept formation has been defined as "the acquisition or utilization, or both, of a common response to dissimilar stimuli" (Kendler [1961], p. 447). The child's first concepts, as seen in these verbal classifications, are often quite general and inclusive. Thus when Candida names things, she "divides her physical world into three large categories—*bottles*, *bocks*, and *oddles*." The concept to which she gives the name *dog* is likewise more general than the one to which adults attach the same label: "She knows Bop is a dog and calls him dog. She calls other dogs, dogs. She also calls horses, cows and ponies dogs." Laurent Piaget used the term *bow-wow* for dogs, chickens, cows, a cowbell, a guinea pig, and a cat. Idelberger's son (Lewis [1936]) used the same term for a porcelain dog, a fur stole, and various feline and canine animals in the zoo, while Stott's [1961] son used it for dogs and horses. All of these children obey the rule which the diarist deduced for Candida's *dog* concept: "Evidently a dog is a four-footed animal."

Observations such as these support the theory, exemplified in the work of Gestalt psychologists, that mental growth progresses from the general to the specific, holding that the child begins with a few broad classifications and discerns successively finer distinctions within each one to form ever narrower concepts—so cats, cows, and horses are distinguished from dogs and each becomes a class of its own. The opposing viewpoint, illustrated in early behavior theory, is that mental growth proceeds from the specific to the general and states, to quote Roger Brown [1958], that "we begin by seizing each thing in its uniqueness, noting every hair and flea of the particular dog" and then gradually learn to ignore specific details and group things into categories. While this theory has trouble accounting for broad concepts such as Candida's dog, it is more in keeping with certain other items in her vocabulary such as *tie*, *puh* (paper), *tok* (sock), and her *dirl* (girl) concept, which has only one instance, Candida herself.

Brown feels that neither theory does justice to the child's cognitive development which, he feels, proceeds in both directions —toward concreteness and toward abstraction—from a middle level which is determined in part by the way adults name things for children (Brown [1965]). He suggests that parents tend to teach children names like dog and flower which are more specific than animal or plant but less specific than terrier or geranium. They do this, he feels, because such terms can be represented by a gesture as well as by a word. The actions of pretending to pet a dog or pretending to sniff a flower transmit these concepts nearly as effectively as do their respective names, while both the more specific Bop and the more general animal defy such nonverbal characterization. Children's learning of the names is aided, according to Brown, by this redundancy of word and action. He draws support from the fact that children themselves tend to define words in terms of actions, for example, "hands are to hold," "a hole is to dig" (Kraus and Sendak [1952]).

Children's concepts differ from adults' in other ways than their concreteness or abstractness. Piaget notes that they are more changeable, citing Jacqueline's almost daily transformations of the meaning of bow-wow. Other differences are indicated in the research and theorizing of L.S. Vygotsky who used an object-sorting task to study concepts in children, adolescents, and adults. The procedure required that subjects sort a group of blocks which varied in size, shape, and color. Vygotsky found that adults tended to settle on a single feature, which they applied consistently as a basis for classification. For example, they might group all of the blocks by color (red in one pile, blue in another, etc.). The classifications made by children were typically inconsistent. Children often switched to a new feature in midstream, having been given no reason to abandon the first. Thus a child might begin with color and place a red square and a red triangle together. However, the next item selected might be a blue triangle, with shape as the new defining feature. Vygotsky called such shifting classifications chain complexes. Another instance of such a chain is the class of objects to which Candida gave the name bottle. Ordinary glass bottles were brought in on the basis of objective similarity (Stern) to her nursing bottle. The next link in the chain was an emotional similarity (Lewis) between the bottle and other items that evoked her desire. Then, since desirable objects were often novel ones, the critical attribute shifted again and novelty became the third link.

One Year Old

Vygotsky drew a parallel between childish chain complexes and the historical evolution, or word meanings, in a language. One example he cites is the phrase "neck of the bottle" which is based on a physical resemblance between the narrow part of a bottle and the human neck. When the term becomes *bottleneck*, the criterion for its application shifts to a functional property of narrow openings. Despite such vestiges in the language, however, Vygotsky believed that adult thought was organized into *concepts* rather than *complexes*. Although the two frequently coincide, thus enabling communication between child and adult, in a concept proper, the defining attribute is an abstract property shared by each and every item brought into the classification. In other words, adult concepts obey the class inclusion properties of formal logic, while children's complexes, though they share the same label, are constructed according to a quite different system. Thus, while we as adults may tacitly assume that children view the world the way we do, especially once they begin to borrow the words we use to describe it, discoveries such as Vygotsky's point out how fallacious this assumption often is. The error of making it inappropriately is known as *adultomorphism*. In succeeding chapters we will encounter other psychological observations (on conservation of invariances, judgments about lying, and so forth), which have helped to point out the implicit adultomorphism in the heretofore commonly accepted view of children.

What makes a child switch to the concepts or word meanings used by adults? Lewis observed that a 19-month-old boy called K understood the difference between *box* and *brick* when an adult used the words, but he himself used the word *ba* to refer to both of them. Lewis wondered why, having developed his own classification system, K would ever be tempted to abandon it. He found the answer three months later in a department store, when K's mother said, "Baby, come and buy some bricks." *Bicki*, *bicki*, K responded eagerly. Henceforth, he used this new word for bricks, limiting *ba* to boxes. It seemed to Lewis that the urgent desire to communicate efficiently with an adult, in this case to obtain a valued toy, led K to adopt the adult classification system.

3
Nearly
15 Months
Old

JUNE 2: Candy has been ill with tonsillitis, a fever, and a rash. Not too seriously, not seriously enough to stay in bed or even indoors. But it has made her cross and given her temper tantrums. Even so, she seems philosophical about them, half ready to call one off if it doesn't seem to be working.

Tonight, for instance, she was put to bed late and got impatient for her bottle. By the time Peggy had bathed her, put her shirt on, and laid her on her back in the crib, Candy was fuming. She kicked and flailed in all directions, and banged her head. When I offered her the bottle she called for Mom to pick her up. Realizing that this would have settled nothing, we decided to wait her out. She slowed down kicking, put her thumb in her mouth, and then accepted the bottle--but from Mom, not from me.

Day before yesterday she used the toilet for the first time and radiantly acclaimed it a wonderful invention. She had been increasingly conscious of the difficulty while sitting in her diapers. Seizing the propitious moment, Peggy popped her on her pot. She needed no second lesson. Yesterday the urge came while she was eating breakfast. She insisted on being taken to the "toe" before she would eat another bite.

Her vocabulary grows daily: "ghi" for drink (because it comes in a glass, at her insistence, just to be sure it isn't milk; milk must be sucked from a bottle); "acka" for phonograph record; "tocka" for tractor or the strap you start it with; "bocky" for bacon which she loves; "eye" for ice, which she likes to handle. She then makes you wipe her wet hand off since she thinks that will wipe the cold away.

She runs rather fast now, and stamps her feet when she's mad. She recognizes babies and dogs in pictures, and enjoys putting one article into another, closing it up, opening it, and taking it out again. She can figure how to open almost anything.

She is very imitative. Often when she picks something up from the floor, she wipes it on her dress. That's what her mother does with anything Candy will put in her mouth again. Almost any new word that means something to her, she immediately tries to repeat. If she is satisfied that her version is close enough to be understandable, she adds the word to her vocabulary. And sometimes she prefers her own version even when she has mastered the original. Blackie, for example, she can now say quite distinctly, but she prefers "Bop." I'm beginning to, myself, and Bop doesn't seem to mind.

Parents encounter many difficulties in trying to raise a child. Not the least of them is the problem of the temper tantrum. Candida, for example, developed tantrums after a bout of tonsillitis and on one occasion, having been made to wait for her bedtime bottle, "she kicked and flailed in all directions, and banged her head." In the past, parents had to chart the course through such difficult situations with relatively little guidance from scientific psychology. Their alternatives were to rely on the advice of experts who could claim more experience with children as a species than the average parent or, like Candida's parents, to use their own common sense: "realizing that this [to give her the bottle] would have settled nothing, we decided to wait her out."

Recently the branch of psychology known as *behavior modification* has turned to the task of bridging the gap between parents, teachers, and child therapists, on one hand, and on the other, the great body of data and theory which a long tradition of experimental research into the elements and principles of learning has accumulated. Historically, this tradition began in the Russian laboratory of Ivan Pavlov [1927] who discovered the process called *classical conditioning*. After repeatedly pairing the ringing of a bell with bringing food to a dog, Pavlov observed that the dog drooled to the sound of the bell even when no food followed. Thus the bell, which had initially been a neutral stimulus to the dog's salivation reflex, had become a conditioned elicitor of salivation through its association with the unconditional salivary stimulus, the taste of food. Pavlov found he could reverse the process by presenting the bell without the accompaniment of food. After many such presentations the bell ceased to evoke saliva and the conditioned response was said to be "extinguished." Thus the general principle behind classical conditioning is *contiguity*. When two stimuli are repeatedly paired—or contiguous—one of them becomes capable of eliciting the response [frequently an autonomic or reflex response such as blinking or sweating] formerly made only to the other. The timing of the pairings is important: conditioning is best when the stimulus to be conditioned immediately precedes the one which unconditionally evokes the reaction.

Classical conditioning is an important process in its own right for child development. Since it is one of the simplest forms of learning, researchers have sought evidence of it very early in the child's life. One investigator (Spelt [1948]) claimed to have observed classical conditioning in human fetuses a month or more before birth. He paired vibration of the mother's abdomen with a loud sound which had been found to elicit movement from the fetus unconditionally. After repeated pairings, the vibratory stimulus also came to elicit movement. His result has since been questioned, however, one question being whether the vibration he used really is a *neutral* stimulus for the fetus. More recently Sameroff [1971] has raised the same question concerning experiments which purport to demonstrate classical conditioning in newborn infants. He concludes that classical conditioning is probably not possible until the baby is at least three weeks old.

By the time a baby is two or three months old, the evidence that it can be classically conditioned is no longer questionable. By this age most babies show conditioned reactions to aspects of their daily feeding routines. For example, Piaget [1952] observed that four-month-old Lucienne opened her mouth when she saw her nursing bottle, the sight of the bottle substituting for the bell in Pavlov's paradigm. Even more clear-cut demonstrations of the conditionability of infants occur when Pavlov's experimental procedures are applied to infants, for example, as clinical tests for deafness (Aldrich [1928]).

The other form of conditioning, called *operant conditioning,* has its own mascot, which is probably as well-known as Pavlov's dog—the rat in a Skinner box. In operant conditioning, reinforcement is made *contingent* upon the occurrence of behavior (which fits the layman's definition for voluntary acts, anything from temper tantrums to reciting numbers) by delivering reward when the behavior occurs and not delivering it when it does not occur. The rat, for example, is rewarded with a food pellet for pressing a lever in the box. As a result of reward, the behavior becomes more frequent: the rat progresses from pressing the bar less than once an hour to pressing it many times a minute.

Operant conditioning goes on, formally or informally, throughout a child's life. Parents reward their children's behavior in many ways—with smiles, praise, a pat on the head, or more explicitly, by giving the child an M&M when he successfully uses the toilet. Operant conditioning can also be reversed by discontinuing the reward, a process known as *operant extinction.* To get the rat to stop pressing the lever, the experimenter simply stops delivering food pellets after the rat presses the bar. Eventually, in the absence of reinforcement, the rat's bar-pressing *extinguishes.*

Behavior modification applies the principles of classical and operant conditioning to the treatment of behavior problems in children, the central assumptions being: (a) the child's behavior is his problem (as opposed to the view that the behavior is a symptom of some underlying conflict), and (b) the problem is due to learning; the child either has learned to do the wrong things or has not learned to do the right things. If he has learned to do the wrong things, extinction is called for, it he has not learned to do the right things, conditioning is called for.

C.D. Williams [1959] describes the use of *operant extinction* to treat bedtime temper tantrums in a 21-month-old boy he calls an "infans tyrannotearus." The boy was seriously ill for the first 18 months of his life. During this time, he developed tantrums, possibly because his illness had placed his parents at his beck and call and had accustomed him to continual attention. When he recovered, the parents understandably felt imprisoned by the tantrums. He required, for example, that they sit in his bedroom with him for several hours each evening until he fell asleep, and if they attemped to read a book to pass the time, he screamed until they put it down.

Williams concluded that the tantrums were being operantly rewarded by the parents' compliance with the boy's bedtime demands. He set up an extinction procedure in which they put him to bed in a relaxed way but left the room immediately and did not return no matter how loudly he cried. On the first night he cried for 50 minutes. He fell asleep promptly on the second night (partly due to exhaustion from his previous night's exertion). Within a week he was falling asleep immediately with no fuss. The schedule was broken after this first week by an aunt who responded to his crying by coming back into the bedroom to see what he wanted. This bit of reinforcement strengthened the tantrum behavior again, and it took another week of extinction to eliminate it a second time. But after this, the parents reported they had no more problems with bedtime tantrums.

A problem which generally ranks ahead of the temper tantrum as a source of difficulty for parents is that of toilet training. Like the tantrum, it is an issue that has received the attention of psychological researchers, largely because of its importance in the theory of Sigmund Freud. Freud's name is associated in most people's minds with the word *psychoanalysis*, a method he invented for treating the mentally ill. In psychoanalysis the patient *freely associates* by relating all the thoughts that come into his mind, without editing no matter how trivial or unworthy they seem.

In the course of psychoanalyzing many adults, Freud made the surprising discovery that most of their free associations dealt not with experiences they had had as adults but with things that had happened to them in early childhood. This finding laid the groundwork for one of Freud's most significant contributions to psychology: the belief that an individual's childhood experiences are critically important in determining the kind of person he will be as an adult, even more important than the events of adulthood.

Another contribution of Freud's, one which has special significance from a historical viewpoint, was the concept of *infantile sexuality*. Freud asserted that the sexual experience does not appear spontaneously with the maturation of the genital organs, but instead has its origins firmly planted in earliest infancy. He went so far as to suggest that babies at the breast (or bottle) experience sexual pleasures not very different from adult orgasm. As revolutionary as this assertion seems today, how much more revolutionary it must have seemed when Freud first made it, in an era deeply emersed in Victorian morality. He himself recollected in his autobiography [1935, p. 62]: "Few of the findings of psychoanalysis have met with such universal contradiction or have aroused such an outburst of indignation as the assertion that the sexual function starts at the beginning of life and reveals its presence by important signs even in childhood. And yet no other finding of analysis can be demonstrated so easily and so completely."

One outcome of the theory of infantile sexuality was the formulation of *psychosexual* stages through which the sexual function must proceed as it develops into mature sexuality. A common feature of all the stages is the existence in each of a central conflict. The nature of the conflict is different in each stage, but its basis is the same: the primitive, hedonistic desires of the child versus the limitations society places on their gratification. Freud conceptualized this conflict in the form of a struggle between three personality structures: the *id*, the *ego*, and the *superego*. The id represents the *pleasure principle*—simple, unadulterated hedonism. The ego represents reality and serves to guide the id to gratification through realistic and appropriate channels. The third structure, the superego, represents "the ethical standards of mankind."

There are five stages in the theory, and each is defined partly by the nature of the conflict, and partly by which area of the body serves as the main pleasure center during the stage. During the first, or *oral*, stage, this area is the mouth. The id is the dominant personality structure at the beginning of the oral stage, when the child is unable to make a distinction between himself and the outside world. But as his needs are not all satisfied instantaneously, an ego begins to develop and manifests itself first in a growing ability to cope with delay. It develops further during the process of *weaning,* which is the first great conflict between the infant and society as embodied in his parents. Freud believed that this conflict was inevitable but felt that parents could intensify it either by undue frustration, through harsh and abrupt weaning, or by undue gratification, through overfeeding or unnecessary prolongation of the sucking stage. Individuals for whom the conflict is thus intensified may develop an oral character and have excessive preoccupations centering on the mouth (a chain smoker or drinker).

The pleasure region shifts to the anal area of the body sometime during the second year of life, giving rise to the *anal* stage. Conflict in this stage centers on toilet training in the form of a struggle between the requirement of hygiene imposed by the parents and the child's impulse to void when and where he pleases. Again, Freud felt that either overfrustration or overgratification would intensify the conflict and potentially lead to an anal fixation, incorporating traits such as messiness, stubbornness and greed.

The genital region becomes the pleasure center near the age of four. During the next year or two, the child is in the *phallic* stage, and conflict, termed the *Oedipal* conflict, is between a sexually tinged love for the parent of the opposite sex and a mixture of jealousy, fear, and affection for the parent of the same sex. The superego develops from a resolution of this conflict and its resolution places the child in the *latency stage.* During this period, which continues until puberty, sexual energy lies dormant, to be awakened again in the *genital stage* as mature heterosexuality.

The three basic issues of conflict which Freud alluded to—weaning, toilet training, and the Oedipal (which will be discussed subsequently)—all have to do with child-care practices and parent-child relations. Freud's theory did not, much as some might have wished it to, prescribe an ideal method for raising children. In fact, according to his theory, there is no such ideal method. No matter which method of toilet training the parents decide on, their child will experience conflict in the anal stage. Although Freud's theory is often taken as a vendetta against the strict child-care practices dictated by

Victorian morality (with the implication that permissive training is the answer), he actually saw as many evils in excessive permissiveness. The best a pair of well-meaning parents can do, according to Freud, is adopt a moderate approach and thereby avoid intensifying their child's inevitable conflict.

What approach to toilet training do parents typically take? Sears, Maccoby, and Levin [1957] asked this question of 379 New England mothers whom they interviewed intensively on many child-care practices, including when they began toilet training, how long it took, how difficult it was, and how the child reacted.

They found wide variation in the methods the mothers reported but were able to rate them on a scale from *mild* to *severe*. At the mild extreme were mothers who reported that the child actually trained himself. The mother simply showed the child when, where, and how to use the toilet and neither punished mistakes nor rewarded successes. This was the method Candida's parents evidently followed, since the diarist writes: "Day before yesterday she used the toilet for the first time and radiantly acclaimed it a wonderful invention. She had been increasingly conscious of the difficulty while sitting in her diapers. Seizing the propitious moment, Peggy popped her on her pot. She needed no second lesson." At the severe extreme, on the other hand, were mothers who reported feeling considerable emotional involvement themselves in whether or not the child used the toilet successfully. Their technique usually involved leaving the child on the potty for lengthy periods, as well as severe punishment for deviations.

When they looked at the effects of these forms of toilet training, Sears and his associates concluded that the more severe the training, the greater the child's emotional difficulty with toilet activities. Emotional difficulty was indicated by a breakdown of partially attained success, by irritability and crying while on the toilet, or by both. Severity of training, however, was not the only factor responsible for emotional upset. In fact, Sears found the warmth of the mother's attitude toward her child to be an equally important one. Warm mothers were those who spoke of their child affectionately in the interviews and gave the impression that they enjoyed the child's company. Sears found that children of warm mothers experienced very little emotional difficulty with toilet training, regardless of whether it was mild or severe, and that children of cold mothers had difficulty even with mild training, although the greatest emotional difficulty was experienced by children of cold mothers who used severe methods.

Still another factor discovered by Sears, Maccoby, and Levin relates to Freud's theory that toilet training has sexual overtones. They found a significant relationship between the mother's own anxiety about sex and the amount of difficulty her child experienced in toilet training. High sex anxiety on the part of the mother seemed to amplify whatever pattern was present already. Thus cold and severe sex-anxious mothers produced the most emotional upsets, and warm, mild sex-anxious mothers produced the least.

Sears and his associates also looked at the age at which mothers began toilet training. Here again, the range was great, from as young as five months to over two years. Looking at the probability of emotional upset, it appeared that training begun very early (5-9 months) or very late (after 20 months) was best, with 15-19 months being the age where the risk of emotional disturbance was highest. The authors explained this on the assumption that the latter period is one during which the child is so active that he resents being restrained on the potty and the diaper habit is well entrenched. They suggested that the improvement at 20 months might be due to the child's greater intellectual maturity, although they doubted from their records that "there is any age after which most children can simply be instructed to go to the toilet when they need to." Candida's successful toilet training at 15 months is exceptional in light of this result. Sears noted a few cases like hers, where the mother achieved almost immediate success by noticing the time of day at which the child regularly moved his bowels and putting him on the potty then.

Freud's stage theory offers an explanation for another aspect of Candida's behavior, illustrated when the diarist wrote: "She is very imitative. Often when she picks something up from the floor, she wipes it on her dress. That's what her mother does with anything Candy will put in her mouth again."

This simple, common occurrence of a daughter imitating her mother has relevance in Freud's theory to the development of the conscience and the sex role. A sex role is a pattern of behavior and attitudes which an individual acquires in the course of being socialized as a member of one or the other sex. This occurs because many behavior and attitudes are culturally sex-typed: they are considered normal and appropriate for one sex but unusual or deviant if someone of the opposite sex displays them. In modern Western society wearing dresses or lipstick, playing with dolls, and openly displaying fears (for example, of mice) are all feminine sex-typed behavior. Masculine behavior includes such things as cigar smoking, wrestling, and playing poker. Most adults conform to the pattern of behavior expected of their sex, and they count on others to do likewise, indicating that they have internalized society's expectations concerning the sexes. Somehow children must acquire both these expectations, or standards, and the sex-typed behavior themselves.

According to Freud's theory, this is accomplished through identification with the parents. He postulated two kinds of identification. Early in infancy, children of both sexes develop *anaclitic* (literally, leaning-against-type) identification. The baby strives to become as much like its mother as it possibly can. The basis for anaclitic identification is self-preservation. The infant's total dependency on the mother for nurturance and survival is a potential source of anxiety which would be reduced could the infant become the mother, or at any rate take over her functions. This is what he strives to do through anaclitic identification.

With the Oedipal conflict, defensive identification emerges. According to Freud, the nature of the boy's love changes during the phallic stage from pure dependency to a love that includes vague sexual feelings. (The boy himself is unaware of all this; the feelings themselves and the conflicts they engender are buried deep in the unconscious part of the mind). The result is a desire for intimacy with the mother, so the boy comes to perceive the father as his rival. Because of the father's power, however, the boy fears a confrontation and, rather than provoke one, attempts to make himself similar to the father through identification. He strives to adopt all of the father's traits including his sex role and moral values. Then, when he sees how much he resembles his father, he comes to experience his father's pleasures and triumphs as though they were his own.

For the girl, the Oedipal (or Electra) conflict is a similar process, except that when her love comes to include unconscious sexual feelings, its recipient also changes. Freud believed that during the phallic stage the girl discovers her anatomical inferiority to boys, blames her mother for it, and shifts her affection to the father, so that the mother becomes both the rival and the model she emulates through defensive identification.

Another theory, called *social learning* theory, preserves the mechanism of identification which Freud introduced but omits mention of an Oedipal conflict. Social learning theorists such as Walter Mischel [1966] prefer to explain identification, or children's differential tendency to adopt the behavior and attitudes of their same-sexed parent, in terms of principles from the theory of learning.

One of the most important of these is the principle of *observational learning*. This simply states that children learn by watching as well as by doing. We have a good illustration in the examples of tantrum behavior previously discussed. The child Williams reported on learned to throw tantrums by doing, through direct reward. On the other hand, Jacqueline Piaget put on a nearly perfect tantrum display after once watching another child throw one. Of course, for tantrums to become an important aspect of Jacqueline's behavior, she too would have to experience reward for them. Mischel suggests that the same is true of the sex-role. A girl, for example, learns the sex-typed behaviors of both sexes through observation, but differential reward teaches her to engage in only the feminine ones. Other properties of observational learning which have been disclosed in experimental studies further support it as a vehicle of sex-role development by suggesting that one of the most likely people for a child to imitate is the parent of his own sex. One such study found that nurturant adults are imitated more than cold and unrewarding ones (Bandura and Huston [1961]). Others have found that children most readily emulate a model they believe is similar to themselves. Since the parent of the same sex as the child typically possesses both of these qualities, he or she is an optimum model.

A third theory of sex-role development, which has been called *cognitive-developmental* theory (Kohlberg [1966]), sees sex-role development as but one aspect of the cognitive development process. The first step in the process is for the child to come to a stable realization of his own gender. This is not as simple as it sounds, since until the age of about seven, children tend to believe that gender is no more stable than haircut or clothing and that a girl, for example, can make herself a boy by cutting her hair short and wearing long pants (Kohlberg). Once the child realizes that his gender is a permanent feature of his personality, he comes to value sex-appropriate objects and activities. Thus because he is a boy he comes to like to wear blue jeans and play football. The sex role is then acquired by means of this positive valuation: because the boy admires the masculine role, he sets about imitating male models and adopting stereotyped masculine behaviors. Finally, as a result of imitating the same-sexed parent in this way, the child becomes fonder of him.

The Cognitive-developmental theory posits a process which is the reverse of Freudian and social-learning-theory identification. In identification the child comes to acquire and value his sex role as the result of an emotional tie to the same-sexed parent. In cognitive-developmental theory he values the stereotyped sex role first, and this leads him to intensify his emotional relationship with the parent of the same sex.

So each of the theories discussed above would have a different interpretation of the incident in which Candida wiped objects on her dress after watching her mother do it. According to Freud's theory, this happened because Candida's mother was nurturant and Candida was anaclitically identified with her. According to social-learning theory, it was because her mother was nurturant and because Candida perceived a similarity between herself and her mother. According to cognitive-developmental theory, Candida's imitation of her mother was a chance occurrence at this age. She would have been equally likely to imitate her father, grandmother, or a stranger of either sex.

Not only do children imitate their parents, parents imitate children. We see an instance of this in the diary when Candida's parents changed the name of the family dog from *Blackie* to *Bop:* "*Blackie,* for example, she can now say quite distinctly, but she prefers *Bop*. I'm beginning to myself, and Bop doesn't seem to mind." Hippolyte Taine remarked on the same thing in a diary he kept of his daughter's language development in 1869 when she was in her second year. He was struck both by the tendency of children to invent words and the tendency of their parents to make use of their inventions. One example was his daughter's word *ham,* which she invented to designate food. Since she was totally French-speaking, the word had no conventional meaning for her parents, and Taine believed she came up with it because it mimicked the sound of eating. He thought "a man among savages" reliant solely on his vocal cords to convey ideas would come up with the same "natural vocal gesture" of snapping up food. The girl's parents picked up the word from her and it thus became an established part of her vocabulary. On the other hand, a word that her parents did not imitate gradually dropped out of her own usage. This was the word *tem,* which she used to indicate a general imperative—it seemed to mean *give, take,* and *look* all in one. Since it corresponded to no unique idea for her parents, they failed to imitate it, so she quit using it.

Taine drew a lesson from these observations: language development is an active process on the part of the child rather than a passive enregistration of adult speech. He felt that a child learns language "as a true musician learns counterpoint or a true poet prosody, it is an original genius adapting itself to a form constructed bit by bit by a succession of original geniuses, if language were wanting, the child would recover it little by little or would discover an equivalent." In view of the child's originality and the parents' tendency to imitate and make use of the child's words, he felt it fair to say that "if it [the child] learns our language from us, we learn its from the child."

It is interesting that this view of language development as an active, inventive process lay dormant in psychology for almost a century, to be activated again, as we shall see, in the psycholinguistic approach to language acquisition.

4
Fifteen
Months' Old

JUNE 13: This record seems to be mainly on the subject of vocabulary. I suppose it interests me because it is the most concrete, or at any rate the most direct, evidence of Candy's thinking. But there are other signs as well. For instance, her ability to classify things:

She knows that Bop is a dog and calls him a "dog." She calls other dogs, "dogs". She also calls horses, cows, and ponies, "dogs". Evidently a dog is a four-footed

Fifteen Months Old

animal. Then there are nuts. I used to think they were a small order of balls because she called the stones in the gravel driveway nuts. But now I perceive that large boulders are also nuts, even when she hasn't been able to feel or lift them. I take it that nuts are all stones and that she can classify stones as such regardless of size. I suppose their apparent texture, together with their irregular size and shape, is the basis on which she groups them.

A beet is a ball. It is still a ball after it has been chopped fine and served to her in a dish. On the other hand, a grapefruit is also a "ball", but not the juice that comes from it. The half rinds that are left are, though.

A flower is a "how". So too are the trees. Her navel, which currently fascinates her, is a button—her own idea; I don't think she heard anyone else call it that. If, however, she did even once long ago and it seemed appropriate, she would remember it. There are many things she knows immediately when their names are spoken, even though she does not yet speak them herself. These include her head, her belly, her foot, her hands, her fingers. And there are many other things she identifies without naming them fully, usually by the sound of the first letter in the name, and often after the single time she heard the thing named.

If you say "mosquito" or "bites," she will slap at her head.

She has a compelling sense of what is proper. The door to the record player cabinet has once or twice been closed on her, to keep her from grabbing at the changer arm. Now she noisily protests whenever she sees it open, insisting it be closed. She will close it herself, too, if you ask her. The same is true concerning articles she has been kept away from, such as the saw. If it is left in her reach, she lectures us about it.

She is just learning to bounce a ball. Formerly she would run after it but had to carry it back and give it to me by hand. She still carries it back, but she has finally allowed herself to drop it in front of me and let it bounce into my hands.

Today she was saying "Dot" and shaking her head. What could it mean? Peggy figured it out. Whenever Candy hears an auto horn she says "Dot," meaning either that it must be I or, more probably, somebody doing what I do when I come home. When it isn't I, Peggy says, "No, that isn't Dot." So now Candy says "Dot" and shakes her head, her way of saying, "No, that isn't Dot, but he's doing what Dot does."

Until recently her vocabulary consisted entirely of nouns or of nouns made to do the work of verbs. "Door," for instance, also means "close the door" or "open the door." Curiously enough, her first word that is not a noun is "why". She loves the word without yet having a clear idea what it means, possibly because it evokes such a satisfactory response from her parents. Hence she says it often and sometimes most appropriately.

JULY 9: An article in Parents Magazine reports that the average child of 18 months has a vocabulary of 75 words, of which about 25 are nouns. Candy speaks at least 100 words and practically all are nouns. Does this mean that the 50 or so non-nouns the writer of the article refers to are cries of various sorts? I can't imagine what 50 words other than nouns a baby would feel called on to speak. Aside from interjections and whatever you call such words as 'bye and 'night, they would practically all have to be verbs. Surely a baby hasn't much use for adjectives, adverbs, conjunctions, prepositions—even articles and pronouns. As for verbs, well with Candy they're practically all nouns used as verbs, or vice versa, such as "door", "ride", and "walk". The only exception I can think of at the moment is "roll". She understands many verbs, of course, but she speaks very few.

Candy's first sentences were single words, and many were negative. Hearing an auto horn, she would say "Dot" and shake her head, meaning, "That isn't Daddy." A dog barking: "Bop" and a head shake, meaning, "That isn't Blackie." Then she put as many as three words together: "Bye Dot Car," meaning, "Daddy's going away in the car."

She understands numbers up to three now and speaks frequently of two. Her reflection she calls Baby ("Bay") and today she saw "Bay" in the dark glasses I was wearing. She is intensely interested in pictures and has taken to pulling apart the magazines again after ignoring them for several months, looking for "dog", "boy", "bay", "dirl", "tar", "tocka", "tow" (cow)—but especially dogs. She can find things you ask her for and has all her toys identified. Today, long after I had put her ball in one of her hollow blocks, without being aware that she was watching me, she suddenly called out "ball" and, though she could not see it, walked straight to the block and pulled the ball out. She pushes my wheelchair to me when I ask her to, hands things to Mom; and today she put a gasoline spout back with the tractor when I asked her to. No gestures or pointing; I just said, "Put it back with the tractor." She also handed me the saw which we had carelessly left out.

JULY 14: Candy has a set of hollow blocks that nest in one another. They are decorated with pictures from fairy tales and other children's stories and rhymes such as Goldilocks, Little Black Sambo, the Three Little Kittens, etc. She enjoys looking at the pictures and identifying the figures. She also tries to put the blocks together and take them apart.

Separating the blocks is especially important, and frustrating when she fails—as she usually does. I have shown her an easier way, by letting the inner block slide out through the force of gravity. She appreciates the improvement and makes an occasional half-hearted attempt to turn the blocks so the inner one will slide, but very soon she resorts again to the direct but ineffectual method of clawing at the inner block with her fingers. I can't help wondering if in matters beyond our ken we don't all behave in this way. Candy is manifestly logical in her methods. Pulling the block with her fingers is the logical way of getting it out for a person still unfamiliar with the mysterious influence of gravity. Sooner or later, of course, she'll learn to let gravity do it, but it will be the result of experience or memory rather than common sense. And so we all cling to commonsense methods and come up against the same frustration. Though we may have occasional brief glimpses of a better method than common sense, and try halfheartedly to use it, we revert to the direct and logical methods that have failed before.

One Sunday afternoon a toddler named Martha came with her parents on a visit to the home of Robert Sears. He described her behavior: "While we had coffee and cookies she thirstily drank down a glass of milk, ate half a cookie, and began an eager exploration of a her surroundings. Toddling most of the time, crawling occasionally, she left trails of crumbs and tipped over cups wherever she went." Martha took special interest in a floor lamp and nearly tipped it over twice. Each time her father put down his cup, leaped across the room to rescue the lamp, and "said clearly and distinctly, 'Now Martha, *don't touch!*'" On her third venture toward the lamp, she deliberately stepped to within a few feet of it, "lifted her arm partly, a little jerkily, and then said sharply, commandingly, *'Don't touch!'*" After an instant of what Sears described as "struggling silence," she fell laughing to her father's feet. Sears remarked to the father that he was fortunate in having overheard "the muted birth-cry of conscience itself."

A similar incident occurred in the diary: "She has a compelling sense of what is proper. The door to the record player cabinet has once or twice been closed on her, to keep her from grabbing at the changer arm. Now she noisily protests whenever she sees it open, insisting it be closed. She will close it herself, too, if you ask her. The same is true concerning articles she has been kept away from, such as the saw. If it is left within her reach, she lectures us about it." This incident also resembles one recorded by Florence Goodenough [1931] in the course of her study of children's anger. One of the two-year-old boys she studied became violently angry when he brought a doll which was always kept in his bed downstairs with him by mistake. His mother reported: "He started upstairs immediately but kept screaming until some time after the doll had been put back into bed. This is an extreme case of his usual behavior when things do not run along in their customary manner" [p. 145]. Goodenough noted anger over changes in routine among other children of about this age, particularly ones whose parents adhered to strict schedules. Candida's behavior with the record player and saw shares elements of this compulsive ordering behavior, as well as elements of the awareness of adult rules which Sears saw as the budding of conscience. In fact, it seems a kind of bridge between the two.

Robert Sears is a psychologist who has devoted considerable time to the study of conscience, especially as it applies to children. In this context he defines conscience as an internal control mechanism which guides the child away from transgression or which, if the child succumbs to temptation, punishes him for having done so. Sears contrasts conscience with two other control mechanisms, both external—fear of punishment and surveillance by parents. Although these also keep a child from misbehaving, they cannot, according to Sears, be considered elements of conscience, since some person other than the child must be on hand to make them work.

It has been found that as children get older, their consciences get stronger. Further, in interviews with several hundred mothers of five-year-olds, Sears, Maccoby, and Levin [1957] discovered that within a given age group there are some children with stronger consciences than others. Although the mothers, by and large, did not feel instilling consciences into their offspring to be one of their parental responsibilities, they were quite sensitive to signs of conscience. One such sign was confession. The child with a strong conscience prefers to own up when he has done something wrong, even when it is something his mother is not likely to discover without his confession. Evidently the possibility of punishment is easier to bear than the sting of a guilty conscience. Some mothers even reported that the child begged her for punishment, not feeling relieved until it was given. Other children are much cagier about confessing transgression. Those with weak consciences tend not to admit wrongdoing spontaneously.

At the extreme of strong conscience, Sears and his associates report on a child whose compulsion to confess was so great that his mother remarked: "Even when he does something outside that he shouldn't do and I don't even know about it, he could very easily not say a word to me. Instead he comes and he says, 'You know what I did?' . . . I should think that if I were a child I'd keep it to myself, but he doesn't." At the opposite extreme, they quote another mother: "He'll admit it if you tell him you're going to take away his television if he doesn't, but as far as getting right up and saying 'I did it,' he's no George Washington."

Sears related both individual differences in strength of conscience and the growth of conscience with age to patterns of child-rearing practiced by the parents, in particular to their style of discipline. He divided discipline into two sets of tactics, calling one *love-oriented* and the other *power-assertive*. In love-oriented control, the mother was seen to make a child feel that her love for him was contingent upon his good behavior. She might, for example, tell the child that if he did such and such, she wouldn't love him any more, or show special affection when he did something good. In power-assertive discipline, mothers provided tangible rewards for good behavior and physical punishment for bad.

Predictably, more evidence of conscience was found in children of mothers using the "love-oriented" tactics than the power-assertive ones, and the difference seemed to increase in proportion to the amount of love manifested by the mother. To explain this, Sears had recourse to the concept of identification, arguing that the mother who is loving, but threatens to withdraw her love when the child behaves badly, makes the child anxious over the possibility of separation from her. To insure against this, he identifies with his mother and internalizes a copy of her moral standards which he no more than she would care to violate. Then, having, in the act of obeying the call of conscience, demonstrated his identification with the person he loves most, he feels good about it, and the good feeling strengthens his resolve to behave well. On the other hand, the child whose mother does not bring love into the business of discipline sees no relationship between good behavior and his attachment to her and, having no strong reason to develop an internalized conscience, resists temptation primarily through fear of the physical consequences if he doesn't.

Coincidentally with what Sears calls the *birth-cry of conscience*, other important aspects of social communication begin to manifest themselves in the human child, notably what is called *holophrastic speech*. We have seen how the infant progresses from the utterance of mere vowels and consonants, through a phase called babbling, and ultimately to true words where a specific vocalization is associated with a specific event or group of events. For a period of time, the child's vocabulary is limited to single-word names which then almost imperceptibly come to do the work of whole sentences. Thus with Candida, "*Door*, for instance, also means *close the door* or *open the door*." The idea that "Children are limited phonologically to uttering single words at the beginning of language acquisition even though they are capable of conceiving something like full sentences" (McNeill [1970, p.1,074]) is the theory of holophrastic speech.

Like speech in general, holophrastic speech has its grammar. This psycholinguistic grammar has its rules, just as the conventional grammar of the school room does. The big difference is that the

Fifteen Months Old

grammar of the school room is prescriptive; its rules define the way one *ought* to speak. The grammar of psycholinguistics, on the other hand, is descriptive; its rules describe the presumed structure underlying the way people have been heard to speak. Another difference is that not all of the latter's rules are known: one of the central tasks of psycholinguistics is to find them.

In holophrastic speech, the rules must incorporate many more elements than the word itself, since, as we have seen, a single word such as *door*, when translated into conventional speech, can produce at least three full sentences: *This is a door. Close the door. Open the door.* In a grammar proposed by David Ingram [1971] these additional elements are found in intonation, gesture, and features of the environment, such as the placement of the speaker in relation to the door. These are combined in various ways. A rising intonation, for example, combined with a word, produces a question: "Is this a door?" The gesture of reaching, together with a word, constitutes a request or command: "Open the door."

Along this line is the holophrastic grammar of Grace De Laguna [1927] who notes: "Even a member of the family often fails to grasp the significance of what the baby is saying if he does not see what the baby is doing" [p. 267]. She therefore includes the nonlanguage context as the subject [*topic*] of holophrastic sentences, the word spoken being the predicate [*comment*]. Evidence of this is found in the diary entry: "When I left for work in the car yesterday she said *Canny* and tried to climb in to." In De Laguna's grammar, the subject of the sentence is *you* (meaning her father); the predicate is *take me* (*Canny*).

In the same way that holophrastic utterances, by concentrating in a single word a sentence-full of meaning, constitute a revolutionary advance in the child's method of communication, so too is there a larger development in the overall behavior of the child, which Piaget characterized as a "veritable Copernican revolution of early childhood." This is the development of the concept of *object permanence*.

This concept is illustrated in the diary: "Today, long after I had put her ball in one of her hollow blocks, without being aware that she was watching me, she suddenly called out *ball* and, though she could not see it, walked straight to the block and pulled the ball out."

What was remarkable about this to the diarist was Candida's

having surreptitiously seen where the ball was put and then, much later, finding it immediately although it was out of sight. To Piaget [1969], on the other hand, the remarkable thing would have been her being able to locate the ball at all, even if it had been hidden in her plain sight a bare few minutes earlier: "The universe of the young baby is a world without objects, consisting only of insubstantial 'tableaux' which appear and are then totally reabsorbed either without returning, or reappearing in a modified or analogous form" [p. 14]. He observed that at the stage described here, his own children found it impossible to search for hidden objects. Although they were physically capable of moving the pillows, sheets, etc., that concealed the objects, the idea of doing so never seemed to occur to them. Jacqueline (8 months), for example, was in the act of reaching for a toy duck when Piaget threw a sheet over it. She immediately stopped reaching. Even when he made her feel through it, she made no attempt to remove the sheet, though she could have easily done so. She behaved, instead, as though the duck no longer existed.

Eventually the baby begins to search for hidden objects, but he searches in a peculiar way. Piaget noted that infants at this stage would only look for an object in a place where they had previously found it. He first observed this while watching his nephew Gerard (13 months) play with a ball. The ball rolled under an armchair and Gerard immediately dropped to his hands and knees and, with some difficulty, crawled in and retrieved it. Later the ball rolled under a sofa, too low to the ground to be crawled under. After watching it disappear, Gerard returned to the armchair and carefully explored the place where the ball had been found before.

Still later, the child learns to look for an object only in the place where it was last seen. Even at this stage, (10 to 18 months),however, the object concept is not complete. What is missing is a concept of invisible displacements. The child refuses to believe an object can change location while it is not visible to him. Children at this stage are easy victims of simple "magic tricks," for example, when one picks up a penny in one's left hand and, behind one's back, transfers it to the right hand. When both closed fists are presented to the child, he will persistently search in the left hand, showing perplexity at not finding it there. He apparently is unable to conceive that it might be in the right hand.

Finally the child learns that invisible objects not only continue to exist, but may even move around while out of sight. Having attained this level of development, Jacqueline Piaget, perhaps in reaction to her father's persistent experiments, contemptuously refused to search in "obvious" hiding places like a closed fist and could manage any number of invisible displacements.

The same hollow blocks with which Candy demonstrated her concept of object permanence allow her to demonstrate another ability: the ability to recognize pictures. The diarist says: "She enjoys looking at the pictures and identifying the figures."

Do children have to learn to see a correspondence between a picture and the object it represents? Hippolyte Taine [1877] discovered that his 12-month-old daughter could not perceive pictures. She had been shown a painting of the infant Jesus and learned to call it *baby*. Later, she used the word *baby* for all kinds of pictures, including still lifes and landscapes, provided they were framed. Taine concluded: "In fact, it is clear that the objects painted or drawn in the frame are as Greek to her; on the other hand, the bright square inclosing any representation must have struck her."

At first blush it might therefore seem that recognition of pictures for what they represent requires learning. Hochberg and Brooks [1962] perfomed an ingenious experiment to test this question. They reasoned that if learning is necessary, a child who has never had an opportunity for such learning, by never having had a picture "named" for him, should grow up unable to perceive pictures.

The little boy who served as a subject for their experiment was deliberately kept away from pictures of any kind from earliest infancy. He was not allowed to look at storybooks, illustrated pamphlets, or magazines. He was never taken to the movies or shown TV. The labels were even soaked off his baby food jars before he came in contact with them.

In spite of these precautions, he glimpsed billboards occasionally while in the car and, during the 19 months that the study continued, he managed a handful of glances at storybooks. Nevertheless, the precautions were considered adequate for the purpose of the experiment: up to the time that the test was given he had never had a picture *named* for him. Meanwhile he had been avidly learning the names of the real objects and people around him. His skill at this, and an inadvertent episode in which he caught sight of a TV and yelled *dog* excitedly at the horse on the screen, prompted the investigators to begin the test.

Fifteen Months Old

They used two sets of pictures—one of line drawings of objects familiar to the child and the other of photographs of the same objects. The child was shown the drawings first and then the objects. All of his naming responses were recorded.

The little boy named the pictures correctly in an overwhelming majority of cases. Thus the skill of picture recognition does not have to be learned separately from object recognition. Extensive exposure to pictures does not even seem to be necessary. And since the child named the line drawings before the photos, it appears that the former are recognizable in themselves, without the mediation of more realistic photographic images. In a similar vein, Piaget [1962] suggests that children may attribute more reality to pictures than adults do. Two-and-a-half-year-old Lucienne remarked of a picture book: "It's very heavy because there's a little girl inside."

Hochberg and Brooks noted one exception to the rule that perception of pictures develops without learning. They included a line drawing of a three-dimensional cube in their test set, and their subject was not able to recognize it. It seems that pictorial perspective cues are not spontaneously interpreted as depicting depth or three-dimensional space. T.G.R. Bower [1964] also found this in testing six-week-old infants' depth vision. Although the infants were able to perceive solid objects in depth and recognized that a 12-inch cube remains the same object when it is moved farther away (reducing its retinal size), they could not perceive depth represented pictorially and treated a photograph of the cube projected on a screen as a new thing entirely. Further support comes from Hudson's [1960] finding that African adults who had had no experience with pictures could recognize pictured objects readily but did not see pictures as representing three-dimensional space.

An interesting corollary to Hochberg and Brooks' results is an observation made by Allen and Beatrice Gardener [1969] of a chimpanzee named Washoe, to whom they taught the sign language of the deaf. When Washoe had learned names for real objects (for example, a live dog), she applied them spontaneously to pictures of the same objects (for example, a drawing of a dog in a book).

59

5
The
Third
Half Year

JULY 19: Today our daughter is 16 months old. She is 31 inches tall and weighs over 24 pounds--above average I believe. She is very much a real person. She talks, in single words, she runs, climbs, gets down by herself, enjoys pictures, likes to close and open boxes, and understands a surprisingly large amount of what we say. She is almost always amiable, is cross only when hungry or tired, or when barred from some place she wants to go. When she is cross, she hollers, but even her hollering is largely a matter of form: if it works, all right; if not, too bad. Except last Friday when she came out of the doctor's office crying as though her heart was broken. It was over a blue plastic duck she had specially selected among the toys made available in the waiting room for children to play with. She kept it all during her examination and bitterly resented having to give it up when she left. For a half hour in the car she cried for her lost "ducko". We got her something else and that made a little difference. Still from time to time she would say "ducko" and sob.

JULY 29: I find it hard to imagine what Candy's world must be like. Simple, surely. When Peggy carried her into the house this evening, still sleeping, I slammed the car door and she woke enough to say "Dot." To her I and an automobile exist together; when she sees a picture of a car or hears a horn blow she associates it with me. Her world has a small radius. Things far away are uninteresting to her, yet the tiniest picture close at hand of a dog, a "pony," or something else she recognizes will at once claim her attention. She delights in the familiar, perhaps because it is relaxing in a world so full of the unfamiliar. She enjoys doing or saying the same things over and over, though when it comes to toys, nothing pleases her more than a new one. What's more, she will know immediately at the first brief glimpse that it is new, that she has not had it before.

    She has now begun to develop her sense of smell, or to realize that she has such a sense. It's mostly still a matter of vigorous sniffing; I'm not sure that she has or recognizes a qualitative response, as between good and bad odors, for instance.

AUGUST 31: Candy still has not forgotten the toy duck she had to leave at her doctor's office. I happened to say that I would be seeing my doctor once a week during August even though I'm on vacation. Suddenly Candy began to cry "ducko." My mentioning doctor had reminded her of it. She didn't weep, of course, as she did the day she had to give it up but it was easy to see that her heart was still sore over it. All the toys and books she had been given in the six weeks since then were unable to take the duck's place in her affections.

The Third Half Year

Her vocabulary continues to grow. She is becoming more interested in verbs and uses quite a few besides "pick," "ride," and "smell," which were on a list I made a few weeks ago and seem now to have mislaid. I can't recall all of the new ones at the moment, but some are: "come," "walk," "go." She uses at least two adjectives: "nice" and "pretty;" and this evening she used the definite article for the first time, saying "duh ball" instead of simply "ball." She also recognizes negative contractions like didn't and wouldn't, and shakes her head, saying "no" when she hears them. "There isn't any more" is easily understood by her, as she shows by a confirming head shake and "no."

SEPTEMBER 10 (nearly 18 months): I can't help wondering what goes on in Candy's head. She catches on to things quickly, a new word, a new object, when she wants to; though it's often hard to tell when she will want to or why she did. And she remembers things tenaciously. Today, for·instance, we looked through a new book of hers, the Golden Book version of "The Three Bears." I identified as a dog a fox shown in the woods with Goldilocks——assuming this would make better sense to her and prevent confusion until she is able to understand why an animal might look like a dog and still be something different.

Peggy later went through the book with her and called it a fox, carefully pointing out its bushy tail in order to establish the distinguishing feature. Candy let her talk about it, then asked her again and again what it was. When Peg finally admitted it was a dog, Candy continued to quiz her, both about it and a bunny that Peggy had called a rabbit.

She likes the nursery rhyme, "Hark, Hark, the Dogs do Bark", probably because she knows that dogs really do bark. When she says, "Hark, hark", I complete the line for her. Then she says, "town" and I fill in, "The beggars are coming to town." Once I substituted "buggies" for "beggars." She questioned, "Buggies"?

She is apparently classifying things into two principal categories: those that change and those that do not. When she points, as she repeatedly does, to a familiar picture in order to have it identified, she is probably testing its mutability. Some things change rapidly; others slowly; some maybe not at all. That's what she proposes to find out.

Dogs, she has learned, may sometimes be puppies. May they also be foxes? Bunnies can be rabbits; lambs can be goats; yes, and boys can be girls. Not too long ago ducks were also chicks, but now she recognizes two entirely different species. Oddly enough, she isn't disturbed over a single word meaning several different things: her own limited control over consonants often makes this necessary. She can easily forgive it in others.

She has only just begun speaking her name. She uses it to indicate ownership or a desire to be included. When I left for work in the car yesterday she said "Canny" and tried to climb in too.

She was openly glad to see her Grandma today, and reminded us several times that the gift Grandma brought her did indeed come from "Dama." She calls her little neighbor Mary Michael, "Mike;" another neighbor, Mr. Newman, "Nume." She dances up and down when you talk of dancing, or of jigs, or playing the fiddle; and also when she hears music; sometimes just when she looks at phonograph records.

Charles Dickens wrote that "language was not powerful enough to describe the infant phenomenon." William James, however, tried to do so and suggested that the infant's world is one in which he, "assailed by eyes, ears, nose, skin and entrails at once, feels that all is one great blooming, buzzing confusion." This would, in all likelihood, describe the world of the adult as well, but for the adult's ability to attend selectively. At a party with a rock band playing and conversation going on all around, it is possible by means of this ability to sift out and attend to what one person is saying and ignore the rest of what assails one's ears.

Each age has its attention-getting stimuli. A two-day-old infant attends to a blinking light, a six-month-old to a lively conversation or a stranger's face; a mechanical rabbit will captivate the attention of a toddler, as will a comic strip that of a school child. For Candida at 16 months it was something close at hand which she recognized. As the diarist notes, "Things far away are uninteresting to her, yet the tiniest picture close at hand of a dog, a *pony,* or something else she recognizes will at once claim all her attention."

The Third Half Year

Jerome Kagan says the thread running through all of these attention-getting stimuli is their being both novel enough to be intriguing and familiar enough to be recognizable. The infant, for example, recognizes his mother's face and is familiar with such slight changes as occur when she changes position from full face to profile. He is intrigued by the discrepancy when she puts on a wig or pair of sunglasses.

Kagan suggests that a small discrepancy from the familiar is the optimum stimulus for attracting an infant's attention. An exact repetition of a stimulus for which the infant already possesses a schema, or mental copy, lacks interest since it provides no new information. The same is true of a stimulus so different from any of the infant's schemas that he has nothing to anchor it to. He finds evidence for this in laboratory studies such as one in which infants were shown pictures of human faces [1970]. In some of the faces, the features were in normal positions. In others, the features were scrambled, a mouth in the middle of the forehead, and so forth. Four-month-old infants paid more attention to normal than to scrambled faces. The mere fact of their being the faces of strangers was sufficient discrepancy for them. By the age of 13 months, however, interest was equal between the normal and the distorted faces, the normal face schema was becoming so well established that distortion was necessary to produce enough discrepancy.

In another study, a group of mothers gave their four-month-old infants daily exposure to a simple mobile. Three weeks later, they were shown a mobile in the laboratory, which was either identical to, similar to, or very different from the mobile they had seen at home. Kagan measured the amount of time each baby spent attending to the laboratory mobile. He found that the mobile which was merely similar to the one at home (rather than identical or very different) was the one that received the longest attention. He concluded that the infants had formed schemas of their home mobiles and that the laboratory mobile was most attractive to those for whom it constituted a moderate discrepancy from the schema.

Candida's lack of interest in objects at a distance might be attributed by some authorities to a lack of acuity of vision, which they contend is not complete until the age of 10. But, then, others maintain that acuity, though imperfect at birth, has attained adult levels six months later. Another visual deficiency of newborns stems from the fact that they do not accommodate the shape of their lens, hence their eyes have a fixed focus set for targets about 8 inches away.

Focusing improves rapidly during the first months of life, and by the age of four months it is quite precise.

As for the other senses, we read of Candida that, "She has now begun to develop her sense of smell, or to realize that she has such a sense. It's mostly just a matter of vigorous sniffing; I'm not sure that she has or recognizes a qualitative response, as between good and bad odors, for instance." This question begins with the neonate and with the very basic question of whether newborn babies can see, hear, feel, taste, and smell. Less than 100 years ago it was believed that human infants, like puppies, were deaf at birth (Preyer [1888]). However, recent experimental studies have shown that babies are born with all sensory systems fully functional. In fact, this sensory precocity, combined with extreme physical dependence, makes the human infant unique among newborn animals.

The presence of sight, hearing, and touch in infants at birth can be demonstrated by eliciting hereditary reflexes which depend on these senses. The *pupillary reflex* causes the newborn's pupil to contract before bright lights, the *rooting reflex* leads its head to turn toward a touch on the cheek, and the *Moro reflex* causes startling when loud sounds are heard.

There are no such simple reflex tests for taste and smell. Nevertheless, Jensen [1932] demonstrated a sense of taste in newborns using a procedure of flavored formulas. He measured the amounts of sugar water, salt water, sour milk, and regular fresh-milk formula an infant would drink and found no difference for any except salt water. Of this, they drank significantly less, proving they did have a functioning sense of taste. The sense of smell has been studied extensively by Lipsitt, Engen, and Kaye [1963]. Using breathing disruption and activity change as indices of excitement, they found that infants became more excited when scented cotton swabs were placed under their noses than with unscented swabs, indicating that odor caused the excitement. The odors used were vinegar, alcohol, anise, and asafetida.

Like Candida's father, these authors wondered whether infants could tell the difference between odors. Using a habituation procedure, they presented the scent of anise again and again until symptoms of excitement were no longer manifested. Then they presented asafetida. The infants became excited again, indicating they discriminated a difference and that a qualitative response to smell is present at birth.

It has been found, however, that this sense, like that of sight,

The Third Half Year

improves with age. Zaporozhets and Elkonin [1971] report on an experiment in which they used learning ability to measure sensitivity of smell. Children from four to seven years of age learned to identify odors: rose, anise, pine, and mint. They were required either to name the odor or point to a hard candy flavored with it. Most of the four-year-olds required more than 10 trials to learn to identify the smells, while the seven-year-olds ordinarily took less than 10 trials.

The improvement with age of sensory and perceptual abilities is attributed by Eleanor Gibson [1969] to what she calls *perceptual learning*. Perceptual learning, as she conceives it, is a lifelong occupation reaching even into adulthood, as, for instance, when an individual becomes a wine connoisseur and gradually acquires the ability to distinguish between different years of wine of the same vintage on the basis of subtleties of flavor.

Perceptual learning is most active in early childhood, as we see in the diary when Candida learns to perceive the differences between storybook pictures of foxes and dogs: "Peggy later went through the book with her and called it a fox, carefully pointing out its bushy tail to establish the distinguishing feature."

The distinguishing, or distinctive, feature is central to Gibson's theory of perceptual learning and, being a dimension of difference between stimuli, constitutes that which is learned. This Gibson contrasts with an older theory of perception in which what she called *prototypes,* or *templates,* constitute the learned material. A human face may be thought of, on one hand, as having distinctive features or dimensions in which all faces vary, such as nose length and breadth, hair color, and size of eyes. A prototype of the human face, on the other hand, is a complex pattern, such as a crafty face or an aged face.

Anne Pick [1965] conducted an experiment to test these two theories of perception. Stimuli were provided by changing three letter-like nonsense shapes in three different ways, for example, line-to-curve (V to U), reversal (b to d), and perspective (A to *A*). Five-year-olds were trained to match the shapes and then were divided into two groups for a transfer task. The first group were again shown the same forms as they were originally trained to match, but these had been changed in new ways—some were larger, some had been rotated 45 degrees, and so on. The second group were presented with new shapes entirely, but they were changed in the same way as the training set (line-to-curve, etc.) Again, the subjects had to match the forms. It was found that the second group of children did better than the first. This result supported Gibson's view that distinctive features, or transformations, are more important for perceptual learning than prototypes, or shapes. The first group could use their original prototype learning but had to learn new distinctive features, and they performed less well than the group for whom originally learned distinctive features remained relevant while prototypes changed.

Candida's need to learn a perceptual distinction between dogs and foxes was brought about by a conflict between her parents in the naming of these animals. Roger Brown [1958] has studied the question of how adults decide which of the many possible names for an object (for example, *Rover, dog, canine beast, quadruped*) to teach a child. He feels that in so doing, they "incidentally transmit the texture or grain of their reality" [p. 14].

Brown believes that in their dealings with one another, adults use the name which categorizes the object in the most commonly useful way. Thus a spoon is called *spoon* rather than *silverware* because spoons are treated differently from knives and forks. On the other hand, a spoon is not, as a rule, given a more specific name like *ill-washed restaurant spoon* or *heirloom sterling silver spoon with a chipped handle* because, for a spoon's usual purpose, a distinction of one spoon from another is not essential. Some things, like spoons, are given the same name by everyone, since everyone, except perhaps antique dealers who specialize in silverware, reacts to them in the same way. Other things, like fathers and pets, are given different names depending on their usefulness to the namer. A man is *Daddy* to his son, *Mr. Jones* to his neighbor, *policeman* when on the job, and simply *man* to a child who happens to see him in the church parking lot. To the last child, he is equivalent to all other adult males, while to the one calling him *Daddy* he is unique.

Brown suggests that while parents frequently teach children the names they themselves find most useful, a parent will occasionally make an effort to imagine the utilities of a child's life. The example he gives is teaching *money* as a name for dimes, nickels, and quarters to a preshopping-aged child who doesn't need to tell them apart. Another example is the diarist's: "I identified as a dog a fox shown in the woods with Goldilocks—assuming this would make better sense to her and prevent confusion until she is able to understand why an animal might look like a dog and still be something different."

Brown suggests that "the most deliberate part of first language

The Third Half Year

teaching is the business of telling a child what each thing is called." At the same time that Candida's vocabulary is growing through these deliberate efforts of her parents, another aspect of her command of language is progressing independently of their explicit teaching. Her grammar has already passed beyond the holophrastic stage recorded two months ago. Now, "she uses at least two adjectives: *nice* and *pretty*; and this evening she used the definite article for the first time, saying *duh ball* instead of simply *ball*."

In combining two words to form the first real sentences, most children use what has been called a *pivot grammar*. Pivot grammar consists of two classes of words, *pivots* and *opens*. The pivot class is small; each word in it is used very often in the child's speech. The open class contains all the remaining words in the child's vocabulary, including his previous sentence-words and most of the new words he learns. Each pivot word has its own fixed position in a pivot sentence. Most pivots occur first (for example, *allgone, more*) but some children also use pivots which can only occur at the end of a sentence (such as *on*). The rule for pivot grammar consists of combining a pivot word and an open word to form a two-word sentence. Since the position of the pivot word is fixed, the open word fits into whatever space is free. Thus sentences such as *allgone shoe* and *shoe on* are formed. All pivot sentences have one pivot and one open word; *pivot+pivot* sentences are almost never heard, and *open+open* sentences occur only later, as a product of a more elaborate grammar.

Candida's sentence *duh ball,* in the diary entry, is probably not a true pivot sentence since, if it were, other sentences like *duh door* and *duh dog* should also have been recorded. On the other hand, her *nice* and *pretty* are probably pivot words, since the diarist's calling them adjectives implies that they were used with different nouns. In the typical child's pivot grammar, both pivot and open classes contain a mixture of adult parts of speech, and adult adjectives, articles, verbs, and pronouns are frequently found within the pivot class.

Martin Braine [1963] has noted that children become ingenious, as well as prolific, with their pivot sentences. One child shot up from a mere 14 to over 2,500 different two-word sentences over a six-month period. A few examples of the pivot speaker's charming ingenuity were: *allgone sticky* (my hands are washed), *allgone outside* (the door is closed), *more page* (don't stop reading), and *more car* (drive around some more). Although none of these sentences is grammatically correct in adult English, they are all understandable outside of the context in which they were spoken, highlighting an important advance of pivot grammar over holophrastic speech.

The pivot grammar is not unique to English. Pivot constructions have been found in the early speech of French, Russian, Japanese, and Samoan children, to name a few. The universality of pivot grammar in the face of such a diversity of adult grammars suggests what is also obvious from the examples given, that pivot sentences are not simplified copies of adult sentences. Instead, children devise and make use of their own consistent grammatical system.

In describing Candida's reaction to the world at the age of 16 months, the diarist reports that "She delights in the familiar, perhaps because it is relaxing in a world so full of the unfamiliar." This is essentially Piaget's explanation of play.

In Piaget's theoretical terms, play is the opposite of imitation. While imitation primarily involves accommodation, play, in his theory, is any activity in which accommodation is heavily outweighed by assimilation. In the beginning, a child acquires a mental or motor skill through hard work (accommodation). But once it is well learned and presents no new challenges, the child may turn it into a game. For example, three-month-old Lucienne learned to cause a mobile over her crib to shake by kicking her legs. At first she studied the phenomenon seriously, apparently trying to understand the relationship between her own movement and the movement of the toy. But later, between four and eight months, when it seemed that she understood the relationship fully, "she never indulged in this activity . . . without a great show of joy and power" [1952]. The same thing happened to Piaget's son Laurent who, in the course of experiments on object permanence, learned to push a piece of cardboard aside to find a toy. He eventually learned the skill so well that, no longer interested in the toy, he would move the obstacle away for the fun of it, laughing all the while. Piaget concluded from these observations that familiar objects and activities are relaxing for the child because they do not require the mental effort necessary to cope with the unfamiliar.

6
18 Months Old

OCTOBER 17: Somebody has written that all thinking, or
at least reasoning, is a matter of discerning
similarities and differences. The repetitious
questions of a child seem to bear this out. Candy asks
over and over to have familiar objects identified. Then
by means of one-word questions (I sometimes wonder how
she manages to compress so much meaning into a single
word), she tries to compare one with another. Monkeys

have tails. So do bears. So does Bop. Does Canny! No. Does
Mom? No. Dot? No. Then around again, again, and again.
Evidently if she gets the same answer repeatedly, this
is something else she can depend on—at least
tentatively.

I say tentatively because it has been her experience
that the answers may change after awhile. The fox in
Goldilocks, for instance. I told her originally it was a
dog, and she sternly corrected her mother for calling it
a fox. But since then, a new book has introduced her to a
fox; she sees quite well how a fox differs from a dog.
Yesterday, going through Goldilocks for the 300th time,
I called it a fox. She passed over it quite
matter-of-factly. Evidently she has secretly known for
some time that it was a fox.

Then there are the sheep. Again, in the interest of
simplicity, we have been calling all sheep lambs. Little
Bo-Peep, however, must needs lose (and rhyme with) her
sheep. And Candy knows the rhyme quite well, for she
filled in the word "sheep" for me this evening. Then I
pointed to the picture of what we had been calling lambs
and said "sheep." There was a fleeting sign of
puzzlement on her face, then she dismissed it. "Of
course," she must have been thinking. "I suspected it
all along."

Still the comparing goes on. Between Bop and the rest
of the family. (She says "not" in relation to Bop,
anticipating the almost certain answer that Bop in this
particular respect is not what we are or does not do what
we do.) Between Dot who has a "tash" (mustache) and Mom,
Canny, and Bop who don't. Between things that she can hold
in her hands and pictures of things that defy her
attempts to hold them and cause her to cry "Hand! Hand!"
while she closes and opens them.

Candy's first thought when she picks up a book that
interests her, or when she gets a new one, is—"Toe;" and
an absolute necessity when she feels like going to the
"toe" is a book. She must have it read to her, or the
pictures explained at any rate; she refuses to look at it
by herself. The text is claiming more and more of her
interest, perhaps because she notices that the books
which interest me are all text. The letter "O" was the
first she was able to pick out of words in titles. Then
"D", "B", and "L". Now she even seems to be taking an

Eighteen Months Old

interest in individual words and what they say.

For some time she has been able to prompt us with key words in nursey rhymes, for example, "Hark", "bark", and "gown". Here is a more recent instance:

Candy (on seeing the rising moon): Cow.
Dot: Hey diddle diddle. The cat and the fiddle. The cow jumped over the moon.
Candy: Doggie.
Dot: The little dog laughed.
Candy: Port.
Dot: To see such sport.
Candy: Dish.
Dot: The dish ran away with the––
Candy: Poon.

Blackie has, of course, been re-christened Bop. Sometimes we forget and call him Blackie, then correct ourselves. Now Candy will occasionally say Bockie . . . Bop, just to show that she too forgets.

I threw barberries at a moth on our porch screen. A little later I took some pictures of Candy. When the pictures were processed, one of them showed her with outstretched arm, obviously issuing a command to her mother. I said it must be to give her a barberry to throw at the moth. Later when Candy was looking through the pictures and came to this, she said Barberry.

Her development, nevertheless, is uneven. Intellectually, as evidenced by her vocabulary and her wide range of interests, she is probably advanced for her age. Her physical capacities, too, seem higher than average. But emotionally she is still very dependent, still very much a baby. She insists on being fed though she is quite able to feed herself. She must have a bottle before going to bed, though when in the mood she can easily drink from a glass. She clings to her mother when visitors come and when she goes visiting. She plays alone only if she really is alone; when one of us is around, she cries Knee, and insists on being shown a book.

The fault is probably ours. It seems so unnecessary not to feed her, not to give her a bottle, not to read to her. It's difficult drawing the line between what is

best for the child and what is most convenient for the
parents.

NOVEMBER 7: Peggy and I went to the Michigan—Indiana
football game last Saturday with the Grissoms, who are
rabid fans. We were gone from noon till six, the first
time we had both been away from Candy at the same time.
Her grandmother stayed with her, took her for a walk
after lunch, and got her to her nap about two. Grandma had
plans for a tea party and when 5:30 arrived with Candy
still asleep, Grandma woke her up. She didn't want the
tea party to be skipped. Candy missed her mother and
asked for her repeatedly before going to sleep, but she
didn't cry. She was happy to see us come home and danced
excitedly and showed off in various ways.

She got the last two or three weeks have brought what seems to
me remarkable intellectual development. She not only
puts two words together, like "big dog," and enjoys
polysyllables like "thermostat" but she has started
forming sentences. Usually they consist of the two or
three most important words, with minor ones omitted in
between. Her memory of key words in nursery rhymes, and
in prose sentences she has had repeated to her, often
surprises me. Repetition can't be the only reason,
however. Some verses she has heard no more than once or
twice are as well remembered as the old standbys.

She gets a special pleasure in demonstrating talents
like this to her grandmother and others outside our
little circle. She enjoys acting, yawning, sneezing,
stretching, shaking at command, even pretending to
sleep. She drops her head on one shoulder and closes her
eyes.

She recognizes the different colors and identifies
them correctly when asked to point one out, but she often
makes mistakes when naming them herself. She counts from
one to six, omitting two and four in the process. She has
a lively interest in written words and asked over and
over this evening to have several words I had typed on a
sheet of paper identified for her. She herself correctly
identifies "ducks," "come," "to," and "farm" in the title
of one of the books she owns.

Lately, too, though still on a limited scale, she has
begun to play by herself, especially if she is left alone

Eighteen Months Old

outdoors. I seem to perceive also more self-assurance in
her contact with other people; so perhaps there was no
cause to worry about that a few weeks ago. What caused my
worry was the contrast between Candy's shyness at 19
months and the highly vocal self-expression of a
20-month-old girl we met at the Art Institute. She
pointed at Candy and shrieked, Girl! All Candy did was
look quietly back at her. And when the other girl
snatched at a rubber toy she was carrying, Candy let her
have it without any protest.

Little by little she is learning the consequences of
certain actions. She is acutely conscious of "hot" and
opposed to having even hot food near her. She holds her
hand over it to feel the heat radiating from it. When she
tears or breaks something, she often cries to have it
"back." At first she seemed to think failure to mend it was
an act of spite on my part, and protested bitterly. But
now she begins to see a connection between the act of
breaking and the less desirable, because it is broken,
thing.

She broke a plastic highball spoon the other day. The
loud snap scared her and perhaps a small piece stung when
it hit her. Anyway, she cried and cried "Back!" and pushed
the broken pieces on me. I tried to demonstrate that they
would not go "back" and at last she seemed to get the idea.
Maybe she was just tired and gave up for that reason.

Back to her memory. She remembers people who call,
like Hugh, Ces, and Fred. We had lunch a week or so ago at
the Fort Shelby with Hugh and Ces. Candy later spoke of
"Hess" and Hugh. I asked her if she remembered the lady
bringing her a high chair. She corrected me: Boy. And it
was a busboy, as Peggy recalled. I had forgotten. I spoke
again of the lady, saying she had put a napkin around
Candy's neck. Candy said, Pin. Yes, she had first tried
to knot it but, failing, had secured a safety pin and
pinned it on.

I suppose it looks as though I considered her
something of a prodigy. It isn't that, really. I do know
that she gets much more attention from both her parents
than most babies do. Few would spend the hours we spend
going through the same books with her, identifying
things, and trying so conscientiously to interpret her
half-formed words and repeat them correctly.
Incidentally, she is very conscious of pronunciation
deficiencies. Sometimes we fail to make out a new word

74

she says, and repeat it the way she says it. She
apparently thinks we are mocking her and she says it
over, trying a little harder to get it right. As it is,
she does unusually well with such tongue twisters as
"drink" and "cream," pronouncing them with hardly a
trace of babyishness. Her grandmother uses baby talk
with her but Candy blithely ignores such foolishness.

Yes, I'm perfectly satisfied that nothing that's
ever happened or ever could happen to me comes within
miles of meaning as much as Candy. I would like to write a
great book, good poetry, a novel, a play; but when I feel
discouraged because I haven't, I think of her and I'm
quite happy. I would like a second child but I know for
certain that the second child would also have to take
second place in my affections.

From the holophrastic speech and pivot grammar of the previous
chapters, with which the infant is believed to begin engaging in
discourse, we find Candida in the diary putting "two words together,
like *big dog*, and then "forming sentences. Usually they consist of
the two or three most important words, with minor ones omitted in
between."

Adults omit minor words from their speech, too, expecially in
newspaper headlines and when each word costs money as when
writing a telegram. Interestingly enough, they agree with the children
as to which words should be left out: articles, for the most part,
prepositions and auxiliary verbs. For this reason the telegram-like
sentences which children put together have been dubbed "telegraphic speech".

An exemplary telegraphic sentence used by Candida is *Bye Dot
car* (Daddy is going bye bye in the car). Roger Brown [1970] cites
others: *he go out* (he's gone out) and *Dog Pepper* (it's not the same
dog as Pepper). Since in each case the words the child retains are
those receiving heavier stress in the adult version, Brown suggests
stress in pronunciation as a reason why children adopt telegraphic
speech. The child would consider lightly stressed words relatively
unimportant, and these would be omitted. By the same token, heavily stressed words would be better remembered due to having been
heard more clearly. Support for this position comes from children's
reductions of polysyllabic words such as *giraffe* to monosyllables

such as *'raffe*. The stressed syllable is almost always the one retained. McNeill [1966], however, takes issue with Brown and points out that in languages with stress patterns different from those in English, children produce telegraphic speech very similar to telegraphic English.

Consequently, a second proposed explanation for telegraphic speech is based on the information content of the omitted words. Candida's *Bye Dot car* communicates information in a way that the words she omitted (*is going* and *in the*) could not. The nouns, verbs, and adjectives that are retained in telegraphic speech are sometimes called *contentives* because their information content is more important than their grammatical function in sentences. The reverse would be true of the omitted prepositions, articles, and conjunctions, which are called *functors*. The idea that children construct their telegraphic sentences to convey the maximum amount of information by means of the fewest possible words implies that they are able to analyze adult words for their information content.

Braine [1970] advances a third supposition, that children's learning of grammar proceeds from the most basic distinctions through successively finer ones. Thus a child who has learned the basic distinction between subject and predicate can produce a sentence such as *Pussycat chair*. Lacking knowledge of more subtle grammatical rules concerning the internal structure of predicate phrases, he cannot yet form the phrase, *is on the chair*.

By means of children's holophrastic utterances and pivot and telegraphic sentences, we are afforded some insight into the way in which young children acquire that most precious of all human abilities—the power of speech. Our next concern ought to be *how* it is done, how children learn to speak not only in words of the language they grow up in, but how they pick up speech mannerisms, intonations, and grammatical rules and turn them into intelligible sentences. We have several instances in the diary: "Blackie has, of course, been re-christened Bop. Sometimes we forget and call him Blackie, then correct ourselves. Now Candy will occasionally say *Bockie . . . Bop,* just to show that she too forgets".

The almost irrepressible urge in children to imitate their parents' habits of speech argues that imitation must be the major, if not the only source of language acquisition. As we shall see (p. 145), the diarist is surprised when Candida, at 21 months, learns a new word without imitating: "Nor did she repeat *dangerous* after me as she often does with words she hears for the first time. (Now that I think of it, she didn't repeat *pretending* either.) Today she climbed up on a small record cabinet, but asked while doing so, *Danger?*"

In this case, it is a question of vocabulary learning, but grammar and other aspects of speech are also thought to be learned through imitation. This theory holds that a child learns to combine words into sentences by echoing the sentences his parents produce.

Unfortunately the theory fails to account for the fact that children often speak sentences for which there is no adult model. Pivot sentences are a case in point. Ervin [1964] found that children appear to be unable to imitate grammatically correct adult sentences unless they are already using the required grammatical rule in their spontaneous speech. A child whose own speech obeys the rules of pivot grammar will convert the sentences he hears into pivot sentences. Hearing his mother say, *The stickiness is gone,* he blithely translates it into *Allgone sticky.* Lenneberg [1969] found it impossible to induce retarded children whose own speech was holophrastic to imitate two-word sentences, although they imitated novel single words with ease.

Since imitation appears to be unsatisfactory as a complete explanation for grammatical development, another theory has been proposed, based on a process called expansion, a process which has been neatly—if perhaps somewhat unjustly—characterized as one in which adults imitate children. Expansion occurs when an adult converts a child's ungrammatical utterance into a grammatical sentence. The diarist notes his own use of this technique: "Few would spend the hours we spend going through the same books with her, identifying things, and trying so conscientiously to interpret her half-formed words and repeat them correctly." Although other parents may be less aware of their use of expansion, Brown and Bellugi-Klima [1964] feel it is almost impossible to avoid doing it: "A reduced or incomplete English sentence seems to constrain the English-speaking adult to expand it into the nearest properly formed complete sentence."

The theory that grammatical development occurs by means of expansions is based partly on their prevalence as a result of this propensity of adults and partly on the effectiveness which should result from their perfect timing and revelance. When a child says *Mommy eggnog* and hears her mother expand it into *Mommy has had her eggnog,* the child can make an almost simultaneous comparison between her own reduced version and the correct adult alternative.

Eighteen Months Old

In addition, she can check the meaning of the two sentences by glancing at the empty eggnog glass.

Courtney Cazden [1965] performed an experiment to test the effect of expansion on a child's growing grammatical competence. Her subjects were nursery schoolers whom she divided into three groups. The children in the "expansion" group had daily conversation hours in which an adult expanded everything the child said. In a second group, called "expatiation," children were exposed to an adult who responded to the child's speech with a related statement. In a third, or control, group, children met with an adult for play that involved no conversation. After three months Cazden tested the children's grammatical progress. She found that the expansion group had improved a little more than the no-conversation group, but the expatiation group had improved far more than either. In other words, simple conversation was more effective than expansion in grammatical development.

More recently, however, Nelson, Carskaddon, and Bonvillian [1973] found that "recast" sentences, which consisted of expansions when the child's own sentence was ungrammatical and an alternative grammatical form of the same sentence when the child's sentence was correct, facilitated grammatical development more than the expatiation treatment of Cazden's second group.

The explanation for the seeming conflict in these results may be that when an adult's expansion misinterprets what the child was trying to say, it does more harm than good, by confusing him. An example of this is the diarist's inappropriate expansion of Candida's *gay mittens* at age two: "Last evening I put the dice boxes on her hands and called them mittens . . . This morning, when she spoke of going outdoors and putting on her gay mittens, I couldn't grasp what mittens she was talking about. She explained further—her cup mittens. Still I didn't know. She repeated *Gay mittens. Day mittens?* I asked foolishly. Candy blew up. Of course she was saying, *Game mittens,* the ones made from backgammon dice cups".

Mistakes of this kind may have occurred more often in Cazden's experiment, where expansions were given for everything the child said than when the alternative recasts of grammatical sentences were also used.

Still a third theory rejects both imitation and expansion as being the major means of language acquisition. It holds that the universal grammar which underlies all languages is not learned, but that "the human nervous system contains a mental structure that has an 'innate' concept of human language" (Chomsky [1967]). Chomsky argues that neither imitation nor expansion, nor any other explanation that attributes grammatical competence to learning, can explain how all children, bright and dull alike, do what no other animal can, and spontaneously master an incredibly complex grammatical system, all within the space of a few short years. The ability to speak correctly must, he holds, like the ability to speak at all, be inherent; that what the child learns at his mother's knee are the peculiarities of his native tongue which distinguish it from earth's other languages.

Following in the footsteps of the poet Shelley who wrote, "He gave man speech and speech created thought, which is the measure of the universe," a look at how children think ought logically to follow our discussion of how they develop the art of speech. It is in this cognitive area of developmental research that Jean Piaget has done his most important work.

One of the first forms of thinking to develop in the child, according to Piaget, is that illustrated in the diary record of Candida's 14th month: "If you say *mosquito* or *bites*, she will slap her head". Again, the diarist noted that at nearly 18 months: "She dances up and down when you talk of dancing, or of jigs, or playing the fiddle; and also when she hears music; sometimes just when she looks at phonograph records".

Piaget called such instances of thinking through action, "motor representation," indicating that motor movement stands for, or represents, the thing being thought about. This evidence of thought is typically manifested when the infant is between the ages of 12 and 18 months.

Thus, when Piaget's own daughter Lucienne was 16 months old, he hid from her an attractive watch chain, concealing it inside a slightly opened matchbox. After trying unsuccessfully a number of times to reach her finger in and take hold of the chain, Lucienne paused, looked attentively at the box and then slowly and deliberately opened and shut her mouth, and again, wider and wider. After this, she pulled the box open and retrieved the chain. Piaget interpreted the mouthing as her way of thinking about the fact that the box was a cavity, the opening to which had to be enlarged. This motor representation constituted visible evidence of her thought as she worked out the solution to a perplexing problem. He wrote: "Due to inability to think out the situation in words or clear visual images she

Eighteen Months Old

uses a simple motor indication as a 'signifier' or 'symbol'" [1952, p. 338].

Bruner, Olver, and Greenfield (1966) see the three forms of thought here identified by Piaget—motor, visual imagisitic, and verbal—as constituting a developmental progression. Like Piaget, they postulate that motor representation, or "enactive representation" as they call it, is the first to develop and predominates in the thought of the two-year-old. This motor symbolism, however, has several limitations. It is bulky; it takes much longer, for example, for Candida to act out a dance than to visualize an image of one. It is restricted; abstract concepts, do not lend themselves to being represented in a motor manner. It is also highly personal and individualistic. The child's motor symbols, unlike those of the professional pantomimist, are apt to be meaningless to other people.

For these reasons, the child is led to develop a second form of thought—Bruner's "ikonic representation"—which takes over many of the functions of enactive symbolism. An ikonic representation is a visual image of the object or event being thought about. It is more like a blueprint than a photograph; some of the details in the image stand out clearly in the mind's eye, while others remain a blur. This form of thought, according to Bruner, predominates around the age of four, after which a third form of thought, "symbolic representation," gradually increases in importance to become the predominant mode of thought for adults. Symbolic representation is epitomized mainly in verbal and mathematical thought.

And observation by Vygotsky [1962] supports Bruner's view that motor imagery develops before verbal thought. Vygotsky had children either describe in words or act out in pantomime the main content of a set of pictures he showed them. The youngest children were able to render the sense of the pictures through action but could not do so in their verbal descriptions.

The predominance of verbal over visual imagery in adulthood is supported by another experiment (Carmichael, Hogan, and Walter [1932]). Adults were shown an ambiguous drawing such as a pair of circles joined by a straight line. One group was told it represented a pair of glasses and the other that it represented a set of dumbbells. Later, when asked to draw the figure from memory, subjects modified the original drawing, the glasses group by bending the line that joined the circles, and the dumbbell group by thickening it. In both groups the visual image had been distorted by memory of the verbal label.

Thus, while Shelley's verse may correctly describe the workings of the adult mind, Piaget's and Bruner's work suggests that speech does not create thought developmentally. Piaget even goes so far as to suggest that thought creates speech, in that certain basic cognitive operations must develop before the child can speak meaningfully.

Support for this position is found in Hans Furth's work with deaf children [1964, 1971]. He found that in many tasks involving cognition, perception, and memory, deaf children performed on a par with normal children of the same age, even though the latter's command of language was far superior. Among those tasks in which deaf children were deficient there were some in which they seemed to develop the same type of thought as normal children but at a slower rate. Furth reported that "investigations seem to emphasize as legitimate the distinction between intellective and verbal skills. The ability for intellective behavior is seen as largely independent of language and mainly subject to the general experience of living. Various sources of empirical evidence confirm the theoretical position that, just as language learning is not closely related to intellectual endowment, so intellective performance is not directly dependent on language" [1964, p. 162]. He concluded that "thinking processes of deaf children are similar to those of hearing children and therefore must be explained without recourse to verbal processes . . . Insofar as Piaget stated categorically that language is not a constituitive element of logical thinking, it is intriguing to consider that the evidence collected in this review provides as strong empirical support as can be expected for this theory" [1971, p. 70].

The ways of thinking that a child uses are each peculiarly appropriate both to his needs and to his environment. As already noted, the motor, or enactive, mode of thought serves the infant well enough in the bosom of his family, who know him so intimately that they can interpret his gestures. As his thinking matures, along with the expansion of his range of experience, enactive representation becomes inadequate, and something like the ikonic becomes necessary to handle his thought's increasing spaciousness. Finally, as the child ventures outside the family circle into the larger social world, among people who cannot be relied on to interpret his gestures and visual symbolism, he finds that nothing but verbal language will serve to communicate his thoughts. Thus thought itself takes on an abstract and symbolic quality.

Expansion of the social horizon begins in infancy. Although an infant's most extensive and important social contact is typically with

Eighteen Months Old

his parents and secondarily with other adults, he will, when given the opportunity, demonstrate a lively interest in other babies. Almost from birth, infants respond to one another's crying; they look closely at one another and show no stranger fear (Lewis and Brooks-Gunn [1972]). There is a rather certain developmental progression in these social relationships, yet, tied with age though they be, they are strongly influenced by social circumstances. Children from large families move much more rapidly up the ladder of social interchange with their peers than do single children such as Candida.

Nowhere is this more poignantly brought out than in the brief encounter the 19-month-old Candida had with a girl only one month her senior. "She pointed at Candy and shrieked, *Girl!* All Candy did was look quietly back at her. And when the other girl snatched at a rubber toy she was carrying, Candy let her have it without any protest".

Maudry and Nekula [1939] studied patterns of interaction in infants from six months to two years old. Their method consisted of putting two babies together in a playpen along with toys such as a ball, which encouraged social interaction. They uncovered three stages in the development of peer social behavior. During the first stage, which lasted from the 6th through the 8th month, the infants were interested in neither each other nor the toys. They spent most of their time looking around the room, and each seemed happiest when the other baby had all the toys.

The second stage covered the 9th through the 13th month and was one of interest in toys. There was still no real social behavior. Infants fought one another to get at the toys, but in fighting, they pushed the other child aside as though he were an inanimate object and they expected no retaliation. True social behavior became increasingly apparent as the infants approached the age of two years. By 19 months there was some smiling, looking, and grasping of the other infant, to an extent which led the authors to conclude that babies were by now more interested in playmates than play materials. The children even made some attempts to coordinate their play, for example, by one child picking up a drum stick when the other was beating a drum.

Harlow [1965] found a similar set of stages for young monkeys and their interactions with one another. He defined these as a *reflex* stage during which the monkeys clung to one another, an *exploration* stage in which each poked and probed the other as if it

82

were an inanimate object, and a stage of *interactive* play which, by involving vigorous roughhousing, might be judged to parallel the second stage of human infant play as defined by Maudry and Nekula.

Mildred Parten [1932] studied social interaction in children from age 2 to 5. She grouped play activity into six categories: unoccupied behavior (no play of any kind), solitary play, onlooker behavior (stands near and watches other children at play), parallel play (children play beside one another, using the same toys, but do not interact), associative play (sharing toys, taking turns), and cooperative play (divide tasks to work toward a common goal). Parten found that as children get older their play progressed through the categories she delineated, from unoccupied behavior to cooperative play. She also found that two-year-olds played mainly in groups of two, while five-year-olds spent a considerable amount of play time in groups of five or more.

7
Almost
Two

DECEMBER 24 (21 months): Even though Candy can have
little notion what it is that she calls Christmas, our
own preparations have had more purpose because of her.
This alone would be enough to make it preeminently a
children's holiday. She will like the Christmas tree,
but mainly I believe for the glass ornaments that, being
balls, ought to be thrown and bounced. She has seen Santa
Claus several times and connects him with this thing

called Christmas. She has even agreed not to open a
Christmas package that arrived in the mail until
"Christmas," after having it in her hands. And when she
sees her new toys tomorrow morning their sheer volume
should make Christmas memorable if nothing else does.

I probably underestimate the amount she is capable
of understanding and remembering about an occasion like
this. The other day she declared, and correctly too, of
something she was doing that it was "pretending." Weeks
ago I explained, briefly and in passing, that we were
pretending she was riding a horse. I had no idea at all
that she understood me even in the slightest degree.
It's the kind of abstract concept that flies in the face
of reality: the notion of doing something you are not
really doing. Yet she evidently did grasp it.

Then I have told her once or twice in the past that
walking on a bed or standing on something high without
support is dangerous. I hesitated to use the word and I
wonder now why I didn't simply say, "You might hurt
yourself," but I didn't. Nor did she repeat "dangerous"
after me as she often does with words she hears for the
first time. (Now that I think of it, she didn't repeat
"pretending" either.) Today she climbed up on a small
record cabinet, but asked while doing so, "Danger?"

There are some round butter cookies that she
especially likes and she calls them "cakes." This is
partly because they resemble the cake pictured in her
pat-a-cake story. We haven't had any in the house for the
past few weeks, but when we last did, she was given the
empty box with the Baker Maid trademark on it. I called
her attention to the baker man (as in the pat-a-cake
rhyme), then corrected myself and said "Baker Girl."
Peggy bought a new package yesterday, evidently under
Candy's eyes. This noon she asked for "Cookies; no,
cakes. Baker man—baker GIRL."

JANUARY 9: Christmas was indeed a special occasion,
taking me all the way back to the days when I was
young—though not quite as young as she—and Christmas
was the one big day of the year. Candy enjoyed opening her
presents and playing with her new toys, especially a
doll that she readily agreed to call Peggy. She got two
bears from outside the family and these were also named
with our help, one Frank, the other Bruno. But to a little

85

Almost Two

dog pull-toy she herself gave the name of Dasher and she also by herself named a reindeer: Cranberry. A hammer and peg toy claimed her attention for a minute or so; unfortunately it was badly put together, so Peggy packed it away, meaning to exchange it. Candy raised no objection, for there were many other things to distract her. Peggy forgot to exchange the toy, forgot indeed the toy itself until suddenly, several days later, Candy began crying for her hammer. What hammer? Nobody dreamed it could be the toy she had played with so briefly. She was shown a couple of other hammers that she used to play with, but Candy stoutly insisted on having a special one. Then a couple days after that, while Candy was outdoors, I remembered the forgotten and still un-exchanged toy and managed to repair it. Candy came in. Nothing was said by any of us. She played with it awhile, then spoke up: "Dot found it?"

Right now she is learning tenses: corrected herself when she had said "Candy see it" to "Candy SAW it," with emphasis on "saw." The mystery to me is how she'll catch on about pronouns. She is always "you" when we speak to her, so naturally "you" to Candy means Candy. On the other hand, when she asks to see "my arm" she means the arm of one of us. She makes up new sentences constantly, plays by herself more than she used to (though she much prefers to have one of us play with her), understands and says in correct context things like "reflection," "following," "please," "thanks." How she learned the special urgency of "please" is hard to explain, except that she must have heard me do it and has turned what is usually an imperative with me into a blandishment by her.

She has become more demonstrably affectionate with me, having long been so with her mother. She enjoys having us draw pictures and likes to try it herself; enjoys dancing too and seems to be acquiring a better sense of rhythm. Wild running and general rambunctiousness are other natural developments, along with climbing. She knows and recites whole nursery rhymes from beginning to end, makes considerable use of "yes"—whereas it was not so long ago that practically her only answer to a question was "no." She has had surprisingly few temper tantrums or other manifestations of the negative phase that girls of her

86

age are supposed to go through. She usually accepts the answer "no" when she asks for something, especially if a reason is given, even though she does not always understand the reason. On the other hand, when she sees her own "no" accepted against our own better judgement, she often changes her mind.

JANUARY 27: This is the time more than any other in my life that I shall look back on with nostaligia. Merely anticipating it, I can feel it as keenly as though the experiences I am living through now were already in the dim and distant past. When I'm playing with Candy and she laughs and gasps out, "No Dot doing that!" I feel a pang as though it were something long ago that I shall never know again. So it is when she pleads, "Mom help you," or, on the other hand, says with so much satisfaction in her throaty voice, "Mom helping you." So it is in a hundred other things she says and does: her languid way of waving good-by or good night; her play at table, holding her spoon in her teeth or sticking her finger in her mouth to pretend she doesn't want to eat; her "no, no" when I ask her something and her repeating "no, no" until I agree that she doesn't have to do it or have it, whatever it is: her banging her doll's head against her own and then saying, "Poor head," so that Peggy or I will caress it (her head, not her doll's); her pushing her face into mine and crying, "Do-ot!" or "Dot-tee!"

MARCH 1: Candy is nearly two years old and we are taking our first vacation trip with her. Being with her all day long, helping her at meals, playing with her, and listening to her chatter in the seat beside me are the nicest thing about the trip. Each day she reveals some new aspect of growth and independence. Today, for example, as we were leaving our motel in Dallas, she climbed in the car by herself. Spring flowers are blossoming down here and trees are coming into leaf. Our pace, except when we were fleeing the ice and later the tree pollen, has been leisurely, and promises to continue so as long as good accommodations can be found spaced near enough together.

Eating out all the time, Candy is constantly meeting new people. As a result she is less shy, more willing to respond when they greet or smile at her, and she enjoys the attention they give her. She mugs at them, even forgetting in her desire to make an impression that her mother and I are at the table.

She is growing ever more inventive in conversation, expressing her own thoughts with original sentences instead of merely repeating sentences we use or sentences she hears from her books or that she herself has used before. These latter still constitute the bulk of her conversation, but the original sentences to fit the occasion are cropping up more and more frequently.

I asked her the other day how she liked one of the motor court apartments which she and her mother had given a preliminary inspection to. She thought awhile and said: "The chairs were nice. The little bed were nice."

One aspect of social behavior that has been noted by many observers over the years is what is called "two-year-old negativism." The response of the typical child in this phase to almost every question, suggestion, or offer of help is *no*. He often uses *no* in ways that would pose a logical contradiction for an adult, as, for example, when he says *no* to an offer to go for a ride in the car and then, when asked whether he would rather stay home, says *no* to that as well.

Not all children pass through the negativistic phase. Candida appears to be one of the exceptions, since the diarist remarks: "She has had surprisingly few temper tantrums or other manifestations of the negative phase that girls of her age are supposed to go through. She usually accepts the answer *no* when she asks for something, especially if a reason is given, even though she does not always understand the reason. On the other hand, when she sees her own *no* accepted against our own better judgment she often changes her mind." Nevertheless, one of the sidelights of negativism is the fact that children learn and use the word *no* before the word *yes*, which is remarked on in the diary: "She . . . makes considerable use of *yes*—whereas it was not so long ago that practically her only answer to a question was *no*."

A number of theories have been advanced to explain two-year-old negativism. One, a learning theory, focuses on the perplexity which logically inconsistent negation produces in the child's parents.

The assumption is that manifestations of this perplexity—such as showing the child extra attention in order to discover what he really wants or trying to talk him into one or another alternative or getting angry—are interesting and enjoyable for the child. The diarist offers such an explanation (p. 84) for Candida's frequent use of the word *why*: "Curiously enough, her first word that is not a noun is *why*. She loves the word without yet having a clear idea what it means, possibly because it evokes such a satisfactory response from her parents. Hence she says it often and sometimes most appropriately."

Another theory explains negativism as a manifestation of growing independence. During toddlerhood the child begins to recognize himself as an individual separate from his parents. Some indication of this development in Candida is seen in her choice of words for refering to herself. From the use of third-person names for herself such as *bay* (baby) and *Canny* (Candy), she progressed through use of the second person *you* ("She is always *you* when we speak to her, so naturally *you* to Candy means Candy") to eventual reference to herself in the first person, as seen at the age of two when she asked, "Have I stopped hollering?" According to the independence theory, when the child first develops a sense of self, he feels compelled to display the fact that he is an independent being on any and all occasions. Thus he says *no* simply to show he is someone different from his parents, with a different viewpoint from theirs. According to this theory, negativism is a healthy manifestation of the developing personality and not necessarily something to be curbed. Such a view would prescribe that parents do as Candida's evidently did and accept the child's *no* occasionally, even when doing so goes against their "own better judgment."

Martha M. Reynolds [1951] conducted an experimental study aimed at verifying the presence of negativism in toddlers and discovering at what age it begins to disappear. Her subjects were 229 preschool children. She examined each of them individually in situations designed to bring out any negativism that might be present. One, called *surrender of personal liberty,* involved placing the child on her lap with no explanation and noting any signs of resistance. In the other three situations, she requested that the child do something (imitate her headshake, build a tower of blocks, or repeat digits) and observed whether or not he attempted to comply.

She found clear indications of negativism at age two and that it gradually decreased through age five. It also appeared that negativism declined with age, no matter how parents attempted to handle it.

Another social phenomenon of infancy to which psychologists have addressed themselves is that of *attachment*. As used in psychology, it refers to a child's striving to be close to, fondled, or spoken to by the particular person he is most closely attached to. Among those who have studied the phenomenon, Schaeffer and Emerson [1964], in their work among Scottish infants, found that under the age of about seven months, infants showed no strong attachment to a specific person. They enjoyed being picked up and objected to being put down, but it made little difference to them whether the one doing the picking up was their mother or a total stranger. Between seven months and a year, the babies formed a single specific attachment, usually to the mother. The strength of this specific attachment did not necessarily depend on the amount of time she spent alone with the child. A more important factor was the speed and efficiency with which she responded to his needs. Ultimately Schaeffer and Emerson found the babies again broadening their attachments to include the father and other members of the family. By 18 months, 88 per cent of the infants they studied were attached to at least two people. We note in the diary that Candida was 22 months old when her father wrote, "She has become more demonstrably affectionate with me, having long been so with her mother."

Various theories have been offered to account for attachment. One, advanced by John Bowlby [1969], equates it with the instinct found in birds, which has itself been extensively studied by the ethnologist Konrad Lorenz [1952]. One of the best known of Lorenz's demonstrations is that in which he separated a group of newly hatched goslings from their mother, after which they began following him around. When he later tried to return them to their mother, they ignored her and continued to follow Lorenz. From the normal behavior of infant geese to follow their mother, Lorenz postulated a process called imprinting, which causes them to follow the first moving object they see after hatching. In Bowlby's analogy, human infants—watching the mother, listening to her, finding comfort in her arms and crying when she goes away—are behaving in a way similar to that of young birds, the principal difference being that, even at seven months, they are still too helpless to follow her around. Another difference is that whereas imprinting gradually dies out as the bird gets older, human attachment strengthens with age and broadens to include new attachment figures.

A second theory of attachment is one based on the Freudian concept of anaclitic identification. In this it is held that the infant's anxiety about what might happen to him should he be separated from his mother prompts him to become as close to her and as much like her as he can. Still another theory offers to explain attachment as due to a conditioning or learning process (for example, Sears [1963] and Whiting and Child [1953]). According to this theory, early in infancy the baby comes to recognize that whenever something pleasant is happening to him—being fed, rocked, or having his diaper changed—his mother is near by. By contrast, when he is unhappy because of cold or hunger, his mother is not around. Thus the infant learns an association between seeing his mother and feeling good, and this learned connection is the basis of his attachment to her. He seeks to relieve unpleasant feelings by drawing close to her.

The Harlows (for example, 1967) whose nearly lifelong study of rhesus monkeys has already been referred to, conducted a series of experiments aimed at disclosing the determinants of attachment in their primate subjects. They concentrated on the two variables of feeding and contact comfort and to this end built artificial mothers for the monkeys. One was made of wire and held a nursing bottle; the other was simply of soft terry cloth. The Harlows found that although the monkeys regularly nursed from the wire "mothers," it was the cloth mothers they became attached to. They clung to them in the cage and turned to them in times of fear, just as a normal monkey does to his real mother. The Harlows concluded that, for monkeys at least, cuddling is a more important determinant of attachment than feeding. It was not just a case of "out of sight out of mind." One year after being separated from their cloth mother, the monkeys remembered her and returned to cling to her. Thus the experiment had the twofold value of throwing light on the subject of attachment and confirming the presence in infant monkeys of a long-term memory which spans up to at least one year.

The memory of human infants and children has also been studied experimentally although unfortunately, not nearly enough. Some 40-odd years ago, C. Buhler [1930] let infants play with a ball which, when squeezed, released a chicken. Later, at varying intervals of time, subjects were shown what appeared to be the same ball, except that when it was squeezed, it failed to release a chicken. By noting whether the infants showed surprise over not finding the chicken, Buhler measured their memory. Her results gave a maximum memory span of 1 minute for infants up to 11 months old, 8 minutes for up to 17 months old, 15 minutes for up to 20 months old, and 17 minutes for up to age 2.

This laboratory method may, however, underestimate the amount a child is capable of remembering about events in his natural environment. Zaporozhets and Elkonin [1971], basing their estimates on diary records, write: "During his second year, the child recognizes familiar people and common objects after several weeks; during the third year, after several months; and during the fourth year, even after a year" [p. 91]. This, we see, was true of 17-month-old Candida: "Candy still has not forgotten the toy duck she had to leave at her doctor's office. I happened to say that I would be seeing my doctor once a week during August even though I'm on vaction. Suddenly Candy began to cry *ducko*. My mentioning doctor had reminded her of it . . . All the toys and books she had been given in the six weeks since then were unable to take the duck's place in her affections."

Although in these and other data, a regular increase in memory span is revealed during the early years of childhood, this is not what psychologists mean when they speak of "short-term" and "long-term" memory. Instead, they refer to two different memory processes, each present throughout the lifespan and each operating according to different principles. The short-term memory covers a span of at most about 30 seconds; long-term memory covers any period longer than that. Short-term memory stores everything a person notices—or to use a technical term, everything that is *encoded*. Long-term memory iş more selective; only information that has been specially processed (by rehearsal) goes from short-term to long-term memory.

The studies cited above indicate that long-term memory span increases with age. A developmental improvement in short-term memory has also been noted. A.S. Starr [1923], for example, found that the average four-year-old can echo back four spoken digits, while the average 15-year-old can echo as many as seven.

Several processes have been found to be important in determining how well information will be stored in and retrieved from long-term memory. One is the memory test. The two most commonly used are *recall* and *recognition*, the difference being illustrated, respectively, by having to supply a person's name or having to pick it out of a list of printed names. Like adults, children find recognition much easier than recall. E.M. Achilles [1920] studied children between 8½ and 11½ and found the ratio of recognition to recall to be 24 to 5 for words, 10 to 4 for forms, and 9 to 2 for syllables.

Almost Two

Using a third method called *relearning*, Harold Burtt [1951] tested the long-term memory of a single child over a period of several years. He began when his subject was 15 months old and continued to his third birthday, reading him passages of Greek tragedy in the original Greek (the child spoke only English). When the boy was 8½, he was required to commit passages from the same Greek play to memory. Some were those that had been read to him in infancy; others were entirely new. The average number of repetitions required to memorize the old passages was 317 compared with 435 for the new ones. Burtt concluded that some memory of the original readings had remained over the five-and-a-half year period. Additional tests were given at ages 14 and 18, and on both occasions new passages were memorized as easily as those previously exposed, indicating a probable total loss of memory of the readings.

Another important factor affecting storage of information in memory is the amount of attention paid to the material to be remembered on its initial exposure. That the need for such attention is generally recognized is evidenced in the surprise the diarist shows over an incident concerning Candida's memory at 20 months: "A hammer and peg toy claimed all her attention for a minute or so; unfortunately it was badly put together, so Peggy packed it away, meaning to exchange it. . . Peggy forgot to exchange the toy, forgot indeed the toy itself until suddenly, several days later, Candy began crying for her hammer. What hammer? Nobody dreamed it could be the toy she had played with so briefly."

The importance of attention in memory is indirectly implied in the analysis of a study concerned with the effect of anxiety on memory (Messer [1968]). One group of third-grade children were made anxious by experiencing failure in a problem-solving task before a story was read to them. Two other groups, one which succeeded in the task and one which did not have to do it, were not troubled by anxiety. When asked to recall details of the story, the anxious group made more errors than the other two groups. Their apparent lapse of memory was attributed to anxiety having distracted their attention from the story's content.

Two processes that are known to facilitate memory are the related ones of *verbal coding* and *rehearsal*. Candida makes use of the first when she remembers a photograph by the verbal code her father applied to it. "When the pictures were processed, one of them showed her with outstretched arm, obviously issuing a command to her mother. I said it must be to give her a barberry to throw at the

93

Almost Two

moth. Later when Candy was looking throught the pictures and came to this one, she said, *Barberry*."

Charles Spiker [1956] suggests that verbal coding aids memory at least partly because a name constitutes a convenient device for rehearsal. Rehearsal, or the act of going over an item in one's mind during the interval between its presentation and an active attempt to recall it, is a powerful memorizing technique. Again, the diarist expresses surprise when, at 28 months, Candida remembers something without this apparent rehearsal: "*Mom,* Candy ordered impatiently, *wash C-A-N-D-Y.* We have spelled her name aloud for her from time to time as we printed the letters. Not very recently, nor did we ever try to get her to repeat it. But there it was in her memory all the time."

Flavell, Beach, and Chinsky [1966] studied verbal labeling and rehearsal in kindergarten, second-grade, and fifth-grade children. In their task, one experimenter pointed to a picture, and the child was required to remember which picture it was for 15 seconds and then point to it himself. During the 15-second delay, another experimenter listened and lip-read for signs of the child rehearsing the name to himself. Very few of the kindergartners, about half the second-graders, and almost all the fifth-graders rehearsed. The ability to remember the pictures increased correspondingly with grade level. Flavell and his associates concluded that the kindergartners' unwillingness or inability to rehearse was responsible for their poorer memories.

The motivation of the child faced with a memory task is stressed by Zaporozhets and Elkonin [1971] who hold that under the age of about four, memory is strictly involuntary, and "the child of this age cannot yet set himself a goal to memorize or recall" [p. 105]. Later, they say, the child begins to show some capacity for voluntary memory but still requires more concrete motivation than the simple instruction, given either by an adult or by himself, *remember this.* They cite an experiment in which a researcher studied children's memory in three situations: laboratory (the child is simply instructed to remember, no reason being given), play (memory is required for success in a play activity such as a treasure hunt), and practical (memory is necessary for the child to fulfill an "important" assignment given him by an adult.) She found that 3- to 7-year olds remembered better in the play task than in the laboratory and best of all in the context of practical activity.

The distinction Zaporozhets and Elkonin make between voluntary and involuntary memory could explain the wide gap between the generally poor showing of young children in laboratory studies of memory (for example, Buhler [1930] and Flavell, Beach, and Chinsky [1966]) and the excellent memory displayed by two-year-old Candida: "Her way of asking questions out of the blue: *What did the little girl have in her hand?*—in all probability something we saw a week or two ago and I have forgotten. But not Candy. I sometimes doubt that she forgets anything." Candida's involuntary memory registers details no adult would set out deliberately to remember and which she herself might well be incapable of memorizing on command.

8
Two
Years
Old

MARCH 21: During the four weeks of our southern trip, as we circled around through Houston, New Orleans, Mobile, Atlanta, and Winston-Salem, North Carolina, where Candy met her grandfather and step-grandmother, I was with her almost constantly. Hence such changes as occurred in her escaped my notice, but as soon as we got home and I could see her against her familiar background, they stood out clearly.

She has grown noticeably taller. Her command of

language, especially in the formation of original
sentences to suit an occasion, is considerably greater.
She is now beginning to develop new ideas. For example,
we were comparing her with Bop, how she could eat with a
spoon and how much smarter she is. She suggested: "Bop
needs to have hands." The idea, I feel, implicit as it may
have been in the spoon suggestion, is still rather
striking. I am sure we have never discussed that basic
difference between humans and animals, nor, I believe,
do people in general consciously see it as a critical
difference, else anthropologists would not feel the
need to remark on it in their books. In Candy's own books,
where animals tend to be humanized, they succeed in
using their paws with as much facility as if they were
hands.

APRIL 6: Candy continues to grow in stature and
self—expression, but her growth is now so gradual that I
can hardly put my thumb on any phase of it. I notice
things—such as her concern over the proper case when
she uses a pronoun—but each of them individually is
rather slight and hardly seems worth jotting down. (That
is what I should do, though.)

I got home early this afternoon. The sun being
bright, even though the air was cold, we drove to the
park. Candy and her mother got out of the car and played
on the grass. After 15 or 20 minutes they returned and
Candy asked to be taken to another spot where she could
play with some more acorns and some more leaves. I drove
to another spot and she and Peggy played for another 20
minutes or so. They again returned to the car and Candy
said, "Go home." She had played enough. It's the same way
about bedtime and her nap in the afternoon. She herself
is usually the one to decide that she wants to sleep. When
she wakes up, she begins talking to herself; if she cries
out it usually means that she is asleep or that she wants
to sleep but something is interfering.

Sometimes, for other reasons than hunger or
weariness, Candy loses her temper. Then the slightest
opposition, especially having to do with something over
which she has had a previous battle, is apt to set it off.
One of these sensitive issues is the game of Alley Oop
that she has long enjoyed playing with. It consists of an

assortment of thin round wooden sticks with little
wooden bulbs attached to one end. She once had her Alley
Oop taken away from her because she was chewing on the
sticks and bulbs. Since then, whenever she plays with
it, she seeks to learn how far she can go in the direction
of chewing before she is told not to. Being told not to,
when one of these sensitive issues is involved, provokes
the explosions.

This happened the other morning. She flew into a rage
and began issuing her commands in a loud voice. Her
mother tried reasoning with her, but Candy only shouted
more. Her mother took the toy away and told her she could
have it when she stopped hollering. There was no
immediate effect. Candy still hollered. Little by
little she quieted down as her interest was taken by
other things and it seemed she had forgotten all about
the disputed toy. Then, with tears still in her voice,
she asked: "Have I stopped hollering!"

She likes to have her feet tickled, first with my
fingers, then she'll call for a piece of paper. After I
tickle her with the paper for a few seconds, she'll say:
"Dat's no dood. Another paper." Mildred, her
step-grandmother whom we visited in North Carolina, was
charmed by Candy's "Ess" for "yes." Already she has
given that up and says "yes" quite distinctly.

APRIL 9: For the past two months or so Candy has been
taken with the concept of "don't." When she sees a
picture of a mother and child, she says: "The mother says
to that little girl, "Don't run away"; or "That little
boy's mother says, "Don't lie on that bed" etc. Mothers,
in Candy's eyes, are preeminently people who say,
"Don't." And yet her own mother doesn't behave in that
way, while her acquaintance with other mothers isn't
really wide enough to give her such an impression.
Actually it goes somewhat beyond mothers: big girls and
boys are also prone to say "don't" to little girls and
boys.

Candy herself is rather free with don'ts when
talking with her dolls Peggy and Louise. Mostly, too,
her don't is for the doll's protection, as when she tells
Peggy, "Don't walk by yourself, Peggy. Hold my hand and
I'll save you from the bees."

Frequently the bees are the pink bees or the yellow
bees--two of her favorite colors for describing
imaginary things. She woke up the other night demanding
to know where Peggy's pink meat was. On the trip she
repeatedly promised to buy Peggy a pink bonnet or a
yellow bonnet, pink shoes or yellow shoes, and a pink or
yellow dress. She correctly names all the principal
colors, but pink and yellow are the ones she likes most to
talk about.

As for buying things, she has a pretty good idea how
that is done. We acquired some sales tax tokens in, I
believe, Missouri and gave them to Candy as her red
pennies. They satisfied her for a few days of planning
what to buy Peggy. But then, all of a sudden she announced
she would get some pennies out of Mom's purse to buy these
things for Peggy. She had evidently observed that was
how the real buying was done--not with sales tax tokens.

APRIL 12: Every so often Candy asks to play a game,
which means she wants the backgammon board, dice, and
checkers. She stacks the checkers up to make a tower just
as she does with blocks. She puts the dice in the dice box
and pours them out. Last evening I put the dice boxes on
her hands and called them mittens. She said she'd make a
snow man with them.

One thing that annoys her, and really annoys her, is
to be misunderstood when she knows she is speaking
plainly. This morning, when she spoke of going outdoors
and putting on her gay mittens, I couldn't grasp
which mittens she was talking about. She explained
further--her cup mittens. Still I didn't know. She
repeated: "Gay mittens." "Day mittens?" I asked
foolishly. Candy blew up. Of course she was saying "Game
mittens," the ones made from the backgammon dice cups.

Later in the morning we looked at a magazine
together. An automatic dishwasher interested her,
probably because her mother uses one. "Where's the
dishcloth?" Candy asked. I walked into it. "You don't
need a dishcloth with a dishwasher." She didn't argue.
She simply asked slyly: "You wipe the table with a
dishwasher?"

APRIL 17: It might be difficult to give a name to the

kissing sound made when you call a dog. Candy has come up
with a good try. She says: "Dot, say 'smuts.' "

APRIL 19: Candy came into my room this morning while I was
sleeping (rather, pretending to be asleep) and said:
"Dot, you hold Peggy while I wake Dot up."

APRIL 20: When Candy was younger, she used to call the
utility room, where furnace, wash tubs, and water heater
are, the "'tility." Perhaps because it's easier to say,
we often used to do the same, but not lately. This evening
Peg slipped and said "'tility." Candy corrected her:
"You mean ME—tility."

   Later, as she was getting ready for bed, she played
with her toys, setting them on the window sill. Some of
the bigger ones wouldn't stay on; her mother said the
sill was too narrow. After awhile Candy tried to put
another toy or doll on the sill. "It's too what, Mom?" she
asked.

APRIL 22: Candy's language has a tendency to be literary
due to her keen interest in books. She says, for
instance, ""I frightened Bop with my running," when
another child would probably have said "scared."

   "Are we to go home now?" illustrates one of her ways
of getting out of verb difficulties. By such means she
also expresses herself more precisely and
economically. Here she not only inquires as to when we
are likely to go home; she also makes clear that she her—
self is ready to go.

   In my wheelchair I have difficulty rolling over
things, especially things like Candy's small toys,
which are also liable to break. I have never mentioned
the problem to her; when I find a toy in front of one of
the wheels I merely reach down and take it away. This
morning I was about to remove a mechanical pencil that
she uses to color pictures with. "I'll get that color for
you, Dot," she said and crawled down under the chair. She
picked it up, backed out, and took it away with her.

APRIL 23: I wish I could describe my feelings this
afternoon when Candy came outdoors after her nap. How
purposeful she was as she clutched a couple of her toys
and declared what she was going to do with them. It seems

that being away from her for just a couple of hours makes everything fresh about her. We dug in the garden and Candy would pick little cones off some pussywillow stems left over from last year. She'd bring them over and say, "I'll give it to Peggy (her doll) to eat and then throw it on the ground." She did it and said it over and over again. She carried stones to the stone pile and sticks to the stick pile. She had great fun with the broom rake sweeping up twigs, them taking them in her hands to the brush pile that she calls the stick pile. She was hungry, as she usually is, and came in readily enough when we went in to get supper.

APRIL 29: Peggy went into the hospital day before yesterday. (It seems much, much longer.) She had an extremely high fever, well over 100 during the night, which seemed an outgrowth of some urological trouble for which she had been taking treatment. Candy watched the ambulance attendants bundle her mother up on the stretcher and carry her out. She was keenly interested but not at all alarmed. I told her that Mom was going to someone else's house for the night and that Grandma was coming over here. She accepted it as a matter of course. We picked up Grandma after supper. Candy had her bath, went to bed with little fuss, and seemed hardly to miss Mom. In the afternoon while she napped in the car I visited Mom at the hospital. One of the doctors, who had served in New Guinea during the war, diagnosed her illness as malaria, an almost incredible conclusion. He said she must have contracted it on our southern trip. Perhaps she did; I recall seeing a mosquito in our motel room in Houston. There is, however, no certain way of telling, it seems, except by means of a blood smear taken during a fever attack. She had such an attack on her first night in the hospital but no test was taken then. Anyhow it would explain why the urologist was getting nowhere.

I told Candy after she woke up that Mom was inside that building and that it was called a hospital: that Mom was sick. "Will she come home when she gets better?" Candy asked. We dropped by the hospital again in the evening and again I told her Mom was there in the hospital and would stay all night.

The next morning she asked Grandma (checking my story possibly), "Where's Mom?" With her old-fashioned

Two Years Old

notions about keeping unpleasant truths from children, Grandma answered evasively and tried to change the subject. "Where's Mom?" Candy asked, more sharply. Still no satisfactory answer. Now she began to get panicky. "Where's Mom?" she cried. I came out of the kitchen and told her, "Mom's in the hospital, Candy." She subsided at once and has shown no signs of worry since. I went to the hospital alone this afternoon. When I returned and Candy was awake from her nap I told her I had seen Mom in the hospital. She said nothing.

Curiously, most of my own concern over Peggy, and it has been extreme, flowed from precisely similar causes. Her urologist had been very close—mouthed about what he thought was ailing her and what he hoped to accomplish by the measures he was taking. Like Candy, I found it worse to be answered evasively than [with what] the harsh truth might have been.

MAY 1: On our way to the hospital to pick up Mom, Candy was in the back seat of the car with her doll Peggy. Her grandmother said, "Maybe Santa Claus will bring you another doll." Candy's answer was: "When I use this doll up, Santa Claus will bring me another." The doll Peggy is far and away her favorite toy. She takes it to bed with her; carries it around wherever she goes; is constantly having to kiss it; talks to it steadily; behaves, in short, as though she considered it human. Evidently she does not, though, since she looks forward to its eventual destruction and replacement matter—of—factly.

She was happy to see her mother, yet anything but demonstrative about it. She settled down with her very naturally in the back seat, just as if she had never been gone. It's good to have Mom home again and Candy wholeheartedly agrees.

When Candida cried over the *ducko* that she was forced to give up in her doctor's office, she was displaying a mixture of emotions, among them, sadness, anger, and affection. These are only a few of the many emotions for which names exist in the language and which adults, as well as children, experience at one time or another.

A central question in the study of emotional development is

which of these emotions young infants experience and whether any or all are present at birth. When infants cry, it is generally believed that they are unhappy; but how about when they are not crying? Are they happy? This was the question, you recall, which agitated the diarist when Candida was less then a year old: "Is Candy happy now? I don't know. She is not unhappy." John B. Watson, who was a pioneer among American psychologists in scientific research methodology and who is sometimes referred to as "the father of behaviorism," was one of the first psychologists to study this question experimentally.

Watson's interest in infant emotion stemmed from at least two sources, a background in classical conditioning and an interest in what in his day was a lively topic of interest—the improvement of mankind. Classical conditioning led him to the view that many specific emotional reactions—and he cited as an example a fear not experienced by the normal infant, fear of snakes—are conditioned reactions which are formed in the course of the infant's life experience. He gave experimental support to this view by conditioning a little boy named Albert to be afraid of furry objects. As we know, children tend to be fond of furry things and this was initially true of Albert in the presence of a rabbit, he approached and petted it when it was placed in his crib. But after several occasions on which a steel bar was hammered each time he saw it, Albert became fearful at the sight of the rabbit itself, without the sudden noise. Fear in the newborn, Watson contended, was the response to only two stimuli: a sudden loud noise or sudden loss of support; all other fears were acquired through having been closely associated with these two (Watson and Raynor [1920]).

Watson's interest in the improvement of mankind led him to study and prescribe better ways of raising children, and here, too, he saw the handling of the emotions as matters of crucial importance. In a book dedicated to "the first mother who brings up a happy child" [1928], he wrote, "Fear behavior can be taught as easily as reading and writing, building with blocks, or drawing. It can be taught well or badly. When taught scientifically the emotional life is then under 'control'" [p. 68]. Of love he wrote, "The mother coddles the child for two reasons. One, she admits; the other, she doesn't admit because she doesn't know that it's true. The one she admits is that she wants the child to be happy, she wants it to be surrounded by love in order that it may grow up to be a kindly, goodnatured child. The other is that her whole being cries out for the expression of love. Her mother before her has trained her to give and receive love. She is starved for love—affection, as she prefers to call it" [p. 80]. In sum, he recommended: "There is a sensible way of treating children. Treat them as though they were young adults. Dress them, bathe them with care and circumspection. Let your behavior always be objective and kindly firm. Never hug and kiss them, never let them sit in your lap. If you must, kiss them once on the forehead when they say good night. Shake hands with them in the morning. Give them a pat on the head when they have made an especially good job of a difficult task. Try it out" [p. 81].

In 1917 Watson and Morgan reported on an experiment which was designed to determine whether there are basic human emotions present from birth or shortly after, and if so, what they are. They placed their infant subjects in situations which are emotion-provoking for adults—for instance, a dark room, contact with a spider, or sight of a smiling face, and looked for signs of an emotional response—fear of the dark or of the spider, happiness at the face, and so forth. From among the many stimuli they tried, they found only four which consistently engendered an emotional reaction in babies. Two of the four—loss of support and a sudden loud noise—produced a catching of the breath and crying, and they labeled this response "fear." Restraint of the infant's movements resulted in stiffening of the body and screaming, and they labeled this "rage." Stroking the baby's skin led to smiling and cooing, which they labeled "love." These three emotions—fear, rage, and love—were the only ones Watson found; it was from them, he contended, by a process of conditioning, that all the other emotions sprang.

Mandel Sherman [1927] repeated Watson and Morgan's experiment, with one modification. A group of observers, consisting of psychology graduate students, instructors, and medical students, witnessed only the infant's emotional reaction instead of, as in Watson's experiment, the stimulus which produced it. These observers were unable to agree on which of the three emotions an infant displayed, or whether there even were three.

Katharine Bridges [1932] proposed a further modification of Watson, stating that there are not three emotions present at birth, but just two—*quiescence* and *excitement*. Neither was quite like an adult emotion, having neither a pleasant nor unpleasant quality. At the age of one month, however, she did find an unpleasant emotion which she called *distress* and, at three months, she found a pleasant emotion which she called *delight*. As an infant grew older, these positive and negative emotions were seen to break up into finer shades of emotion, so that by six months there were three new distress reactions—fear, anger, and disgust—and, by age one, two new pleasant emotions, elation and affection. Still branching out, like the budding shoots of a tree, from her two original proto-emotions of excitement and quiescence, Bridges found two-year-olds experiencing the emotions of fear, disgust, anger, jealousy, distress, excitement, delight, joy, elation, affection for children, and affection for adults.

So also at two—and not in all likelihood for the first time—we observe in Candida the typical rise and fall of an outburst of anger: "She flew into a rage and began issuing commands in a loud voice. Her mother tried reasoning with her, but Candy only shouted more. Her mother took the toy away and told her she could have it when she stopped hollering. There was no immediate effect. Candy still hollered. Little by little she quieted down as her interest was taken by other things and it seemed she had forgotten all about the disputed toy. Then, with tears still in her voice, she asked: *Have I stopped hollering?*"

Florence Goodenough [1931] studied the seven-month to eight-year-old children of 45 mothers who kept a record of their anger outbursts. When she analyzed what form the outburst took, she found that infants under age one lashed out indiscriminately when angry. They might kick, flail, and shout, but that was about all. As they grew older, their anger showed more direction and less explosiveness. By age two they made threats and, like Candida with her Alley Oop sticks, retaliated directly against anger-provoking authority. By the age of four, children made use of indirect methods of retaliation, such as refusing to speak to the one they were angry with.

Goodenough reports that anger episodes became more and more frequent with age and reached a maximum at age two. They then began to decline in frequency and the decline was more rapid for girls than for boys. She found that the duration of anger episodes changed very little as the child got older, but the duration of after-reactions, such as sulking, increased.

Goodenough also tallied the causes of anger in children. Under age one, most anger occurred in connection with routine physical habits such as bathing, feeding, dressing, and being put to bed.

Two Years Old

Between ages one and two, a new cause was added: direct conflict with an authority prohibiting something the child wanted to do. Between the ages of two and three, social conflict with playmates became another important source of anger and remained so during the period studied.

Goodenough's mothers made note of the time of day when an anger outburst occurred. Peaks were found just before bedtime and just before meals, with sharp drops right after meals. The diarist also noted this, by implication when he wrote, "Sometimes, for other reasons than hunger or weariness, Candy loses her temper."

The mothers in Goodenough's survey reported more anger episodes on days when the children had colds, constipation, and other illnesses than when they were feeling well. So too in the diary when Candida was 14 months old, we read: "Candy has been ill with tonsillitis, a fever and a rash . . . it has made her cross and given her temper tantrums." And in a later entry: "Whatever the cause, she is a most miserable little girl right now with a sore throat, dry cough, running nose, loose bowels, and a general ill temper."

In the view of John B. Watson, as we have seen, anger or "rage" in infants was an instinctive response to physical restraint and was activated as the baby grew older by the tightly restrictive garments infants are often made to wear. Similarly, from his theory that a sudden loud noise produced the instinctive response of fear, he was able to deduce that fear of lightning resulted from the clap of thunder that accompanied it. He extended this to the concept of *don't*, noting that "the parents' 'don't' is the most potent factor of all in producing both fear and negative responses" [p. 57]; It was nevertheless undeniable that "the simple word 'don't' has no power in itself to produce either a negative or a fear reaction in the child. It must borrow its power." The power, Watson contended, came from the powerful voice of the father. "Just at the moment the child starts to reach for something or to perform some act not desired by the father, he yells 'Don't!' You have everything ready to produce a conditioned fear reaction. The powerful word 'don't' takes the place of the steel bar in our laboratory experiment" [p. 58]. Eventually, according to Watson, "Because of the frequency with which we use them, 'don't' and words like it soon become the ruling forces in the life of every child" [p. 59].

The diary record seems to bear this out: "For the past two months or so Candy has been taken with the concept of *don't*. When

106

she sees a picture of a mother and child, she says: *The mother says to that little girl, "Don't you run away"*; or *That little boy's mother says, "Don't lie on that bed."* etc. Mothers, in Candy's eyes, are preeminently people who say *don't*. And yet her own mother doesn't behave in that way, while her acquaintance with other mothers isn't really wide enough to give her such an impression. Actually it goes somewhat beyond mothers: big girls and boys are also prone to say *don't* to little girls and boys."

In addition to being a word which, according to Watson, inspires fear, *don't* is also a negative word or, properly speaking, the contraction of two words, the verb *do* and the negative *not*. The use of the negative is a highly important development in the field of language, comparable in many ways, if not in degree, to the use of language itself. It is, after all, one thing to say that which is and quite another thing to the literal mind of the child to say that which is not. Why not refrain from saying anything at all?

Roger Brown [1964] and his colleagues at Harvard studied this question in the language development of three children. For the purpose of the study, all three were given Biblical pseudonyms. Adam, the son of a Boston minister, and Sarah, the daughter of a clerk, were 27 months old when the study began. Eve, whose father was a Harvard graduate student, was 9 months younger. Each child was separately and periodically tested in his own home and everything said by and to him was tape recorded. The interviews continued until Adam was 42 months old, Sarah 48 months, and Eve 26 months. The children's speech was analyzed into three stages based on the average length of the sentence spoken, chronological age itself not being considered an accurate index of speech development.

Taking the data Brown collected and using his three stages, Edward and Ursula Klima [1966] found that in the first stage a negative expression was created by the simple addition of *no* or *not* to the beginning or end of an otherwise affirmative sentence. When Candida was 22 months old, she spoke a sentence typical of this rule: *No Dot doing that*. At an earlier age she formed negatives by prefacing a holophrastic sentence with a headshake. Thus when she was 15 months old, the diarist wrote, "Today she was saying *Dot* and shaking her head. What could it mean? Peggy figured it out. Whenever Candy hears an auto horn she says *Dot*, meaning either that it must be I or, more probably, somebody doing what I do when I come home.

Two Years Old

When it isn't I, Peggy says, *No, that isn't Dot.* So now Candy says *Dot* and shakes her head, her way of saying *No, that isn't Dot, but he's doing what Dot does."*

During the first stage, the Klimas doubt whether children comprehend embedded negative contractions (such as *That isn't Dot*). But during the second stage, which comes some two to four months later, not only are embedded negatives understood but the child begins embedding his own negative words inside the sentence. Thus the Klimas' rule for stage-two negation consists of inserting a word between the subject and predicate of the corresponding affirmative sentence. Two new negative words, *can't* and *don't,* are added to the *no* and *not* of the previous stage. In this second stage, however, these words are used only in the negative; *can* and *do* do not appear in affirmative sentences.

Candida's comprehension of embedded negatives suggests that at 17 months she may have attained this second stage: "She also recognizes negative contractions like didn't and wouldn't, and shakes her head, saying *no* when she hears them. *There isn't any more* is easily understood by her, as she shows by a confirming head shake and *no* ."

Finally, in the third stage, which develops from two to six months after stage two, the child's negatives come much closer to those used in adult speech. Instead of employing undifferentiated negative elements, the rule includes manipulation of both modal auxiliaries (*can* and *do*) and the negative morpheme (*not*) as separate words. Thus the stage-three child's speech includes both affirmative sentence, "I can do it" and the negative, "I can't do it." Candida's *don't* sentences might be the product of stage two or stage three in the Klimas' system. The sample of her speech at this age is not broad enough to determine whether she uses *do* without the negative element.

Similar work to that of Brown, but done with seven children ranging in age from 1 year and 10 months to 2 years and 10 months, was conducted by Susan Ervin [1964]. One of her most interesting findings was one she called *overgeneralization,* a tendency of children to apply regular rules or patterns in place of irregulars which are both gramatically correct and have previously been learned. Ervin observed this in children's use of past tense and plural inflections.

Initially the children she studied formed the past tense correctly. Like Candida at 22 months—when the diarist noted, "Right now she is learning tenses: corrected herself when she had said *Candy see it* to Candy SAW it, with emphasis on *saw*"—these children produced past tenses for the irregular verbs *came, went, was, had,* and so forth. Then a few weeks later, they began making errors on these same verbs, saying *seed* where they had said *saw, comed* for *came,* etc. At the same time, they began using the regular past tense formed by adding *ed* to the present, as in *walked* and *helped.* Ervin reasoned that the first correct irregulars were learned by rote, but that when the children discovered a rule for the past tense of regular verbs, the rote gave way to the rule. The children also overgeneralized plurals. Having learned the rule, "add *s,*" which applies to most nouns in English, they extended it to irregulars and came up with plurals such as *foots, feets,* and even—by analogy with plural forms such as *glasses* and *boxes*– *footses* and *feetses.* Since these forms are not used in adult speech, their use by children constitutes additional evidence against the view that language is acquired through simple imitation.

The diary discloses no evidence of these types of overgeneralization—past tense of verbs, plurals of nouns—in Candida's speech. Interestingly enough, however, it brings to light a new one, as the following extract shows: "When Candy was younger, she used to call the utility room, where furnace, wash tubs, and water heater are, the *'tility.* Perhaps because it's easier to say, we often used to do the same, but not lately. This evening Peg slipped and said *'tility.* Candy corrected her: *You mean Me-tility.*" A few weeks before this entry was written, Candida's difficulty in using the pronouns *me* and *you* was remarked on. She, for example, said *Mom is helping Candy.* Now she seems to have gone overboard in the other direction and wants her mother to make the you-to-me reversal for a word that doesn't involve *you* at all, but merely has the same sound.

The diarist also remarks on the fusion of thought with speech in connection with 15-month-old Candida's learning of words: "This record seems to be mainly on the subject of vocabulary. I suppose it interests me because it is the most concrete, or at any rate the most direct, evidence of Candy's thinking." According to L.S. Vygotsky [1962], the functions of speech and thought are quite separate in the very young child. The infant thinks without speaking, as Bruner's theory of motor and ikonic representation implies, and he vocalizes without thinking—for example, when he babbles and cries. As the child grows older, the separate lines of speech and thought come together. Vygotsky quotes William Stern [1914] who, like the diarist, places their meeting point at around age two, "when the child 'makes the greatest discovery of his life', that 'each things has its name'" [p.

Two Years Old

43]. Vygotsky suggests that once speech and thought meet, they develop together through a series of three stages which he labeled *external speech, egocentric speech,* and *inner speech.*

During the stage of external speech, the child talks as an accompaniment to activity. But his speech is not yet of any real help to him in solving problems which come up in the course of activity. Linguistically, external speech does not differ in any fundamental way from the social speech which the child addresses to other persons.

A.R. Luria [1961], a follower of Vygotsky, studied the external speech of preschoolers through a series of experiments. He noted that when a two-year-old who is in the act of putting rings on a post is told "Take the ring off," the meaning of the command has no influence on his behavior and he continues to put the ring on, perhaps with greater gusto. Luria taught three-year-olds to give themselves the verbal instruction *don't squeeze* every time a green light came on. Later he put a squeezable bulb in their hands. They squeezed vigorously when they saw the green light, even while giving themselves the contradictory command. In other words, speech as yet had no control over action.

Vygotsky postulated that egocentric speech gradually emerges from external speech as the child passes from age three to age seven. Unlike external speech, egocentric speech differs importantly from the social speech by which the child communicates with others. It is less grammatically complete, contains idioms understood only by the speaker, is briefer, sometimes less audible, and is often incomprehensible to an outsider. It resembles external speech, however, in being produced to accompany activity. The following diary entry probably illustrates the beginning of egocentric speech: "How purposeful she was as she clutched a couple to toys and declared what she was going to do with them . . . We dug in the garden and Candy would pick little cones off some pussywillow stems left over from last year. She'd bring them over and say, *I'll give it to Peggy* (her doll) *to eat and then throw it on the ground.* She did it and said it over and over again."

Again, egocentric speech differs from external speech in being of real help in the solving of problems. Vygotsky found that when nursery school children were faced with frustrations and difficulties such as not finding paper and pencil when getting ready to draw, the amount of egocentric speech they engaged in almost doubled. When the child is beginning to use egocentric speech, the speech at first occurs after the action to which it relates. As the child gets older, his speech moves forward in the chain of events, toward the middle, and eventually to the beginning of the activity, where it serves a planning function. Thus a small child makes a drawing and decides after it is finished what it represents; slightly older, he names it while drawing; and finally, he decides what he will draw before picking up his pencil. Vygotsky observed the transition to the planning function of egocentric speech in a five-year-old who was in the midst of drawing a picture of a streetcar when his pencil broke. After exclaiming, *It's broken!* he threw the pencil away and continued the picture with water colors. This time, though, he drew a picture of a streetcar which had been in a crash and was "broken." It seemed that his exclamation about the pencil had changed his plan for the picture.

The final stage of inner speech occurs when egocentric speech becomes inaudible. Rather than "talking to himself" out loud, the older child thinks to himself in words, just as he moves with age from counting on his fingers to adding in his head. According to Vygotsky, inner speech is briefer and less grammatical even than egocentric speech: "Inner speech is to a large extent thinking in pure meanings. It is a dynamic, shifting, unstable thing, fluttering between speech and thought, the two more or less stable, more or less firmly delineated components of verbal thought" [p. 149].

9
Two
and
a Quarter

MAY 13: Candy doesn't cry much even when she hurts
herself or when she's angry. I was surprised last
evening to see her cry over a story in a book. It's a story
most familiar to her about a little duck called Flibbity
Jibbit. Flibbity Jibbit lives with a funny little man
called the Key-Keeper whose duty it is to lock and unlock
the doors in the king's castle. The Key-Keeper loses one
of his keys and is taken to the prison tower. It was here

that Candy began to cry, and so seriously that I had to skip over the rest of the suspense and get the Key—Keeper released at once. Then she was all smiles again.

Candy and her mother picked wild flowers yesterday and Candy remembered and said their names: trillium, mayflower, violet. She calls out "forsythia" when we pass them in the car, along with the water towers that she "spots." She knows colors perfectly and manages to paint, with approximate accuracy relative to the outlines, in her coloring book. She is beginning to be interested in numbers, counts to four, and says the other numbers pretty much at random.

She asked about some colored paper recently. I told her it was for wrapping presents and if she liked she could wrap one of her toys and give it to her mother. Then it would no longer be her toy but Mom's. She liked the idea, only as it turned out there were few if any toys she wanted to part with. However, she finally settled on one.

One of her favorite pastimes is scribbling on a piece of paper and asking one of us what it is. If we see a resemblance to something, we identify what she has drawn. This evening I called one a false face. "Where's the falt?" asked Candy. Obviously, if there was a falt's face there must also have been a falt.

She is very much in the "why" stage now, though without actually saying "why." She uses "if" instead. "What are you doing with that bandage, Dot? I'm putting it on my sore finger. And if you don't put the bandage on? My finger will get dirty. And if it gets dirty? My finger will get sorer than ever. And if it gets sorer than ever? It will hurt. I may have to go to the doctor."

She also investigates the opposites of things. She saw me adjusting my removable dental bridge and asked what I was doing. "Loosening my bridge. And if it is tight?"

MAY 23: "What is Peg?" Candy asked.
"What IS Peg? You tell me," I countered.
"My doll and Mom," said Candy.

MAY 24: Mom went up to the attic to rummage around for some things. She didn't take Candy with her. Candy hollered up:

Two and a Quarter

"Mom, you don't like to see a lot of junk but I do!"

JUNE 12: We were driving home last evening on
Schoolcraft Road when we approached the Consumers'
Power Company gas storage tank that has a blinking red
light atop. Candy always recognizes this as one of the
"water towers" that she takes such pride in "spotting."
So I asked her what she saw up ahead. She said she
couldn't see anything. Each time the tank appeared
through the trees I asked again but still Candy
couldn't see it, or so she said. Then when we were past
she said, "What were you trying to show me, Dot? Was it a
tree?" "No, it wasn't a tree." "It wasn't a water tower
either," said Candy, still teasing me.

JULY 2: She likes to dawdle, which I understand is normal
for children of her age. Even when she is hungry, she will
stall around rather than get ready to eat. She is
reluctant also to get into her bath and equally slow
about getting out. We resort to various strategems, and
one of the best is to offer her a choice. "Which would you
rather do, wash your hands at the basin or with a washrag
at your table?" "With a washrag at my table," she says,
climbing promptly in. Last evening she was sitting at
her table while her mother dawdled at getting the
washrag ready. "Mom," Candy ordered impatiently, "wash
C-A-N-D-Y."
    We have spelled her name aloud for her from time to
time as we printed the letters. Not very recently nor did
we ever try to get her to repeat it. But there it was in
her memory all the time. So it will be with innumerable
strange words and expressions; and when she utters one
of these we usually say, "Where did you hear that?"
Yesterday, Candy herself asked the question.

JULY 20: Last evening she moved the stool from the
bathroom to the bedroom and climbed on it to get
something off my desk. She could have done it before. In
fact, I think she carried the stool around months ago but
until now it never occurred to her to use it to increase
her reach. The idea must have been hers; at least I don't
know where she could have seen anyone else do it.
    Pogue, her doll (the one that used to be Peg; the
transition from Peggy to Peg to Pogue seems to have been

114

imperceptible), is in some ways her playmate, in some ways her other self. When she has Pogue along to give her moral support she will talk quite freely to people outside the family, even to strangers. Without Pogue she is extremely shy. On the other hand, if I ask her a question that she can't or doesn't want to answer, she turns to Pogue, seeking her help; and yet she never forgets that Pogue is only a doll. She knows very well that she can bite and pull at Pogue without hurting her and looks ahead to her eventual replacement.

We nearly lost Pogue at the zoo a few weeks ago. Candy and Mom set her down so that Candy could feed peanuts to the ducks. Mom remembered her quite a while later and went back to find her. Candy then realized she was lost, but if she was seriously concerned she didn't show it. Mom reported seeing the doll near the lake but on the other side of a high chain wire fence, having apparently been thrown there by someone who tried to pitch it into the lake. The problem now was how to recover her, and while we wrestled with this, Candy kept saying, "I want Pogue," but not insistently. She seemed confident we would eventually get her. I think if the doll had been lost Candy would have been pacified with the promise of another, but I'm not sure a new doll would ever take Pogue's place. She often talks now about Pogue being lost and enjoys looking at the zoo map and pointing out where she was found.

For some time, months I should guess, Candy has been talking a blue streak. From 6:45 a.m. when she calls out, "Mama! I'm all finished sleeping!" until 8:30 p.m. when she at last goes to bed, she talks almost continuously. Her favorite themes: what she is doing at the moment, what she is going to do, "Why?" which she repeats incessantly, dialogues with Pogue, and conversations with Peg and me——in about that order. Every so often, in the midst of her own running chatter, she'll suggest, "Let's have a conversation."

Lately she has begun making up long stories, mostly having to do with imaginary adventures of herself or Pogue. She tells how she found a bee in the house; how Pogue wanted to walk through a fish pond, only the fish would bite her, so she walked around it; how Pogue climbed way up high. (Meanwhile, thanks to her proficiency in moving and climbing on the bathroom

stool, there is scarcely anything in the house too high
for her to reach.)

She has two Pogues now. I bought her a new doll as much
like the old as I could find, thinking it would be a
replacement. She liked the new Pogue but she liked the
old one too, although it is little more than a battered
wreck and is rapidly losing all its rubber stuffing. To
postpone the time when it will be nothing but a hard
plastic head and empty flabby rubber skin, we proposed
that she play with the new and sleep with the old; and the
dolls have become, respectively, "playtime Pogue" and
"sleepytime Pogue" who long ago lost her voice. Even so,
she still occasionally plays with her sleepytime Pogue
doll. She says it is "nice and brown and nice and old."

Next to talking--and reading, of course--she likes
best to pick flowers. There are vases of them all over the
house. Each morning, as I leave for work, she picks a
zinnia for my buttonhole. Speaking of reading, I started
bringing a paper home two months ago and reading Candy
the funnies. She went for them in a big way, especially
the Sunday ones in color. She learned them all quickly
too. By the second week she was identifying each one as
soon as I turned the page--a trick I doubt I could have
performed without the title to read.

And Candy can't read--not yet. She does know some of
the alphabet: all the letters in her name, M for Mom, B
for Bop, O and T as in Dot. Her color recognition is
perfect. She knows practically all the familiar animals
and many flowers by name. She says "Aren't I?"--a
contraction Peggy and I never use.

There are so many things about her I should like to
record so that I may remember them. How she greets me when
I come home: "Did you bring any funnies home, Dot?" How
she says goodnight: "Good night, Dot," and goodby: "Bye,
Dot. Come home early." Her invariable injunction when I
pick up a sharp knife: "Don't cut your finger like Mom
did." Her way of asking questions out of the blue: "What
did the little girl have in her hand?"--in all
probability something we saw a week or two ago and I have
forgotten. But not Candy. I sometimes doubt that she
forgets anything.

A favorite game of hers in reading books is to pick up
the things she sees in the pictures: flowers, marbles,
or what not. Pages later, she will still have her fists

clenched. "Where can I put these marbles?" she'll ask.
We'll find a cup or a box. "Will this do?" "Yes," she'll
say, opening her hand and letting the marbles fall in.

A special treat is to find a package to open, just the
package, nothing in it: untie the ribbon, take off the
paper, lift the box cover. "What's in it, Dot?" "A fire
engine." "A fire engine! Clang! Clang!" and off she goes
through the house. Imaginary books inside these
packages have to be opened and read. They all tell
stories of Candy and Pogue and she listens with rapt
interest. Oh yes, and she likes to brush her teeth. She
especially enjoys something containing sugar—jam,
peaches, cookies, ice cream—not alone because it is
sweet but because then she'll have to brush her teeth.

OCTOBER 5: Candy has the same attitude toward nursery
school as toward a new food. She'll take a bite, taste it
thoughtfully, swallow it and say, "It's good." That's
the faint praise that damns. She'll have no more of it.

In the planning stage of nursery school, she looked
forward to it eagerly, and she went off bravely and
expectantly with her mother the first morning. But the
teacher would not allow Peggy to stay and Candy, never
having played with children before, cried when she saw
her go. When Peggy returned for her at noon she learned
she had made a couple of tentative tries for some of the
toys only to have them snatched away by one of the other
children. This was enough to discourage her and she
spent the rest of the morning standing in silence.

Nevertheless, she declared after her nap that she
had enjoyed herself and wanted to go again. The next
morning, however, she insisted on a condition: Mom must
stay. This was Mom's intention, to stay for a short while
at least; but no, the teacher said she must leave
immediately. Again Candy did almost nothing except
watch the other children play. The teacher gave her some
carrot peelings to feed the rabbits and Candy told us
about that with enthusiasm. Yes, she liked nursery
school and wanted to go again.

A weekend intervened. Monday was rainy so she didn't
go. Tuesday she didn't want to but she'd go tomorrow. She
went shopping instead and chattered with her mother
about nursery school and how she'd go tomorrow and "I
won't cry when you leave, Mom." All Wednesday afternoon

and evening she maintained that nursery school was fine;
she wanted very much to go the next morning.

But the next morning at breakfast I mentioned it and
her face fell. No, she stated flatly, she didn't want to
go to nursery school. "All right," I said as before, "you
don't have to go if you don't want to." That was fine with
Candy. "How would you like just to go, say hello to the
teacher, and come right home?" I thought if she went thus
a few mornings, she'd get over the strangeness and could
be left for gradually lengthening intervals. Candy
agreed but the teacher didn't. The only proper course,
she said, was to have her stay all day, though how she was
to be taken to school in the first place, against her
will, she didn't say. It is true, of course, that Peggy is
stronger than Candy.

This was the same position taken at another school we
had inquired about; they would only enroll a child for a
minimum 30-day period, saying it did no good unless he
came regularly. And I've no doubt they are right; Peggy
must leave her alone if Candy is going to begin playing
with the other children. She has none of her own age
around home to play with. She wants very much to play with
them and looks forward to it, but when the time for going
is upon her, she gets scared. The other children
frighten her.

This morning we said nothing about school. When the
time approached for me to leave there was the usual
discussion about which car I would take, the Olds or the
Chevy. "What car will we go in, Mom?" Candy asked. "You
and Mom will go in the Olds," I answered, purposely
failing to say where. Candy didn't ask. Later there was
some talk about Mom getting some tissues at the
drugstore.

They drove to Plymouth and into the residential area
where the school is. "There's no drugstore around here,"
Candy said. They parked on a street near the school.
"Mom," Candy protested, "there's no place to go here."
They walked a block. "Let's go in the gate," Mom said. The
teacher took her. Peggy left. Candy wept but not so long
this time; and late in the morning she got up nerve and
played a little. As usual, this afternoon she said she
enjoyed it and wants very much to go tomorrow.

OCTOBER 19: Candy: What did Chicken Little say?

Mom: She said, "Oh, the sky is falling."
Candy: She should have known better.

After two weeks she is thoroughly reconciled to
nursery school. She'd rather go than stay home. She even
stayed for lunch last Friday but wouldn't sit down with
the others or eat anything, having established this
policy at the mid—morning snacks. After three days
lunching at home she decided again yesterday to have her
lunch at school, and ate heartily. She is now getting
ready this morning to go and stay through lunchtime. I
think her quickness to accept and even welcome something
that had previously frightened her proves once more that
the best policy is one of not forcing. I doubt she would
have been won over sooner by taking and leaving her
against her will, and I greatly doubt that her
enthusiasm would be as real as it is.

She has told us the names of several of her playmates
and some of the things they do together. Marching with
flags to the music of a piano is evidently her favorite.
She hasn't spent nap—time there but she probably will
next week. Besides filling a large gap of social
companionship in her life, her school experience and her
way of welcoming it seem to prove that a child will
himself do what is best for him when he is able clearly to
see the alternatives.

OCTOBER 27: How things can change in a few weeks or even
days. It's raining this morning and Candy's nose is
stuffed up. So when Peg talked of getting ready for
nursery school, I suggested perhaps she ought to stay
home today. She had been dawdling as usual. Now, faced
with the prospect of no school, she allowed herself to be
dressed in record—breaking time and is on her way. She
will stay for lunch. She'd much rather eat there than at
home.

She doesn't tell us much of what happens. Yesterday
she pushed herself on the swing. Another time she rode
the see—saw. Usually when I ask her she says, "We
played." She mentions names: Maureen, Jerry, Billy,
Barry, and number of others. She has two separate lives.
At school, play and companionship, learning the rules of
social behavior. At home, mostly reading and
conversation. She counts with no trouble at all up to 10,
probably higher. Her interest in words continues; she

Two and a Quarter

recognizes that written words have meaning. She knows
perhaps a dozen letters of the alphabet, maybe more. Her
drawing is becoming controlled. She said yesterday, "I
won't play with Pogue because I'm so angry to eat." "You
mean anxious." "Yes, I'm so anxious to eat."

Second only to language as a means of communication is communication through pictures. Much of what we know of the thinking of primitive man is conveyed to us by paintings on the walls of caves. The ancient civilizations of Assyria, Egypt, and China used picture alphabets to preserve thoughts and transmit ideas. Since virtually every child draws and paints, a question often asked is whether his drawings, too, is an attempt to communicate, either with others or with himself (cf. Vygotsky's *egocentric speech*). A related question is whether child art is meant to depict reality as the child sees it or whether the pictures he draws are merely esthetic ends in themselves.

The diarist speculates that both aims may be present in Candida's drawing when he writes in March, just before her sixth birthday: "She continues to be interested in art. She spends much of her time drawing, painting, and coloring with crayons. Sometimes she does representations of real things which she can describe fully and in detail, indicating how true her representations are in her own eyes. This morning in her 'scrapbook' we looked at some drawings she had made before Christmas. Without hesitation she was able to tell me about each one, just as though she were looking out the window and describing what she saw. Sometimes when I ask her about a picture, she says it is just a *design*. Occasionally there is evidence that a *design* is a realistic representation that went wrong. Other times it would appear that she aimed at an abstract design in the first place."

G.H. Luquet [1927] theorizes that children's drawing is always realistic in intention, though the child is not always able to represent reality realistically. After making every effort to shield his young daughter from outside art influences, adult or child, he preserved all the drawings she made between her fourth and ninth years. On the basis of this collection, he outlined four stages in the development of drawing, each coming one step closer to artistic realism as adults know it.

In the first of these stages, called *fortuitous realism,* he found the child's artistic activity to consist mainly of scribbling. The meaning of the scribble is discovered only while, or after, making it. Such a stage would be that in the diary when of Candida, age two, it is reported: "One of her favorite pastimes is scribbling on a piece of paper and asking one of us what it is. If we see a resemblance to something, we identify what she has drawn."

During the second stage, which Luquet calls *failed realism,* elements of the drawing bear a resemblance to real objects, but the child has a *synthetic incapacity.* He cannot depict appropriate spatial relationships between objects, nor can he coordinate individual elements into a whole figure. Thus he draws a man with a hat a few inches above his head or coat buttons alongside his body.

Calling his third stage *intellectual realism,* Luquet describes it as one in which "the child draws what he knows rather than what he sees," and pictures conceptual attributes with no concern for visual perspective. Thus he draws a profile with two eyes and "x-ray" pictures showing hair through a transparent hat or potatoes under the ground or inside a man's stomach; while his drawing of a model before his eyes is no more literally accurate than when no model is available.

In Luquet's fourth and final stage, called *visual realism,* the laws of visual perspective are adhered to. Objects grow smaller with distance and the artist adopts a fixed point of view in which objects in the background are shown to be partly concealed behind objects in the foreground. So it is with the sun and the cannon balls in a drawing by Candida at age six and a half: "She does pictures of the beach and ocean, and one that she drew last evening of a sailing battleship (her own version) with flags (stripes against the pole and stars to the outside edge) and cannons. The cannons (two) are shooting big cannon balls straight out from the ship. The sea under the ship is a regular succession of waves, and the sky overhead has pink clouds and a white moon. At my suggestion she drew a setting sun on the horizon, but that became almost obscured by the cannon balls."

A critical assessment of Luquet's theory would have to take account of his ability to effectively screen his child from outside artistic influences, particularly in the view of the difficulty which Hochberg and Brooks had in denying their infant subject exposure to pictures. While not raising this essential question, Rhoda Kellogg [1967] takes issue with Luquet in the belief fundamental to his theory, namely that children strive to communicate reality in their drawings. She contends that "the child's purpose is not drawing what he sees around him" [p. 35].

Accepting the premise that children from two to seven are relatively free of adult art influence, Kellogg, too, outlines their development in a series of four stages beginning with a *placement stage* in which childish scribbles reflect an awareness of figure and ground relationships. At around age three a *shape stage* occurs, during which children draw six simple shapes: circles, rectangles, triangles, crosses, X's, and odd forms. This, in turn, is followed by a *design stage* during which the child combines two or more of these shapes into a single design, as yet nonrepresentational. During the final *pictorial stage* Kellogg believes that the child gradually becomes conscious of resemblances between his designs and real objects and at the same time begins to feel increased adult pressure to produce accurate replicas of what he sees in "the real world."

Florence Goodenough [1931] sees the art of the young child neither as an attempt to depict reality nor as an attempt to create something that is esthetically beautiful, but instead as a *graphic language* through which the child expresses his own ideas and concepts. She states that, like other languages, child art is symbolic. Just as the infant's holophrastic "door" communicates a full sentence's meaning, so too a pair of lines in a child's drawing may symbolize both trousers and the legs inside them. As the child develops his skill in drawing, the symbol becomes more detailed, but it remains somewhat idiosyncratic. One child may symbolize clothing by drawing buttons, another by drawing pockets.

For Goodenough, this view of art as language holds up to the early grades of elementary school, at which time it undergoes a transformation of function. Most children then give up drawing, while those few with special talent who continue to draw and paint no longer use art as a means of communication—speaking and writing have by now far surpassed it in efficiency—but instead adopt the aims of adult artists and strive to render interpretations of what they see in esthetically pleasing ways.

However, art is not viewed as a special talent in nursery school. Virtually every nursery schooler draws, paints, and models with clay. As attempts at communication, these nursery school art productions offer an as yet largely untraveled avenue into the content of children's minds. This is not to suggest that there has been any lack of observational work by child psychologists within the nursery school environment in general. Quite the contrary, studies have been made ranging over a wide area, including one issue very pertinent to the problems voiced by the diarist—the orientation of the new child into the school.

Schwarz and Wynn [1971] studied the effect of the mother's presence on a new child's adjustment to nursery school. This, as the diary reveals, was the question over which Candida's mother and her nursery school teacher were at odds: "In the planning stage of nursery school, she looked forward to it eagerly, and she went off bravely and expectantly with her mother the first morning. But the teacher would not allow Peggy to stay and Candy, never having played with children before, cried when she saw her go. . . . The next morning . . . she insisted on a condition: Mom must stay. This was Mom's intention, to stay for a short while at least; but no, the teacher said she must leave immediately."

In their experimental study, Schwarz and Wynn compared the effect of (1) having the mother remain a short while, as Candida's mother proposed to do, (2) having mother and child visit the school in advance of opening day, (3) doing both (1) and (2), and (4) doing neither, the child being simply dropped into a room of strange children as Candida's teacher insisted. Judging by the child's emotional reaction over the mother's departure, the experimenters concluded that courses (1) and (2) were about equal in orientation value and that, contrary to the opinion of Candida's teacher, her emotional reaction to being left at school would have been less had her mother been allowed to remain a short while. However, course (3) was no better than course (4), which Schwarz and Wynn explained on the assumption that the combined procedures activated stronger dependency feelings than either one by itself.

Rather predictably, Schwarz and Wynn also found that children who had had experience playing with other children before coming to nursery school showed fewer signs of emotional upset than those who had had no such experience. They explained it as due to the fact that children naturally fear a very strange situation. For those children who have never played with others of their own age, a nursery school playroom can be frightening, and this we find confirmed in the diary: "She wants very much to play with them and looks forward to it, but when the time for going is upon her, she gets scared. The other children frighten her." Schwarz and Wynn similarly reasoned that the previsit and the mother's presence were effective to the extent that they reduced the strangeness of nursery school, the previsit by accustoming the child to the physical surrounding of the classroom, and the mother by being one familiar element in the midst of strangeness.

One important reason for enrolling a child in nursery school, recognized alike by thoughtful parents and child psychologists, is the opportunity it affords for social contact with age-mates, especially for children like Candida who have no other opportunities for meeting and playing with their peers. As the diarist notes: "She has two separate lives. At school, play and companionship, learning the rules of social behavior. At home, mostly reading and conversation."

Adults are often poor teachers of social behavior to children because they are apt to require either too much of the child or too little. They may demand on some occasions unquestioning obedience to their authority; on others they may excuse breaches of acceptable social conduct as being those of a mere child. Children of the same age, on the other hand, lack the authoritarian status of the adult while at the same time holding to stricter rules of social behavior.

It is thought that the two main ways in which children teach one another the rules of social behavior are by reinforcement and by modeling. The effect of reinforcement on 3-and 4-year-olds in nursery school was the special study of Charlesworth and Hartup [1967]. Basing their approach on the ideas of B.F. Skinner, they looked for four types of social rewards. The first of these was attention and approval, as when one child watches while another shows off; the second, submission, such as adopting another child's suggestion; the third, affection; and the fourth, a tangible reward. All four types were effective reinforcers of the behavior they followed. Four-year-olds used them in the order listed, while three-year-olds used submissive rewards more often than attention and approval. Four-year-olds tended to be more generous in the dispensation of social rewards than three-year-olds, and some children in both age groups tended to be more generous than others. These were the children who were also apt to recieve the most reward.

In an earlier laboratory experiment, Hartup [1964] compared the effects of reinforcement on a preschooler when offered by a peer he liked or one he disliked. Two groups of children were set to work on a task of transferring marbles, one by one, from one container to another. Each child in one group was given verbal encouragement (*good, fine*) and attentional reward by one of his best friends. Children in the other group received the same kind of reward from a peer they disliked. Counting the number of marbles dropped over a 6-minute test period, it was found that reinforcement from a disliked peer was more effective than from a friend.

A similar experiment by Titkin and Hartup with children in the second and fifth grades [1965] compared the effectiveness of reinforcement when offered by a popular classmate, an unpopular classmate, and a socially isolated classmate whom none of the subjects knew very well. The unpopular peer was found to be the most effective. The rate of marble-dropping increased under his reward, while it remained constant under the reward from the social isolate, and declined slightly under the popular peer. A third experiment by Ferguson (reported in Hartup [1970]) showed that peers of the same age as the subject were less effective agents of reward than older or younger peers: fifth graders dropped marbles faster when reinforced by second graders; the reverse was true of second graders.

Hartup deduced from all of these studies that the unexpected in peer reinforcement is what determines its effectiveness. Children tend to expect rewards from their friends and take them for granted, whereas a good word from one they dislike is rare enough to be highly valued. Much the same is true of popular versus unpopular rewarders since, as we have seen, popular children are on the whole more lavish with their rewards; the rule would also hold for age-mates versus children as different in age and interests as second graders and fifth graders would be.

Modeling, the second after reinforcement of the two main ways in which children teach one another the norms of social behavior, reaches beyond reinforcement. Reinforcement, as we have seen, has its main effect on behavior already within the child's repertoire. With modeling, new behavior may be added to the repertoire. In peer modeling, the child imitates behavior he observes other children engaging in. Behavior susceptible to the influence of peer models covers a wide range, including antisocial behavior such as aggression; prosocial behavior such as sharing; resistance to temptation such as not cheating on a test; courage; and problem-solving.

Experimental investigations of the factors contributing to the effectiveness of peer modeling include one by B.S. Clark [1965], who found that children copied more problem solutions from a rewarded than from a nonrewarded model; and another by Hartup and Coates

Two and a Quarter

[1967], who found that the preexperimental reinforcement history of both subject and model was also important. They singled out two groups of preschoolers, one of which, in the course of their daily interactions with their peers, gave and received social rewards with high frequency. The other was just the opposite. They found that the high-reward-frequency children modeled better from a high-reward-frequency model and that the reverse was true of the low-reward-frequency children. They concluded that children are more likely to emulate those they perceive as being similar to themselves.

The behavior being modeled in the Hartup and Coates study was one called "altruism." First, the model, and later the subject, received trinkets as prizes for maze completion. There were two bowls into which the trinkets could be placed, one to keep and one to be donated to a preschooler whom the subject did not know. The model always donated five of the six prizes he received to the other preschooler. Subjects who watched the model gave away more trinkets when it was their turn to play than subjects who did not see a model.

In another altruism study, Bryan [1969] investigated the influence of both the practice and the influence of both the practice and the preaching of a peer model. Elementary school children were exposed to one of four models: a *hypocrite*, a *cynic*, a *generous model*, and a *greedy model*. Each child imitated his own model appropriately in both word and deed: those exposed to the hypocrite verbally urged generosity but in practice kept all their winnings for themselves, those exposed to the cynic spoke well of greed but actually donated a large proportion of their winnings, those exposed to the generous model preached and practiced generosity, and those exposed to the greedy model preached and practiced greed. The children exposed to the hypocrite and the cynic seemed unaware of the contradiction between what they said and what they did. When asked to rate the models after the experiment, the consensus was that the hypocrite was a "nicer person" than the cynic.

It would appear that not only in the laboratory but in real life as well, the habit of altruism is acquired by peer modeling. Evidence of this appears in the diary. Two-year-old Candida, who had not as yet played with peers, was not noticeably generous: "She asked about some colored paper recently. I told her it was for wrapping presents and if she liked she could wrap one of her toys and give it to her mother. Then it would no longer be her toy but Mom's. She liked the idea, only as it turned out there were few if any toys she wanted to part with." However, when Candida was four and a half the diarist wrote: "Lately her great enthusiasm has been giving things, especially to her friend Merry. *Wasn't I generous?* she asks, and I don't know whether the pleasure comes from giving or the praise she expects for it. Anyhow, she devotes much time and thought trying to decide what to give Merry next time they meet. The other day she told me she had given Merry her best teddy bear, Frank, given to her one Christmas by Frank Bayer. The same Christmas, she received another and much cheaper bear, Bruno, but it, perversely, has always been her favorite. So I could appreciate why she gave Frank away."

Support for the view that children learn generosity by modeling comes also from an effort to determine the natural causes of generosity in children, in which Rutherford and Mussen [1968] gave a group of preschool boys a series of tasks designed to find out about them and their home environment. In one task the boy was asked to act out several family scenes with dolls. The way in which he represented the father doll was seen to reflect his perception of his own father. Other tasks measured generosity (how many candies out of a group of 18 he chose to give away to his friends) and competitiveness (how fast he pushed his own doll in a "race" against the experimenter's). Predictably, the more generous boys were seen to have generous fathers to model from, but they were also seen to be less competitive and, on a rating by their teachers, less gregarious.

10
Two
and a Half

OCTOBER 29: "Bop woke me up."

"What did Bop do to wake you up?"

"He unwoke himself, came into my room, and told me breakfast was ready. So I told Mom to shut the water heater on and get me up."

NOVEMBER 2: Hallowe'en, as usual, was a parade of kids in masks and costumes to the front door with bags open to

receive gifts. "Help the poor!" they cried. A year ago it
marked Candy's beginning awareness of people outside
our circle. She watched the kids at a respectful
distance almost as though they were visitors from
another planet.

This year at the outset she very nearly seemed ready
to go out begging herself. She helped her mother shop for
the apples to be given the kids; helped me cut the
jack-o-lantern to go in the front window; saw and was
fascinated by a parade of Plymouth school children in
their costumes in the afternoon. Yet when the children
came to the door she would not help to pass out the
apples. When we ran out of apples, however, and started
on hard candy, she pitched right in—putting the candy
into bags, handling and looking at it between their
visits. Nursery school is responsible for her newly
acquired taste for candy. It's not simply that she had
little knowledge of it before; other youngsters,
prizing it as highly as they do, have given her an
enhanced idea of its value.

She balked yesterday morning at going to school.
This seemed strange considering how much she had come to
like it. She didn't go. At breakfast this morning she
happened to think of it, plainly showed her worry, and
said, "I don't want to go to school." Something had
happened evidently, but all she would say was, "Alan
said I don't sit straight." It was plain she wanted to go,
but she had a stronger reason for not wanting to. Hence
her worry—and it really was worry, which might be
defined I suppose as mental agitation over a problem
a person realizes he has to solve for himself.

I told her not to bother thinking about school, but
she continued just the same. Then, still at breakfast,
a light broke through. She wanted very much to go—"I'll
sit in the table by the wall, the red and blue table."
Peggy assured her she could, supposing she meant at
lunch time. As they walked into the school yard Candy
said hopefully, "Maybe Alan didn't come today."

Peggy told Mrs. Hulett there was something Alan had
done that bothered Candy, she didn't know what. Yes, it
seemed one of the other little ones had also been picked
on by Alan yesterday when Candy wasn't around.
Two-year-old Alan—a month or two younger than Candy but

Two and a Half

far wiser in the ways of the world--is something of a
bully. The table by the wall is his table, since he eats
lunch on it, and he would not allow Candy to play on it. It
was comic, but almost tragic for Candy: a full-size
worry.

DECEMBER 6: During the past few weeks I have been jotting
down sentences Candy says when (1) they seemed to reveal
something about her current aptitude in speaking and (2) I
had pen and paper handy. Here is one of the earliest:

"Dot, are you expecting me to have these?'

A few days later:

"Do you mind if Mom puts this toothpaste away?'

Once when we were driving home in the evening she
asked, "Why are the trees moving?" Of course, looking up
out of the car windows and seldom if ever seeing the
ground go past, it must seem to her that the trees are
moving.

"I tore the picture by accident."

"When I get to be a big girl, can I color my fingers
red?" She was asking about that again last evening. She
had got beet stains on her fingers and didn't want to wash
them off because she wanted to be like a big girl.

"Don't put anything on my chicken fats. I like to
scratch them."

She had the chicken pox just before Thanksgiving, on
top of considerable trouble with her nose, throat, and
coughing, the result of allergy. Exept for the itching,
the chicken pox hardly troubled her, but the allergy did
seriously. She has almost forgotten how to breathe
through her nose. She had trouble learning to blow and
never did acquire either a liking or facility for it. As
for nose drops or nose spray, she detests them both. We
took her to the doctor a few times when her cough sounded
especially bad, but, except to agree it was allergic, he
could only say that many children go through a whole
winter with stuffed up noses.

"Mom, why are your eyes like fish and mine are like
fish and Bop's are round?"

"Why aren't I going in the first grade?" Another sign
of impatience with the time it takes to grow up.

"Dot, I'm curling my hair."

"Are you?"

130

"Yes. And when I go to the store people will say, "Why Candy! You curled your hair nice!""

She returned to nursery school after a long absence. When I asked her what she did, she said she hadn't played with any of the things. The others played and she watched them. She was happy to go back.

"I have everything perfectly right." This may have referred to the game she plays in the evening after her bath, using the backgammon board with its dice and checkers, a set of Alley Oops, and a set of miniature dominoes. Playing that game is a nightly ritual and an inducement to hurry with her bath.

"Pogue's my friend, so she let me eat her peanut."

Christmas is coming and Candy is ready for it, poring over the mail order catalogs for toys and, especially, candy. Her favotite toys in actual use are those that afford opportunity for imaginative play: cooking, eating, sweeping, doing things with and for her dolls. Other toys, including the educational ones, produce a quick, immediate enthusiasm and then she wants nothing more to do with them. Her toy chest is full of relics.

DECEMBER 14: One of Candy's dearest pastimes is her evening game. She builds what she calls "sandwich towers" (checkers and dice alternately in a stack), knocks them down, scatters them, snaps and unsnaps the dice cups, and talks incessantly. She values only reading and perhaps drawing any higher in the way of entertainment. Its charm is in part its regularity, in part its postponement of bedtime.

JANUARY 4: When I got home this evening, Candy had a new song to sing. She had asked her mother earlier in the day if there wasn't a song about a rocking chair. There is, to be sure, but we haven't played it for months and never often. Evidently it remained in Candy's mind, as so many odd words and expressions do, and the sight of her own little rocking chair recalled it. Peggy put on the record, and Candy said she would sing it for Dot when he got home, but Mom must promise not to sing it. I had been home only half an hour when she said, "Dot, I have a new song for you," and she sang, in tune:

"Old rocking chair got me . . . ."

Two and a Half

A little later, she showed me a picture of a toy with something wrapped around it which I guessed must be the paper rope used for Christmas decoration. "I think it's beads," said Candy.

"Maybe it is," I agreed. "In this dim light, I can't see it too well." I thought that ended it. But no; after going to bed two hours later, she happened to think of it and asked to go back on the toilet. There she turned again to the picture and asked, "Mom, is this beads or paper?" "Beads, I think." That satisfied her. She went back to bed.

I suppose I should say something about Christmas, but there really isn't much to say. She enjoyed the preparation, had definite ideas on what she wanted and stuck to them; she helped pick out the tree and trim it, put stickers on presents, was happy with everything she got, including three or four dolls, a toy piano, a wagon, a sled, and incidentals. Of it all, I think she liked the candy canes the best, although she really eats very little candy; and, now that Christmas is well in the past, her favorite toy is still her poor beat-up shell of a doll that she calls Sleepytime Pogue (Slider, for short) to distinguish her from Playtime Pogue (Skidder, for short).

She now recognizes and can name most of the letters of the alphabet and knows several of the numerals. While lying awake in her crib she recites all of "Sing a Song of Sixpence" or "Rock a Bye, Baby," or hums a tune of her own composition. She likes drawing and modeling in clay (which she calls "play") and draws quite well I think.

JANUARY 18: It is foggy this morning. Bop began barking at something he saw or thought he saw. Candy went out into the living room to check up. "He's barking at the fogness," she said. The concept of fog as both a substance and a state apparently offended her sense of logic. We have near and nearness, late and lateness; obviously there must be fog and fogness.

We have a new game called playing store. She sells me things, I sell her things, and we count out the money in each other's hand. She counts up to six with no trouble and yesterday discovered with some slight surprise that she has five fingers on each hand, five toes on each foot, two eyes, cheeks, ears, and hands, and one nose, chin, and forehead.

She continues to find things to worry about. Now it is her next visit to the doctor, scheduled for March. Every so often out of the blue she'll say, "I don't want to go to the doctor in March!" At nursery school she alone of all the kids won't go outdoors to play. She would like to because she sees how much fun the others are having. Why not go out then? "I was afraid Mrs. Hulett would close the door tight and I couldn't get back in." Now she has agreed to ask Mrs. Hulett not to close the door tight. It remains to be seen whether she does or prefers to hang on to her worry. And who am I to point the finger? I also worry over trivialities that could be taken care of by relatively slight action on my part, fearful to take that action because of the new worries that might rise in the old ones' place. Two months to go till Candy's third birthday.

JANUARY 29: I was running the power sander on some wood. "That's a cold sound," said Candy. "I'm shivering!"

Tonight she asked, "What is a boy and what is a girl?"

"A boy's a boy and a girl is a girl."

"No. A girl is a female. What is a boy?"

FEBRUARY 10: Candy has been ill so much this winter that, looking back, it seems the days she was well were the few and unusual ones. I don't know whether to blame this climate, or the possibility of contagion at nursery school, or a persistent infection that subsides to give her a few days' relief only to break out in some new way. Whatever the cause, she is a most miserable little girl right now with a sore throat, a dry cough, running nose, loose bowels, and general ill temper. "Why do I cough?" she asks. Each day we hope she'll begin eating again because when that happens she is on the road to recovery.

FEBRUARY 18: Here is Candy talking to herself as she lies in her crib before napping:

"Well, we first put them in a big pink pile."

"Do you know how to do it?"

"Yes, I know how . . . " and so on, in a continuous dialogue from subject to subject.

Two and a Half

"Did you get any money?"
"Yes, we got it . . . "
"All the purple stamps used up?"
"Yes."
"Well, you'll have to get more."
"Here's some more letters."
"Some more purple ones?"
"He would have to pay you . . . "
Some of the words are intelligible, some half
muffled by yawns. Now the sentences become only
occasional. Then a flurry of words.
"There's nothing in there. There's nothing in
there."
"What do you mean, there's nothing in there?"
"Well, I mean there's no animals or stuff like that or
people."
"Oh, that's what you mean."
Now the talking stops. An occasional kick. Is she
going to sleep? No. A sing-song of gibberish. More talk.
"Don't you think you better . . . "
"She wanted it . . . "
The dialogue still goes on, but I can hardly make out
any of it. Perhaps her mouth is covered.
"Maybe it would be she. Maybe it would be he. We'll
call it he . . . Oh he ate the . . . too. He must have
pretty . . . "
""She's supposed to be there at five o'clock and she
might want to . . . "
"Well, you'll have to take her . . . "
"If they don't come, well, I'll just go in there. The
other ring was here. Well hi! That was another story too.
It happened to get their list of what she takes into
kettle. That's what I want. Forty. Sixty. We'll be a
flat. She come by grape juice. Te dum de dum. Like that:
we'll play. And that's how rusty . . . We'll sit by the
rabbit and the rabbit will——(Yawn. Whisper.) That's a
good joke. The one about the window. Two days she'll look
out two windows and four days she'll look out six windows
and . . . All by himself 'cause . . . she was the one who
. . . so the girl will have to buy it all by herself.
She'll have to go all by herself to buy it. So if she
appreciated well they would buy it. Appreciated.
Appreciated. We were passing one night . . . (Yawn.)

That was a good story . . . "
     And so on and on and on. But she finally did go to
sleep.

FEBRUARY 22: She told her mother today, "I was looking in
the recipe book and it says you should give children
crackers and cheese EVERY DAY."

Long before the violence depicted in movies and television
caused worry among parents and educators, psychologists saw a link
between the aggressive model and the aggressive child. Children are
peculiarly susceptible to aggressive modeling, having little if any
knowledge of the feelings of the victim, and the younger the child,
the truer this is. An infant in arms, for example, has no conception
whatever of the pain he may cause merely by pulling his mother's
hair. One relatively early experimental investigation of the effect of
adult models on nursery school subjects was that conducted in 1961
by Bandura, Ross, and Ross, involving three groups of children.
Group one watched a model beat up a rubber clown; group two
watched a model play quietly with a construction toy; group three
was provided with no model to watch. All three groups, in turn, were
given an opportunity to play with the clown. Group one proved the
most aggressive, group two the least; and group three, which had no
model, fell between the others.
     Using a similar procedure, D.J. Hicks [1965] tested for both im-
mediate and delayed effects of aggressive modeling. Four groups of
preschoolers were shown a film, each film featuring a different aggressive model: male adult, male child, female adult, female child. In
a test immediately after the film, each of the groups displayed a high
level of imitative aggression, those who watched the aggressive male
child displayed the most. In a retest six months later, none of the
groups showed much imitative aggression, including the one that
had watched the male child; but the group that had watched the
aggressive male adult showed somewhat more aggression than the
others.
     Reinforcement has been found to play a part in fostering aggres-
sive behavior, as well as modeling. In the face of such aggressive actions in nursery school, hitting another, taking away toys, invasion of

Two and a Half

territory, threats, and name-calling, Patterson, Littman, and Bricker [1965] observed such responses as passivity, crying, yielding toys, taking up a defensive posture, telling the teacher, recovering property, and retaliation. Not surprisingly, a victim who opted for a submissive reaction (first four types) and thus rewarded peer aggression, was most often subjected to the same kind of attack again. Counterattack measures, on the other hand (the last three types), usually resulted in the aggressive child changing his victim, his manner of aggression, or both. Counterattack of this kind was exceedingly rare in the Patterson study, however. In up to 97 percent of the cases, the victim of aggression rewarded the aggressor. Thus it would seem that a child who enters nursery school moderately aggressive has a strong chance of becoming more so by virtue of reinforcement from his peers. An initially nonaggressive child may or may not become aggressive, depending on whether he is victimized by an aggressive child, and, if so, how he responds. Should he counterattack, the study would seem to predict a good chance (67 percent) of his being successful and hence learning to be more aggressive.

An example of aggression reinforced by submissive behavior is recorded in the diary: "Something had happened evidently, but all she would say was, *Alan said I don't sit straight.* It was plain she wanted to go, but she had a stronger reason for not wanting to . . . Then, still at breakfast a light broke through. She wanted very much to go—*I'll sit in the table by the wall, the red and blue table.* Peggy assured her she could, supposing she meant at lunch time. As they walked into the school yard Candy said hopefully, *Maybe Alan didn't come today.* Peggy told Mrs. Hulett there was something Alan had done that bothered Candy, she didn't know what. Yes, it seemed one of the other little ones had also been picked on by Alan yesterday when Candy wasn't around. Two-year-old Alan—a month or two younger than Candy but far wiser in the ways of the world—is something of a bully. The table by the wall is his table, since he eats lunch on it, and he would not allow Candy to play on it."

This incident illustrates another rule concerning aggression in children: aggression appears to be more prevalent among boys than girls, and this very largely on account of the greater vigor of boys' play. R.M. Oetzel [1966] summarized the results of 12 studies, or 14 separate observations, in which preschoolers were observed in natural interaction with their peers. Nine of the 14 observations concerned primarily physical aggression, and boys predominated;

but in the remaining five, where verbal quarreling was the rule, boys and girls were about equally aggressive. Similar results were obtained in another 10 studies in which mothers, teachers, and peers rated preschool and elementary school children's aggressiveness, as well as in an additional set of five modeling studies. Oetzel also surveyed seven studies which measured fantasy aggression in preschoolers through their play with dolls. In all seven, boys surpassed girls in physical aggression, whereas in two that additionally measured verbal aggression, girls surpassed boys in one and the sexes were equal in the other.

For approximately three decades, following on the heels of the often-quoted frustration-aggression hypothesis of Dollard, Doob, Miller, Mowrer, and Sears ("Aggression is always a consequence of frustration" [1939, p.1]), psychologists have debated the question. Is frustration both a necessary and the only cause of aggression? Is aggression both a necessary and the only consequence of frustration?

The diarist may have some thoughts along this line when he wrote of 16-month-old Candida: "She is almost always amiable, is cross only when hungry or tired or when barred from someplace she wants to go"; and when she was age two, "Sometimes for reasons other than hunger or weariness, Candy loses her temper. Then the slightest opposition, especially having to do with something over which she has had a previous battle, is apt to set it off."

Barbara Merrill [1946] observed a group of mothers and children and afterward criticized half the mothers for failure to bring out the full capabilities of their children. The criticized mothers reacted in a subsequent session by restricting and directing their children's activities. The children, in turn, reacted by being more aggressive than the children of the noncriticized mothers, which supports the frustration-aggression hypothesis.

However, in another and somewhat earlier study (Barker, Dembo, and Lewin [1937]), regression rather than aggresion was the primary consequence observed when two- to six-year-old children were frustrated by being denied access to a set of highly desirable toys. The children responded to the frustration simply by playing in a less mature and constructive way with the few toys remaining to them. The play of some six-year-olds regressed to the level of three-year-olds.

Other nonaggressive consequences of frustration which have

Two and a Half

been observed in children are withdrawal; apathy; expressions of guilt, shame, remorse, embarrassment; nagging; and efforts to evade, rationalize, or explain away the issue (Jersild [1954]).

J.R. Davitz [1952] demonstrated the importance of training in determining whether or not a child will respond aggressively to frustration. Half of his seven-to nine-year-old subjects engaged in group pursuits (for example, painting a mural together) and were given encouragement for helping one another. The other half of the subjects played vigorous competitive games (one in which the object was to crush one another's ping pong balls) and were praised for aggressiveness. After this training, all of the children were frustrated: an exciting film they were watching was stopped just before the climax and candy they had been given was taken away. In their subsequent play, the children's activity reflected their training: the aggressively trained group were aggressive, while the cooperatively trained group were cooperative, showing less aggression, in fact, than they had in a play session prior to both training and frustration. It would seem, therefore, that aggression is not an inevitable consequence of frustration. Children's games provide an important training ground for the cultivation of aggressive and altruistic behavior: aggressive from an emphasis on winning at any cost, and altruistic, from the collective spirit fostered by teamwork. Indeed, as Piaget [1948] has shown, a self-contained moral system free of adult influence and involving, besides altruism and aggression, a whole gamut of moral behavior, may be traced in a simple game of marbles. Over 100 Swiss boys ranging in age from 3 to 13 were observed by him, first at their play and then individually as he took each one aside and asked to be taught the rules of the game. In addition, of course, he watched his own children at play with marbles and proposed, on the basis of all his research, a series of stages in the development of marble play.

In the first, or *motor and individual*, stage, up to age two or three, the child handles marbles more or less randomly according to the dictates of his desires and current skills. He may develop a set of rituals through continued exposure to them, but these are not rules in the strict sense, since they have no social component. Each child's rituals are his own individual invention. Thus when Piaget gave Jacqueline marbles for the first time at age three, she first examined them closely and then incorporated them into her play: she bounced them on the carpet, stuffed them into hollows in a chair, piled them into a pyramid, put them into a toy saucepan and pretended to cook dinner, and so on. She did the same things with them day after day, indicating a ritual.

At age two, Candida had developed similar rituals incorporating the equipment of an adult board game: "Every so often Candy asks to play a game, which means she wants the backgammon board, dice, and checkers. She stacks the checkers up to make a tower just as she does with blocks. She puts the dice in the dice box and pours them out. Last evening I put the dice boxes on her hands and called them mittens. She said she'd make a snowman with them."

During Piaget's second, or *egocentric,* stage, from age 3 to 6, the child begins to observe rules introduced from the outside and to turn them to his own purposes. He is as happy to play alone as with others, and when with others, he sees no need to take turns. He makes no attempt to win and believes that all players can win at the same time. Even the rules which he borrows are distorted in his play, although he is not aware of it. In observing children of this stage playing marbles, Piaget noted that a player might shoot from whatever place he wished and his partner would make no attempt to correct him.

Piaget's stage of *cooperation,* beginning at about age seven, is marked by an urge to win, coupled with the desire for an official set of rules to be observed, even though the general understanding of these rules may still be rather vague. Thus even children who play together constantly are apt to give each a different version of the rules, and they manage to get along by omitting those in dispute and playing a simplified game.

During the final stage of *codification of rules,* which begins at around age 11, every detail and possible variation of each rule is fixed and known to all. Moreover, the children devise new rules to cover every conceivable contingency, likely or not. In this connection, Piaget observed a group of boys who, simply in order to throw snowballs at one another, spent quite a bit of preliminary time electing captains, fixing the voting procedure, deciding on teams and distances, and setting up sanctions of rule-breaking.

In addition to his four stages in the use of rules, Piaget saw a sequential development in children's understanding of what a rule is. This begins with an utter lack of consciousness of the meaning of rules, and proceeds, toward the end of the *egocentric* stage, to a view of them as sacred and unalterable, invented by God or the first men. During the stage of *codification* in marble play, the child begins to view rules as the product of mutual agreement among the players.

Two and a Half

At the beginning of the *egocentric* stage, at a time when the rule concept was being acquired, the children saw nothing wrong with adding a new rule or even changing all the established rules. This casual attitude toward the invention of rules is illustrated in a conversation Candida had with her mother just before her third birthday: *"There is a game where you run down the sidewalk and run back up again.*

Oh, said Mom, *where did you learn about that game?*

I didn't. I just thought it up.

You thought it up? Then you can teach the game to the other kids, can't you?

Yes. And when other kids play it, one kid runs down the sidewalk while the other kid runs up the sidewalk."

Piaget, however, draws a distinction between the four-to five-year-old's easy attitude about changing rules and the more mature view of the 11-year-old that rules can be altered by mutual consent of the players. He contends that the young child is simply unable to distinguish conceptually between an old and a new rule, and that once he does, he will necessarily pass through a period of seeing rules as fixed and absolute.

The egocentric stage in marble-playing is for Piaget part of a more central egocentric quality in young children's thought. The egocentric child is defined by Piaget as one who cannot take another person's point of view, cannot conceive of the possiblity that a point of view other than his own exists (his usage thus differs from the usual one implying selfishness or calculated unconcern for others). To demonstrate this, Piaget performed an experiment in which children were seated facing a diorama of a mountain range, shown a set of pictures, and asked to pick out the picture which showed what the mountains would look like to a doll moved from point to point around the room. Preschoolers picked the same photo no matter where the doll was positioned: the one which showed the view the child himself saw. Their opinion did not change even after practice going around and taking a look from where the doll was. This is similar to the soldier on parade who insists that everyone is out of step but him.

Egocentrism is often manifested in the questions children ask. The diary, for instance, notes: "Once when we were driving home in the evening she asked, *Why are the trees moving?* Of course, looking up out of the car windows and seldom if ever seeing the ground go past, it must seem to her that the trees are moving." Candida's egocentrism consists of inferring movement from her own perception without being aware of the viewpoint of someone standing among the trees.

In studying the questions of a six-year-old boy as recorded by his governess, Piaget [1926] found evidence of egocentrism in the fact that the questions were often worded in a way that anticipated a magical or illogical answer. For example, the boy asked, "Does the butterfly make honey?" "No." "Then why does it go on the flowers?" According to Piaget, the young child expects natural pheonomena to be explained in terms of wishes, ambitions, and strivings, because he cannot distinguish the rules of nature from the rules that govern his own behavior.

Further confirmation of this view came when Piaget [1930] posed similar *why* questions to children of about the same age as the little boy. He asked, for instance, why the clouds move and received the answer that the clouds want to follow us as we walk. Or when he asked why water in rivers moves, that the men with oars push it along. He also found that, like Candida with the trees although for a different reason, the children believed that the apparent movement of the moon when they walked at night was real and that the moon moved along so as to follow them and light the way. Piaget concluded from the children's explanations of natural phenomena that their egocentrism causes them to attribute to inanimate objects like the moon and clouds the same kind of consciousness that they are aware of in themselves.

Another common question, the "if" question, is one Piaget called a "question of imagination." For example, the six-year-old boy he studied asked, "And if I had gone away?" "She would tell the police." "And if the police did not find me?" "They would find you." "But if they didn't?" And so on [1926, p. 211]. Similar questions were asked by Candida when she was 26 months old: *"What are you doing with that bandage, Dot? 'I'm putting it on my sore finger. And if you don't put the bandage on? My finger will get dirty. And if it gets dirty? My finger will get sorer than ever. And if it gets sorer than ever? It will hurt. I may have to go to the doctor."* Piaget related this type of question to imagination because in asking them, the child performs imaginary experiments. He alters reality and asks what would happen under the new conditions.

The egocentrism Piaget saw in childish thought is expressed not

Two and a Half

only in questions but in general speech. Like Vygotsky, he observed that when children are together, particularly when they are engaged in common activity such as drawing, they talk out loud but do not seem to be trying to communicate. This is egocentric speech. So, too, is the presleep monologue which Candida was heard to utter when 2 years and 10 months old. The main point on which the presleep monolog differs from other egocentric speech is in not tolerating a listener: if someone enters the room, the child stops talking. The linguist Ruth Weir managed to record the presleep monologs of her 2½-year-old son Anthony in spite of this problem, by turning on a tape recorder in his room whenever she put him to bed. She reported the monologues and her linguistic analyses of them in her book, *Language in the Crib* [1962].

In a preface to this book, George Miller commented on some of the psychological implications of presleep monologues, stating that their existence disproved the view that language learning is just like any other learning—a matter of being rewarded for correct responses and not being rewarded for incorrect ones. Weir had noted that Anthony would correct his own pronunciation in the course of a monolog and drill himself in difficult pronunciations such as consonant clusters. Candida also practiced pronunciation: *She'll have to go all by herself to buy it. So if she appreciated well they would buy it. Appreciated. Appreciated."*

Miller observed that only the pleasure of hearing himself speak with increasing fluency can serve as the child's reward for the diligent practice of pronunciation and grammar he undertakes in presleep monologs, and that the child's ability to correct himself indicates he knows much more about language than appears in his casual speech.

Impressed by the poetic quality of Anthony's presleep monologs, Roman Jakobson noted that the child often seemed to forget the meaning of what he was saying, in favor of assonance, alliteration, and rhyme. In Candida's monolog, too, there is evidence of concern over the sound of language independent of its meaning: *"It happened to get their list of what she takes into kettle. That's what I want. Forty. Sixty. We'll be a flat. She come by grape juice. Te dum de dum."*

11
Three
Years
Old

MARCH 19: Three years old this morning. We haven't said anything about it being her birthday, although she has known for some time that it was near. The idea was that Pogue would be all better by now, but styles in dolls change rapidly these days and others exactly like Pogue are no longer carried in the shops. We asked a dealer to order one, but it still hasn't arrived. Hence, no Pogue, no birthday.

Three Years Old

MARCH 26: Candy (while her mother holds her and her father puts drops in her eyes): "Let me out of this position! This is a very bad position!"

We found another Sleepytime Pogue and so we were able to bring her favorite doll back from the hospital all healed as good as new. She even had her voice back, which was marvellous to Candy. It was missing before she lost and arm, damaged her eyes, broke her head, or suffered her numerous other ailments. Since Sleepy's return, Candy is hardly ever separated from her. She even holds her on her lap while being read to on the toilet.

In a way, she is beginning to read to herself. What I mean is, she will have a comic book read to her two or three times. Then a day or so later, she'll stand and study the comic book. Every so often, she'll pipe up: "Mom, why did Uncle Wiggily say . . . ?" or: "Why did Nancy tell Sluggo . . . ?" She sings, too, little tunes that she makes up herself, and hums very sweetly.

APRIL 22: Candy: "This bell won't ring. It must be a dumb bell."

MAY 8: Candy: "I just made up a song. Would you like to hear it?"

Dot: "Yes, I would."

Candy: "Book, book
Tra la la
Nice book
You're a nice book
Tra la la
Book, book"

This the first of her songs I have heard that has something of a formal pattern. As I write now (her mother is in the hospital again), she is showing me a picture she has drawn and colored. Here, too, she is beginning to put form into her work.

A week ago she showed me a picture consisting of a yellow and green field with a long black mass across the top of the page. I supposed she wanted my interpretation. I was about to turn it over and tell her the black was the earth and the yellow and green were flowers growing in it. But before I could begin, she proceeded to explain it to me. The yellow and green were a picnic and the black mass was an umbrella to keep the picnickers from getting wet.

Parties and picnics are her great interest these days. They fill her imaginary play, and her dolls all come to them. Some have to be invited by telephone and she tells them: "My name is Candy Clifford. I live on Stark Road, eleven nine two five." Then she tells of the long drives by car or bicycle that her dolls must take to come.

JULY 5: Candy: "How do people say their cigarette is irritating?" And another time: "Camay. Buy it today."

Much has happened since my last entry. Peggy was seriously ill with a ruptured ectopic pregnancy that might have cost her her life if by chance I had not come home extra early that afternoon. She was suffering so much from shock that she had not been able to telephone. But they rushed her to the hospital and operated on her. With the loss of her second tube she has now to give up the idea of any more children.

While Peggy was away, Candy stayed alone with me. We went out for dinner and managed on light breakfasts and lunches at home. After her nap, Candy stayed with a neighbor while I visited Peggy in the hospital. Candy said once, "Dot, I don't need Mom as long as I have you to take care of me." Just the same, she was pretty happy to see Mom come home. And I certainly was.

Later on, Candy herself was ill with an infected throat. She had just gone back to nursery school, and it seems she's fated to catch something whenever she goes there.

SEPTEMBER 23: Candy (in bed, on requesting a drink of water): This looks like the middle of the night, Mom.
Mom: It's practically the middle of the night.
Candy: Almost, you should have said.
Mom: (correcting herself): Almost.

I find I have neglected this journal. Many incidents occurred that I meant to put down as signposts of Candy's development, but now I'm afraid they're forgotten. The best I can do is summarize.

She has been attending a story hour at the Detroit Public Library nearly every Wednesday and, by

Three Years Old

borrowing, has had many more books to read. She now enjoys a book on the first reading, whereas not so long ago she had to have it read to her two or three times before she took to it. Notwithstanding all of the excellent books she gets, however, her real favorites are the comics, especially Nancy, Donald Duck, and Mickey Mouse. Other things being equal, her favorite characters, in comics or standard literature, are little girls--preferably mischievous ones.

She brought a school reader home last time and recognizes two or three words in it. What continues to amaze me, however, is her ability to recite 24 hours later, word for word, a long passage in a book I have read to her just once. It comes out in the form of a question: "Why did--" and then the passage.

Speaking of why, she has a rather sure sense of what to ask why about. A new word, for example, will sometimes interest her immediately and sometimes not. If not, it is usually a word I myself would seldom use.

Two little neighbor girls, one exactly her age, were here this morning to play with her. Both are far ahead of her in social development. She has still not learned to play with children and can only stand around and watch them.

OCTOBER 11: Little Baldy, Candy's tiny rubber doll, represents the devil in her universe. He frequently gets into mischief, the kinds of mischief that Candy herself would like to at least try, and so serves as a doppelganger. By telling what Little Baldy has done, Candy can learn, and perhaps weigh, the consequences. Little Baldy is also quite contrary. She (all Candy's dolls are girls) deliberately does things in the opposite way to what is proper. Thus, also, Candy experiments, and she learns why things are done in a certain way from the consequences when Little Baldy does the opposite.

JANUARY 24: Candy: What will we do the day after tomorrow?
    Mom: Saturday?
    Candy: Maybe it will be a sad day.
    Mom: Why?
    Candy: SADDER day.

Three Years Old

Much has happened since the last entry and much about Candy I neglected to record as we travelled to the West Coast and back. Almost my only journal notation, apart from the trip's events, was of Candy renting a ride (her first) on a pony in Yuma, Arizona, too late in the afternoon, I noted regretfully, for picture-taking. Her greatest thrill was over the pony's name—Trigger. For the next several days she dictated postcards to friends back home telling of riding a horse named Trigger.

FEBRUARY 4: When Peg and I quarreled, as we did frequently under the time pressure of the trip, Candy tried to stop us. At first she would holler but, finding this did no good, she tried striking me in the face, with no more effect. Once, after we had been home a few days, we stopped at a grocery store for eggs. It was close to supper time and I was hungry. Peggy and Candy went in while I waited in the car. They were gone for over half an hour with me getting more aggravated by the minute. When at last they came out, having done a weekend's shopping, I bellowed at Peg, she bellowed back, and Candy began hitting me in the face with a cellophane bag of peppermints. I snatched the bag and pitched it out of the car window. Candy was desolate over the loss of her pink peppermints. I brooded, realizing the delay in the store wasn't her fault, and stopped at last at a druggist's to let her buy some more. Since then we have had no quarrels, but I should say Candy makes no distinction between quarrels and arguments. Now she has decided to work on her mother when she feels an argument has to be stopped. This morning she brought the subject up and advanced the theory that Mom is the one at fault when arguments or quarrels occur. I told her perhaps so, and the thing she should do is put her arms around Mom and that would stop her. Candy seemed interested in this approach to what is evidently a vexing problem, but it remains to be seen whether she can learn from advice (few adults can, after all) or whether it will be necessary to stumble on the solution by herself.

A similar problem is that of adults monopolizing a conversation; in fact, I think it may be the heart of her objection to our arguments and perhaps even our quarrels. When she and her mother go visiting, all the

Three Years Old

talk is over her head. Last week this happened at a
neighbor's house, so when they got home, Candy insisted
on being allowed to go back and visit for awhile by
herself. Again, when they called on another neighbor,
she asked to stay for a brief period after her mother left.

At home, when there are no arguments, she initiates
practically all conversation, and the topic is usually
her imaginary adventures with her dolls: with Sleepy,
her favorite; with Sleepy's mother, Louise, who often
leaves Sleepy with Candy either because she has to go to
the movies every day (rose-colored movies) or because
she has a job; and with little Baldy, the mischief-maker.
On the trip Peggy and I were the responding voices when she
telephoned Louise and Susan back home, as we have long had
to speak for Sleepy when Candy converses with her.

She starts a new nursery school today, one that her
mother has been waiting months to get her into. It is more
a real school than the one she used to attend in Plymouth,
less a baby-sitting service. Candy will probably like it
better because her activity will be more directed, more
purposeful. Whether undirected play wouldn't be better
for her who has so little of it, is of course the question.

The ordinal position which a child occupies in the family, along
with the number of brothers and sisters he has, is thought to influence the kind of person he becomes (Altus [1966]).

In a family of two or more children the eldest is presumed to have
certain advantages. One is the chance of becoming an eminent person. As early as 1874, Sir Frances Galton found that there were more
first-borns among famous British scientists (Fellows of the Royal
Society, etc.) than would have been expected by chance. Havelock
Ellis [1926] found the same was true of 975 eminent men and 55
eminent women who earned lengthy listings in the British *Dictionary
of National Biography*, and H.E. Jones [1954] found evidence that
first-borns' chances of becoming a name in *Who's Who* (and *Who's
Who in America*) are greater than those of younger brothers and
sisters.

Intellectually and academically, the eldest has also been seen to
have a lead on his younger siblings, by doing better in school (Forer

[1969]), earning higher verbal intelligence test scores (Altus [1966]), and more often attending colleges with stringent admission standards (Altus [1966]). Laosa and Brophy [1970] found him more creative in kindergarten and, also in kindergarten, Helen Koch [1965] found him more articulate.

Against this array of advantages, Jones found the eldest child to suffer somewhat poorer physical health than his younger brothers and sisters, and Helmreich and Collins [1967] saw him also tending to be fearful of physical dangers and reluctant to take part in sports and athletics, while Rosenow and Whyte [1931] detected in him a tendency toward such nervous symptoms as shyness, emotional tension, and hostility. They judged him a more likely candidate than his younger brothers and sisters for treatment in child guidance clinics.

Various explanations have been offered for these findings, all centering on the unique position of the first-born—that of being the eldest in a family of other children. For one, the fact that for a period of time the eldest enjoys the exclusive attention of his parents—who talk and read to him and answer his *why* questions—is seen to account for some of his presumed intellectual superiority over younger siblings who receive many expanations and examples of speech from brothers and sisters only slightly more knowledgeable than they.

Another theory holds that competitive pressures within the family urge the first-born forward intellectually. He has only adult standards ahead to measure his achievements against, and all the younger siblings, who themselves see him as the standard, to keep ahead of.

On the other hand, the fact that the eldest has less experienced, and therefore more cautious, parents than his younger siblings is thought to explain his greater timidity in the face of physical danger, while his susceptibility to emotional maladjustment is attributed to the anxiety and guilt he has suffered over the sibling jealousy an only child experiences when a new arrival comes to claim part—often a large part—of the parents' care.

As for the only child himself, we note from the following passages that this was to be Candida's fate: "Much has happened since my last entry. Peggy was seriously ill with a ruptured ectopic pregnancy that might have cost her her life if by chance I had not come home extra early that afternoon. She was suffering so much from shock that she had not been able to telephone. But they rushed her to the hospital and operated on her. With the loss of her second tube she has now to give up the idea of any more children."

While attributing to the only child some of the advantages enjoyed by the eldest, such as good grades in school and good chances of going on to graduate study (Forer [1969]), psychologists tend, on the whole, to have a rather low opinion of the only child's chances. Charlotte Buhler [1931], on the evidence of several German psychologists (for example, Blonsky, Buseman), finds him unpopular, antisocial, timid, dictatorial, and sad. Another German psychologist, Walter Toman [1969], interviewed 264 psychiatric patients and 135 personal friends and from these interviews drew a picture of the male only child as a self-centered, immature ingrate. Of the female only child, he drew an even sorrier picture. She was more selfish than other girls, she passionately demanded whatever she set her mind on; she was a nuisance at work, lazy, insubordinate, and unable to get along with others. As for marriage, Toman says: "Friends of the couple may sometimes think of him as a fool or masochist"; while as a parent, Toman writes: "Should her husband be an only child too, they will, with great likelihood, remain childless; the few exceptions tend to prove that they should have" [p. 119].

Yet, notwithstanding G. Stanley Hall's airy judgement that "being an only child is a disease in itself," psychologists have been found who take a more optimistic view of the subject. Guilford and Worcester [1930] conducted a systematic inventory of the only child's personality and intellectual status relative to children with siblings. Their subjects were 162 junior high school students, 21 only children and 141 non-only children. The measures they used were based on school records, ratings by at least six different teachers, and a report from a community group on each child's extracurricular activities.

They found that only children had better health attitudes and habits and received higher marks in school, that they were superior in self-control, initiative, truthfulness, dependability, courtesy, and industry. On the other rated traits—IQ, cooperation, obedience to law and order, sense of fairness, and voluntary participation in extracurricular activites—they found the only child to be at least equal to children with siblings.

The only child's unusual situation is also seen to be reflected in his play life—with only children engaging in more imaginary play and less social play than those with brothers and sisters. Piaget [1962] divided children's play into four categories, including these

150

two, and labeled the first of the four to develop, *exercise* play, consisting, as it does, of repeating an activity over and over for the simple pleasure of doing it.

Candida's ritual with the backgammon set is an example of exercise play. More mature forms include tag, bean bag, catch, climbing trees, and jumping rope—where much of the enjoyment comes from the practice and perfection of motor skills. According to Piaget, exercise is the only form of play of which subprimate animals and children under two are capable. Dogs do not pretend to fight off an enemy when they mouth their masters' fists, nor does a kitten chasing a dry leaf or ball of yarn imagine them to be mice.

This form of play is what Piaget calls *symbolic* and includes playing with dolls, playing school, store, and cowboys and Indians. Piaget's theory is that children use symbolic play to satisfy both emotional and intellectual needs, neither of which can be satisfied completely in a social world of elders with separate interests and in a physical world which the child in only beginning to understand.

In the form of symbolic play, where the intellectual motive is paramount, the child attempts to come to grips with a perplexing experience by acting it out. Lucienne, for example, was puzzled and somewhat frightened while walking through a village by a loud sound which she was told was the ringing of church bells. The next day, she stood beside her father's desk, stiff as a ramrod, screaming loudly. When he tried to stop her, she pushed him away, explaining that she was a church. Similarly, Piaget once discovered Jacqueline lying on the couch, so still she was thought to be ill. She was pretending to be a dead duck which, with some alarm, she had seen earlier in the kitchen.

In other cases the child neutralizes strong emotional feelings by turning them into play. Once, for instance, when Jacqueline was crying with temper over something she couldn't have, she began imitating the crying of her infant sister, and this consoled her. On another occasion, three-year-old Lucienne was frightened by owls hooting in the trees and described how her pillow went out with hobnailed boots to scare them away. Candida, at age two, neutralized a fear in play by warning her doll, *"Don't walk by yourself, Peggy. Hold my hand and I'll save you from the bees."*

Another instance in the diary of symbolic play made to serve intellectual, and perhaps emotional, ends was described when Candida was three: "Little Baldy, Candy's tiny rubber doll, represents the devil in her universe. He frequently gets into mischief, the kinds of mischief that Candy herself would like at least to try, and so serves as a doppelganger. By telling what Little Baldy has done, Candy can learn, and perhaps weigh, the consequences. Little Baldy is also quite contrary. She (all Candy's dolls are girls) deliberately does things in the opposite way to what is proper. Thus, also, Candy experiments, and she learns why things are done in a certain way from the consequences when Little Baldy does the opposite."

Jacqueline invented an imaginary character named Marecage who resembled Little Baldy in going contrary to the dictates of Jacqueline's parents. For example, when Jacqueline was made to take a nap, she protested that Marecage never took one. However, instead of viewing this as the diarist would have—as being an attempt to learn the consequences of disobedience—Piaget saw it as an attempt to gain emotional satisfaction through what he called *compensation*. According to Piaget, the child finds vicarious enjoyment, through compensatory play, of a pleasure that is denied him in real life. So Jacqueline vicariously enjoyed Marecage's pleasure in taking no naps. In another instance, after Jacqueline had been told she could not hold her newborn sister, she began rocking a pretend baby in her arms. The imaginary baby apparently provided at least part of the satisfaction she would have felt by holding the real one.

As still another example of compensation, Piaget cites two-year-old Jacqueline's disparagement of a friend of her mother's while the three of them were walking together: "'She's naughty' . . . 'she can't talk' . . . and especially, 'I don't understand what they're saying'" (1962 [p. 133]), followed, when Jacqueline was in bed, by an imaginary walk in which Jacqueline herself conversed with the friend. Here Jacqueline's real handicap of being unable to understand adult speech was overcome in her imagination.

The imaginary character Marecage, however, also served a purely intellectual function in Jacqueline's play, through what Piaget called *anticipatory symbolism*. At four and a half, Jacqueline was walking on a narrow mountain path and had been warned not to tread on loose stones. She then made up a story in which Marecage slipped on a stone and hurt herself badly. According to Piaget, Jacqueline couldn't understand the warning when it was presented in the abstract. However, when, through anticipatory symbolism, she visualized a concrete happening in her imagination, its meaning became clear to her.

According to Piaget, *games with rules* become one of the most important forms of play after the age of seven, when symbolic play begins a slow decline. The reason, for rule games' relatively late appearance and for their persistence even into adulthood (chess, cards, sports, etc.), he believes, is that they are social. Their importance increases in proportion to the widening of the child's social horizons.

Piaget's fourth kind of play, *games of construction* , also makes its first appearance later in childhood. Games of this type begin as symbolic play when the child makes things—doll houses, wigwams, forts, etc.—to serve as props for imaginary scenes. Gradually, however, construction becomes an end in itself. Laurent invented the make-believe country "Siwimbal" as a setting for imaginary adventures with his toys. But later, at age eight, he eliminated the imaginary characters and devoted himself to drawing maps and charts of Siwimbal. He also set out precise details of climate, terrain, and population—which he was then learning about in school—for sections of the country, which he distributed to his sisters and friends.

At age four and a half, construction was already becoming as important as symbolism in Candida's doll play: "She also cuts out paper dolls and dresses them. Her choice of a doll for this Christmas was based on the clothes Candy saw her in. She also constructs figures with a fork, pieces of paper napkin, and a ribbon to tie them together. They have vari-colored dresses and hair of shredded paper."

Of the four kinds of play Piaget described, symbolic play seems more than any other to have captured the attention of psychologists, and several explanations have been advanced for it. One of the earliest was G. Stanley Hall's doctrine of recapitulation, which states that children relive in their play the important life activities of their evolutionary ancestors. According to Hall, girls (and boys when they were permitted to) play with dolls because a vestige of their forebears' penchant for idolatry has been transmitted genetically to them. He felt it was necessary for children to work these tendencies out through play so that they would not encumber their adult lives.

Karl Groos expressed the more traditional view that play is a necessary preparation for adult life, but as a form of training, rather than as the kind of purging it was for Hall. According to Groos, the girl's play with dolls prepares her to be a better mother when she grows up, just as the boy's play at war prepares him to become a better soldier.

Three Years Old

Freud agrees with Piaget in viewing symbolic play as a means of neutralizing strong emotions. But unlike Piaget, he sees the emotion involved as a deepseated and unconscious aspect of the personality, stemming from the conflicts encountered in each psychosexual stage. According to Freud, the motives underlying the conflict are expressed through play, and the child thereby experiences symbolically some of the pleasure denied to him in real life.

Thus in his view, a girl might play with dolls because she subconsciously envies her mother or because she covertly wishes she could go back to being a baby herself. Followers of Freud have used play as a diagnostic technique with child patients, finding in it the same links with the unconscious that dreams and free associations reveal to skilled psychoanalysts of adults.

When Jacqueline Piaget criticized the speech of her mother's friend, she was not only engaging in compensatory symbolic play, but was also giving voice to a prevalent complaint of young children: inability to understand adult conversation. Candida expressed this complaint at age three when the diarist wrote: "A similar problem is that of adults monopolizing the conversation; in fact, I think it may be the heart of her objection to our arguments and perhaps even our quarrels. When she and her mother go visiting, all the talk is over her head. Last week this happened at a neighbor's house, so when they got home, Candy insisted on being allowed to go back and visit awhile by herself. Again, when they called on another neighbor, asked to stay for a brief period after her mother left."

In view of children's difficulty in understanding adult conversation, Catherine Snow [1972] studied the question of whether adults normally modify speech addressed to the very young child. Her subjects were 12 mothers of 10-year-olds, 24 mothers of 2-year-olds, and six women who had no children. Each mother was asked to explain something, describe something, and tell a story to her own child and to one of the other age. She did it once with the child present and once into a tape recorder to be played to the child at a later time. The nonmothers only made tapes for the two-year-olds.

In comparing speech addressed to 10-year-olds to that addressed to 2-year-olds, Snow found that mothers had modified the latter significantly. They used shorter sentences, fewer third-person pronouns, etc. to the very young child's need for simplicity: they used simpler speech to 2-year-olds and more complex speech to 10-year-olds than did the other mothers. However, practice at talking to young children was not an absolute must. While the non-mothers tended to use slightly more detailed, precise, and formal-sounding speech than mothers, Snow felt that her most important finding was the similarity of the speech of the two groups of women when they addressed the 2-year-olds. She concluded that the pervasive tendency to modify speech for youngsters serves not only to stimulate the child's interest and comprehension but also aids his learning of his native language.

12
Four
Years
Old

MARCH 23: "We changed around husbands yesterday. I married Bruno, which Louise married, and Louise married Frank, which I had married." A rather complex sentence but not at all unusual.

Last Wednesday was her fourth birthday. She is taller by three inches than most four-year-olds, huskier too, though in play with other children she has not learned to take advantage of her strength. She still

lets boys smaller than she hit her without hitting back.
Intellectually, too, I think she is advanced for her
age, evidenced mainly by her grasp of language and her
understanding of story plots. Socially she is still
backward. She leans heavily on her closest friend Merry,
even refusing certain foods she normally likes when
Merry does. At her birthday party Thursday with two
other less intimate playmates, she and Merry were
cliquish, excluding Peggy and Glenn. At nursery school,
without Merry, she has not learned how to play with
children in a group or, I suspect, even to make a
temporary friendship with a single child. Most of her
play consists in doing things at a table, like painting
or modelling in clay.

Peg has been reading Alice in Wonderland to her in
installments and she likes and seems to understand most
of it. On television she prefers the dramatic programs
including, of course, Westerns and mounted police
stories. She had no liking whatever for yesterday's
symphony program with Toscanini, said the music was too
noisy.

Better than anything on television, better than
anything at all except perhaps playing with Merry, is
still playing with dolls. Last week when she was asked to
choose her birthday present, notwithstanding the
multitude of dolls she already owns--and every one
named--she looked at all the toys in the store and picked
out twin rubber dolls. Her second choice would have been
a Tinker Toy because the pieces were colored. The Tinker
Toy might conceivably have been her first choice had the
colors been pink and green.

She was disappointed in the birthday cards she got,
threatened angrily to tear them up because they were not
pink and green. She reacts in the same way to her name
being written in lower case letters on a drawing or such.
She takes such treatment from the teachers at nursery
school, but when her mother--working there one
morning--did it, it made her angry. She has learned her
name in capitals; with considerable effort she can even
write it that way. She resents seeing it written
otherwise.

"Ah ha!" I hear the educators chortle. "Just what
we've been saying. She'll have to unlearn the capitals

Four Years Old

before she can learn how to read." I say tommyrot. She
knows many lower case letters, with no effort on
anyone's part to teach her. She prefers capitals for the
same reason, I guess, that sign painters do and the
Greeks who invented the alphabet: they're simpler, more
legible, and easier to learn to write. Lower case print
is two steps down the scale in these respects. It
represents a standardization of handwriting which for
its part derived from the original capitals.

I don't worry about Candy having to unlearn
something. This fear confuses education with training
and applies mainly to performing animals and the mastery
of manual skills. For a thinking child the important
thing is to learn how to learn, and this involves an
orderly progression from the simple to the complex,
unlearning as he goes.

JULY 7: No doubt about it, the development of a
four-year-old is less spectacular and noteworthy than
that of an infant or a child of two or three. Candy is tall
and growing rather thin, though she does weigh over 40
pounds. Her belly, that used to protrude so much, is
almost flat. She is more skillful with her hands,
keeping her crayon marks inside the outlines, cutting
rather exactly with scissors, threading buttons. She
has started to assemble the Tinker Toy herself. Her
dolls receive less attention than they used to and when
she does play with them, it is mainly to dress them. From
merely picking flowers and giving them to her mother,
she assembles them herself in vases. She also likes to
put the tracks together for her train. She enjoys
wearing jewelry and prefers frocks to overalls. She is
particular about the things one buys for her, and her
usual first reaction now is to declare she doesn't like
it; a new doll or animal seldom get named any more. As her
acquaintance with other children has widened, she has
acquired certain childish habits she didn't use to have,
notably crying and whining. Lately, too, she has been
screaming at her mother, but this may be due to illness
and confinement to the house. She is getting over a case
of the measles and her umpteenth case of tonsillitis.
Last evening, after a long session of crying about
nearly everything, she went for a walk and was quite
cheerful when she returned.

Intellectually she continues to grow. She can now enjoy having a book read to her while she is not looking at the pictures, although she still prefers picture books of course. Her enunciation and her speaking vocabulary are practically identical with our own.

JULY 9: Fellow down at political headquarters told me yesterday of some friends of his discovering that their four-month-old baby was blind. He thought it was horrible. It was my view that it was less horrible for the child to have no sight to begin with than to lose it and realize what he was missing. This led naturally to a discussion of perception in general and how much of it we all lack without realizing, never having known it. And from that to the seat of all perception, the brain, and how for nearly every one of us that organ—so much more wonderful than the eyes—is all but unusable. If a child grows up without the use of his eyes we think it tragic, but if a child grows up without the use of the greater part of his brain we think nothing of it, for that is the way all but one out of a thousand children do grow up.

I wondered why, amidst all the studies of child development I have read, none has been given to brain development. The brain is, after all, much like any muscle: it needs to exercise in order to grow. Whether a child will want to exercise his brain, whether he will discover that there is pleasure in it—just as there is pleasure in racing and climbing a tree—depends on the amount of exercise he gives it in his earliest years. But what form shall this exercise take? Solving problems? How tough shall the problems be, how much help shall the child be given, and to what extent, if any, shall the child be forced to work on them?

I remember giving Candy a Playskool toy when she was two or younger. It was a wooden duplicate of a nut and bolt and she was supposed to turn the nut off the bolt. I showed her how and let her try, but she always wanted to pull the nut off the bolt rather than turn it. When it would not budge, she got mad and insisted I take it off for her. My problem was whether to keep taking it off until she learned to do it by rote. If I had done that, I am sure she would have grown quite skillful at taking nuts off bolts, but I can't see how it would have encouraged her to solve other problems. So I tried

letting her do it by herself, and of course she gave up.
Merely getting the two things apart was not enough
incentive for the mental effort it required. There were
other thing to play with.

Should there have been more incentive: her food
perhaps? That is how animals are encouraged to solve
problems. But she had long ago learned a better method of
getting fed, and that was to set up a holler. A child has
never had to be resourceful in the search for food. Human
parents have always fed their infants when they could;
and when they could not, the children starved. Perhaps
if Candy had been deprived of all other play resources
except the nut and bolt, she would have worked at it until
she got it apart. Perhaps with nothing better to
stimulate her, she would have become apathetic.

Lord knows there is enough in print about child
nutrition, training to be a polite and considerate
person, psychological (which is to say, emotional)
development, and muscle-building. Why not give some
thought to helping young children to a full realization
of the capacities of the human mind? Or have I simply
missed it?

In the literature of psychology, the concept of *transfer* refers to
the effect previous learning has on later learning. *Positive transfer,* or
facilitation, occurs when subsequent learning is made easier as a
result of earlier learning. *Negative transfer,* or *interference,* is said to
occur when subsequent learning is made more difficult than it would
have been had no previous learning taken place. The diarist expresses doubts about the validity of negative transfer, both in the specific
case of Candida's learning to read capital letters before small ones
and in general: "I don't worry about Candy having to *un*learn something. This fear confuses education with training and applies mainly
to performing animals and the mastery of manual skills. For a thinking
child the important thing is to learn how to *learn,* and this involves an
orderly progression from the simple to the complex, unlearning as he
goes."

In the psychology of children's learning, there is far less evidence of negative than of positive transfer. Charles Spiker [1960] has
attempted to demonstrate negative transfer among sixth grade chil-

dren, using the *paired-associate learning method*. One group was given six learning trials on four word pairs (for example, *sled-clown*). Another group was given 15 trials to learn the same four pairs. Then both groups had to learn another eight word pairs. Half of the new pairs (old-new) retained a word from each of the old pairs (for example, *sled-cup*); the other pairs were entirely new. Spiker assumed that original learning would interfere with the learning of the old-new pairs and, in addition, that the group that had more original learning should show more interference.

Spiker found the net transfer for old-new pairs on the first two trials was "negative, changing to positive after the third trial." The six-trial group did better than the 15-trial group in these same two trials, but overall, there was no difference between the groups in learning the old-new pairs. The 15-trial group did better than the six-trial group in the pairs in the second list, which were entirely new, suggesting that the extra trials of original learning had enhanced their general ability to learn word pairs.

Positive transfer is a frequent occurrence in children's learning, particularly when older children and verbal processes are involved. A procedure often used in this connection is the *discrimination shift* developed by Howard and Tracy Kendler [1962].

In initial learning the subject in a shift study is trained to distinguish between members of two pairs of stimuli which vary in two respects (such as size and shape). The subject might, for instance, see a large square and a small triangle and learn to pick the large square. In other trials, seeing a large triangle and a small square, he might learn to choose the small square. In other words, he learns to ignore size and always choose the square.

Then a transfer task is given. In one kind of transfer, called a *reversal shift*, the same dimension remains relevant, but its values are reversed. So the subject would learn to choose the triangle, still ignoring size. In the *nonreversal shift*, on the other hand, the previously irrelevant dimension becomes relevant. Thus the subject might be taught to pick the large stimulus regardless of its shape.

When rats are given this kind of problem, they learn nonreversal shifts more easily than reversal shifts (Kelleher [1956]). So do most nursery school children (Kendler, Kendler, and Wells [1960]). By kindergarten most children are split about equally; half still learn nonreversals more easily, while the other half learn reversals faster than nonreversals (Kendler and Kendler [1959]). The ease of learning reversal shifts increases from then on, until by college age reversals are learned much more readily than nonreversals (Kendler and D'Amato [1955]).

The Kendlers explain these results in terms of a developmental change in the learning process. The first kind of learning to develop is what they call *single-link* and applies mainly to infrahuman animals and very young children. It is thought to consist of direct associations between external stimuli such as the square and overt responses such as pointing.

The second kind of learning to develop is called *mediational* and includes a symbolic representational response which mediates between the external stimulus and the overt response. Sometimes this mediating response may be a name the subject says to himself; in other cases it may be perceptual or even strictly conceptual with no overt analogue. In the discrimination shift, this mediating response represents the dimension of the stimulus which determined reward in the initial learning phase (the dimension of *shape* in the example of the large and small squares and triangles). Since the same dimension remains relevant during a reversal shift, reversal learning is facilitated through positive transfer for a subject who mediates. On the other hand, shape is irrelevant during the nonreversal shift, so there is no opportunity for transfer of the mediating response, which explains why mediating subjects take longer to learn nonreversals than reversals. According to the Kendlers' theory, as children grow older there is a gradual transition in their mode of learning from simple single-link to more complex mediational learning.

Thus there is some experimental support for the diarist's "commonsense" notion that the child's learning proceeds in "an orderly progression from the simple to the complex, unlearning as he goes." In voicing his skepticism concerning negative transfer, the diarist also voiced a belief in what he called "learning how to learn." This phenomenon, which has also been called *learning set* in psychology, is another kind of positive transfer that has been studied extensively among animals and children.

Harry Harlow [1959] developed a procedure for studying learning set in monkeys. He presented a series of discrimination problems one after the other, each for a fixed number of trials. For example, he might have given the monkey a choice between a tin plate and a spoon for the first six trials, with food always hidden under the spoon. In the next six, he might have let it choose between a leaf and a bead, with food under the leaf.

Using this procedure, Harlow found that the monkeys' learning improved during successive problems. Even though each problem offered a choice between entirely new objects, the monkeys' learning of which member of the pair to choose did not start from scratch. They found the food sooner and more consistently in later problems in the series and eventually (after more than 100 problems) most adult monkeys came to require only one trial.

The learning set procedure has been applied to children with essentially the same results. Reese [1965] found that, on the average, preschoolers acquire learning sets which enable them to solve discrimination problems in one trial after learning just one problem satisfactorily. Harold Stevenson [1970] summarized the findings of several researchers, which showed that children as young as three acquire learning sets faster than do adult monkeys and that older and brighter children acquire them faster than younger and duller children.

Several theories have been advanced to explain learning-to-learn. Harlow [1959] suggests that the improvement which occurs over successive problems is due to the elimination of what he calls *error factors*. According to this view, the subject enters a learning set experiment encumbered with tendencies which impede his ability to learn—for example, the tendency to always pick whatever item appears on the left rather than always choosing a particular object. As the learning set experience accumulates, these tendencies are proven inefficient and are gradually eliminated, thus explaining the steady improvement.

Another theory, proposed by Levinson and Reese [1967] and Levine [1959], is that during learning set subjects develop strategies, or *hypotheses,* such as one called "win-stay, lose-shift," whereby the subject stays with an object after being rewarded for choosing it but shifts to the other object when he fails to get a reward. According to Levinson and Reese, these strategies develop piecemeal in the young child, so that a preschooler might always shift after an error but not always stay with an object after a win.

Stevenson [1970] offers additional explanations for improvements in learning as a result of the learning set procedure: development of appropriate observing responses, attention to relevant properties of the stimuli, changed expectancies concerning the difficulty of the problem, and improved strategies for extracting and remembering information after each response.

Just as Harlow's studies of learning in monkeys led to important

Four Years Old

discoveries about children's learning, the work of the Gestalt psychologist, Wolfgang Kohler [1925], on problem-solving in chimpanzees has provided new impetus for studies of human reasoning and how it develops.

Gestalt psychology emphasizes the quality of wholeness or unity in perception and thought, stating that a whole experience is more than the sum of each of its individual parts. For example, the taste of vanilla ice cream is held to be more than a simple aggregate of coldness, smoothness, sweetness, softness, and a vanilla aroma (Katz [1950]). Support for the Gestalt position was drawn from simple perceptual phenomena such as the tendency to hear the first two taps in a "tap-tap, pause, tap-tap" sequence as a unit (but not the second and third taps), or the tendency to view men in marching formation as a group, while scattered pedestrians appear as individuals.

The Gestalt theory of thinking applies the rules that explain these perceptual phenomena to the organization of mental processes. Koffka [1935], for example, suggests that tendency which causes a triangle to be perceived as a closed shape rather than as three separate lines also explains the intellectual urge to settle an *open question*.

Kohler studied thinking in chimpanzees by providing them with detour, barrier, and reaching problems. In one demonstration he hung bananas from the ceiling of a chimpanzee's cage. There was also a box in the cage. After some minutes of futile jumping and stretching toward the bananas, the chimpanzee paused and scratched its head as it slowly eyed the whole situation. Then it pushed the box under the bananas, climbed on it, and pulled them down.

A similar problem solution was recorded in the diary when Candida was 28 months old: "Last evening she moved the stool from the bathroom to the bedroom and climbed on it to get something off my desk. She could have done it before. In fact, I think she carried the stool around months ago, but until now, it never occurred to her to use it to increase her reach. The idea must have been hers; at least, I don't know where she could have seen anyone else do it."

According to Kohler, the chimpanzee's solution to the reaching problem involved *insight*. In contrast to the trial-and-error groping with which it began its attempt to get the bananas, insight required a restructuring of perception of the situation. Kohler assumed that before solving the problem, the chimpanzee saw the box as an object blocking its path, or perhaps as a container, but saw it neither as a stool nor as being in any way associated with the bananas. After insight, perception of the situation changed to include the potential relation between the food and the box, the box being a tool for obtaining the food. This is made clearer by contrast with a chimpanzee who did not use insight and did not solve the problem. Even though he had watched other chimpanzees, he imitated only part of what they did: he climbed on the box, and even pushed it, but never to the right place. He seemed unable to perceive a connection between the box and the fruit he wanted.

According to Gestalt theory, the same kind of insightful restructuring occurs when humans solve problems, for example, when a man needs to drive a nail and cannot find a hammer (Katz [1950]). He may improvise with a pair of pliers or, if pliers are not available, he may resourcefully remove his shoe and use that. Perception of the shoe is temporarily restructured from being seen as something to wear on the foot to being seen as a makeshift hammer.

From his observations of the chimpanzees, Kohler contended that the process he denoted as insight has to occur, for the following three reasons: (1) he doubted that his apes had ever climbed on boxes to retrieve objects before or watched others do it and therefore, their solution could not result from instrumental or observational learning; (2) dismissing the possibility that random activity chanced to bring a successful solution, he called attention to the "smooth and unchecked movement" involved in the solution activity, such as pushing the box beneath the fruit and climbing on it; (3) he noted that the animal typically paused and surveyed the situation just before solving the problem, and he assumed that perceptual restructuring went on during the pause.

A more recent study by Birch [1945] focused on the necessity for previous experience with manipulating the objects in order for chimpanzees to solve problems insightfully. Birch used the stick problem, in which the animal must rake food into the cage by means of a stick. Unlike Kohler, Birch had information on his six chimpanzees' previous contact with sticks: only one of them, Jojo, had used a stick as a tool before the experiment. Only two chimpanzees solved the stick problem, Jojo and a chimpanzee named Bard who had previously pulled strings to drag food into the cage. Here, too, the

Four Years Old

previous experience seemed to have been crucial: Bard happened to observe the stick in the same position relative to the food as the string had been earlier, so he "pulled it in with the same technique as that which he had used in string-pulling." Birch's other four chimpanzees did not solve the problem spontaneously, but they all managed to do so after three days of experience with sticks.

The fact that experience in manipulating the objects that must serve as the tools for insightful problem-solving is a necessary prerequisite, has a bearing on a question that puzzled the diarist: "I remember giving Candy a Playskool toy when she was two or younger. It was a wooden duplicate of a nut and bolt and she was supposed to turn the nut off the bolt. I showed her how and let her try, but she always wanted to pull the nut off the bolt rather than turn it. When it would not budge, she got mad and insisted I take it off for her. *My* problem was whether to keep taking it off until she learned to do it by rote. If I had done that, I am sure she would have grown quite skillful at taking nuts off bolts, but I can't see how it would have encouraged her to solve other problems. So I tried letting her do it by herself, and of course she gave up." Birch's observations suggest that in order for Candida to apply insight to this problem, she would at least need experience with other turning objects such as, perhaps, wheels or doorknobs.

Candida did not achieve an insightful solution of the problem of separating the nut from the bolt, nor did she of one described when she was 15 months old: "Separating the blocks is especially important and frustrating when she fails—as she usually does. I have shown her an easier way, by letting the inner block slide out through the force of gravity. She appreciates the improvement and makes an occasional half-hearted attempt to turn the blocks so the inner one will slide, but very soon she resorts again to the direct, but ineffectual, method of clawing at the inner block with her fingers. I can't help wondering if in matters beyond our ken we don't all behave in this way. Candy is manifestly logical in her methods. Pulling the block with her fingers is the logical way of getting it out for a person still unfamiliar with the influence of gravity. Sooner or later, of course, she'll learn to let gravity do it, but it will be the result of experience or memory rather than common sense. And, so we all cling to common sense methods and come up against the same frustration. Though we may have an occasional brief glimpse of a method better than common sense, and try half-heartedly to use it, we revert to the direct and logical methods that have failed before."

The fact that in two situations where insight was obviously called for, Candida failed to show any signs of it, not to mention the diarist's personal opinion that adults do not show insight very often, raises the question of just how prevalent insightful problem-solving is among young children. The Kendlers [1967] conducted a series of experiments addressed at this question.

Modeling their procedure on the problems Kohler gave to apes, the Kendlers devised tasks in which children had to integrate two behaviors, each of the two having been learned separately. While Kohler's apes had to integrate the behavior of pushing and climbing on a box with reaching for bananas, and Candida integrated moving a stool with climbing on it, subjects in the Kendler experiments had to integrate the more economical responses of pulling strings, pushing levels, and pressing buttons. In the final version of their procedure, the child initially learned three separate behaviors: to press a button on a red panel to obtain a glass marble, to press a button on a blue panel to obtain a steel marble, and to drop the steel marble down a chute to obtain a toy charm. Then with no marbles in view, the child was asked to get himself a charm. A solution required that he perform the two relevant behavior segments in the proper order.

The Kendlers found that when kindergarteners were given this seemingly simple problem, more than half of them were totally unable to solve it. Most of those who eventually achieved a solution did so indirectly. For example, they frequently pressed both buttons, handed the marbles to the experimenter, etc., before dropping the correct marble down the chute. By the third grade, on the other hand, over half achieved direct and correct solutions: they obtained the steel marble and immediately dropped it into the chute to release the charm. The proportion of third grade nonsolvers was between 12 and 22 percent. By college age, all subjects were able to solve the problem, and 92 percent did so directly.

The experimenters felt that these results indicated that inference, or insight, is infrequent among young children and that the capacity to use it increases with age.

One of the factors involved in its development was discovered in another experiment by the Kendlers. Using the same basic procedure, they had one group of kindergarteners name the marbles (*steel* or *glass*), both when they emerged from the panel and when the relevant marble was dropped down the chute. This naming resulted in more correct integrations by the children. The Kendlers proposed that the name had served as a mediating response similar to the ones they postulated to explain improvements in reversal shift learning with age. According to this view, the child must first develop the ability to represent to himself the two behavior segments which must be joined by inference. Then, because he represents them identically, his chances of joining them together are increased.

In describing the problem of the Playskool nut and bolt, the diarist wonders whether Candida might have solved it if her reward for doing so had been greater: "Merely getting the two things apart was not enough incentive for the mental effort it required. There were other things to play with. Should there have been more incentive: her food perhaps? That is how animals are encouraged to solve problems."

The type and amount of incentive offered have been found to play an important part in children's learning and problem-solving. At least three different kinds of incentives have been studied: *informational, material,* and *social.* An informational reward consists simply of the knowledge that an answer is correct. In the case of Candida and the nut and bolt, seeing that she had gotten them apart was an informational reward. In learning experiments, informational incentives usually consist of buzzers or signal lights, which come on only after a correct response. A material incentive is any reward that is tangible. Food is the most frequent one used in learning studies. Animals often earn their entire day's ration in such experiments, but children merely supplement their diet, mostly with candy, sometimes with raisins or peanuts. Other frequent material incentives for children are trinkets and pennies. Social incentives typically consist of expressions of praise or approval from another person, such as a nod, smile, or the word *good.*

Studies have been conducted to determine which of the three types of incentives produce the fastest learning by children. The results of such studies are somewhat equivocal. Terrell and Kennedy [1957] found that preschool and elementary school children learned a discrimination nearly twice as fast when the reward was candy as when it was praise. Horowitz found that praise resulted in faster learning than a buzzer signal. But Rosenhan [1967] found that children who had had 15 minutes of social interaction with the experimenter before beginning the learning task did better with a signal light than with a social incentive.

When material incentives alone are used, their scarcity seems to increase their effectiveness. Stevenson, Weir, and Zigler [1959] gave children either 5, 10, 20 or 40 colored stickers prior to the experiment. The only children to show clear evidence of learning were those who began with the fewest stickers (5 or 10) and, in addition, had to give back a sticker after each error. The subject's personal preference for an incentive also determines whether the incentive will aid learning. Bisett and Rieber [1966] had 6-year-olds and 10 year-olds rank their preferences for eight rewards. Each age and sex had different orders of preference. One group of children then received their most preferred incentive as a reward in a learning task; the other group received the one they least preferred. Not surprisingly the most-preferred group learned faster. In a similar study (Brackbill and Jack [1958]), kindergarten children learned better when the reward was of their own choosing than when it was one assigned arbitrarily by the experimenter.

In sum, it would appear that the value of a reward as an aid to learning is determined essentially by the one who receives it. A social reward loses its effectiveness on a child who has been sated with social approval, as does another material token on one who already has many. A half dozen M&M's would seem a relatively handsome reward to a preschooler but not to a college student, and the reverse would be true of a pair of theatre tickets.

Even this conclusion must be qualified by the results of two studies comparing informational to material reward. Miller and Estes [1961] divided 9-year-old boys in a discrimination learning task into three groups. One group received 50 cents for each correct response, another received 1 cent, and the last group saw only a signal light. The group that received 50 cents learned no better than did those who received 1 cent, and both groups did significantly worse than the light-only group.

Similarly, middle-class children were found to learn faster when correct responses were followed by a light than when they were followed by a light plus a piece of candy (Terrell, Durkin, and Weisley [1959]). It appears from these results that Candida might not have solved the nut-and-bolt problem any better if her incentive for doing so had been something material such as food.

13
Four
and a Half

AUGUST 18: At nearly four and a half Candy is still rather tightly tied to her mother's apron strings. She is still shy with other children, except Merry when Merry is alone, refuses to play with them and no longer plays by herself as she used to. We took a short trip up to Glen Haven with the trailer a few weeks ago. Merry's parents were vacationing at the State park up there, and we thought it might be nice for Candy if we should join them.

Candy did too and for once was eager to start on a trip. All the way up she talked of seeing and playing with Merry. But when we got there and Merry and her sister Kim came to play with her, Candy would not leave her mother. Since our return we have let Candy stay all day with her grandmother a few times and I am convinced we should do more of it. Peggy, however, prefers to have her mother come out here and help with the work. So actually, for one reason or another, it is Peggy more than Candy who ties the apron strings.

SEPTEMBER 9: We have some new neighbors next door, or will have when they finish building their house. They come on weekends to work on it and their little boy, aged 6, has become a favorite playmate of Candy's. She looks forward eagerly to his coming and, despite the difference in their ages, they get along very well. He lets her tell him what to do, which is all Candy wants; but at the same time, being older and more adventurous, he widens her own field of experience.

She learned how to fly an airplane that you shoot with a rubber band, after having owned it for months. When she first got it I tried to show her how to shoot it and she tried to learn, but it just wasn't interesting enough. Last evening we dug it out of a box of her junk; I fixed up a rubber band on a tinker toy stick; showed her once how to do it and she took right over. I coached her a bit more to prevent her shooting herself with it and she was on her own.

Lately she has been playing what she calls her "lying down game." She gets out of her own bed after waking up and climbs in with me. She's waking now, as a matter of fact. I'll soon hear her call, "I want to get up now." She has become more demonstrably affectionate in recent months; often says to her mother or me, "I like YOU"; and often hugs us as tightly as she can. Here she comes now to have her nose blown.

SEPTEMBER 20: We took our annual trip to the zoo last week and made some movies this time, of the animals, the flowers, the pond, and of Candy walking around looking at them. These pictures are fine records of her physical growth--and we have a fairly complete sequence from the

Four and a Half

age of ten days—but they still leave untold her mental
and personality development. To some extent this
journal does that, but to a very limited extent. I should
like to show with examples her continued growth in the
grasp and expression of ideas. Unfortunately the exact
wording often escapes me, and without her exact words
the flavor is gone.

I recall the other morning when she brought in a small
bouquet of flowers: asters, zinnias, and calendula. She
told me their names and, when I asked her, explained how
each differed from the others. The calendula were
usually yellow or orange. The asters were more
rose-shaped. She smelled one of the asters and said, "It
doesn't have a very deep smell." The use of "deep" to
describe a smell is just such an example I would like to
preserve of her aptness and originality in choice of
words.

She has returned to nursery school: goes mornings
Wednesday and Thursday. One of the rooms has a piano and
some other furniture in it. The children were asked,
after their summer's absence, if they noticed anything
different about it. Only Candy did: the wallpaper. I
have often observed this talent for observation she has,
how she will describe down to the last detail the
appearance and apparel of some person at the time of her
last encounter. But it, like others, has gone
unrecorded.

I had meant to recall an instance of another talent:
her recognition and use of the different meanings of a
word or two words with the same sound. Thus she will pick
up a sentence, alter it slightly to use the central word
in a different sense, and produce a pun. But I can't
remember one to quote.

DECEMBER 9: With Merry she is off today to a
pre-Christmas party at one of the Detroit Library
branches. I think the main reason she likes parties is
because she can dress for them. Her clothes
consciousness extends to her dolls, and Sleepy, who used
to be regularly exposed to summer's sun and winter's
winds (Candy preferred her unclothed), is now decently
dressed most of the time. She also cuts out paper dolls
and dresses them. Her choice of a doll for this Christmas
was based on the clothes Candy saw her [the doll] in.

The people she draws are all elaborately clothed and
the belly button that was once an inevitable part of
every human figure is gone. I'm rather fond of her
portraits with their wide up-curving mouths and large
round eyes. If the hair is curly she draws it so—a halo
of tight round curls. If it is straight, it is really
straight, straight and flat across the top and down in
two straight clusters of lines on each side.

She also constructs figures with a fork, pieces of
paper napkin, and a ribbon to tie them together. They
have vari-colored dresses and hair of shredded paper. So
far as I know, these and the picture abstractions she
does with paints in nursery school are her own idea.

Lately her great enthusiasm has been giving things,
especially to her friend Merry. "Wasn't I generous?" she
asks, and I don't know whether the pleasure comes from
giving or the praise she expects for it. Anyhow, she
devotes much time and thought trying to decide what to
give Merry next time they meet. The other day she told me
she had given Merry her best teddy bear, Frank, given to
her one Christmas by Frank Bayer. The same Christmas,
she received another and much cheaper bear, Bruno, but
it, perversely, has always been her favorite. So I could
appreciate why she gave Frank away.

Still I didn't think it was the right thing to do and
tried to explain why. The bear, I told her, was a present
and she should keep it because the person who gave it
wanted her to have it. It didn't sound too convincing
even to me so we ended up with a little game of going
through her things, deciding what she could and what she
ought not give away. It turned out that most of the things
it was proper to give she could not, either (1) because
she wanted it herself, (2) because Merry already had one
like it, or (3) because Merry had given it to her.

A few weeks ago she was busy deciding to give
something to Merry. I've forgotten what it was but after
she had said for the umpteenth time (saying a thing once
or twice is never enough), "I'm going to give this to
Merry because I don't want it any more," I protested
mildly:

"Well, don't tell her you don't want it or Merry won't
want it either."

"Oh no, I won't," she enthusiastically agreed. "I'll
tell her I want it. I'll tell her I want it, Dot. I'll tell

Four and a Half

her I want it." How easily the diplomatic lie is
cultivated! I suggested she not say anything at all,
because if she told Merry she wanted it, that would not be
true.

In March she will be 5 and would be able to enter
kindergarten if we lived in Detroit. There is no
mid-year entrance in Livonia. Last evening she tried her
first lesson in reading, more as a game than anything
else. I don't much care whether she learns to read
especially early, but if she wants to I can't see any harm
in it.

She continues to show her affection, and
disaffection, more openly. She hugs her mother and me,
telling us how much she likes us--"better even than a
walkie talkie doll!" But when she gets the least bit
angry, she says, "I don't like you." Then in the next
breath, she'll say, "Like!" and reach out her arms for a
hug. She's rather proud of how tightly she can hug, too.

The esthetic, representational, and communicative functions of
children's drawings were discussed in an earlier chapter. In addition,
certain psychologists have put children's art to the more controversial purpose of measuring something called *intelligence*, or *mental
age*. Florence Goodenough [1926] devised one of the first of such
tests; it simply required the child being tested to "draw a man." The
rationale for this was based on the observation that drawings of the
human figure change fairly systematically as the child gets older. The
diarist noticed this when Candida was four and a half. "The people
she draws are all clothed and the belly button that was once an
inevitable part of every human figure is gone. I'm rather fond of her
portraits with their wide up-curving mouths and large round eyes. If
the hair is curly she draws it so—a halo of tight curls. If it is straight, it
is really straight, straight and flat across the top and down in two
straight clusters on each side."

Goodenough noted other changes with age, for example, that
many four-year-olds regularly omitted bodies on the people they
drew and attached the arms and legs to the head, ears, or hat brim. At
a slightly older age they still did this, even though they now drew the
trunk. By age eight, she noticed, the body parts were usually all
joined in the right places, but legs tended to show through trousers,

heads and feet were disproportionate to the rest of the body, and profiles appeared in impossible contortions.

Goodenough came up with a series of 51 points, based on such age regularities in the drawings of many children, forming a scale which she considered to be indicative of mental growth. The Draw-a-Man test determines a child's "mental age" by the number of points out of the set of 51 which his drawing earns. Some of the points include correct location of elements, realistic proportions of parts of the body, and the number of body parts shown. None of the points are designed to measure artistic ability per se, although dexterity and control of a pencil is one of the points.

Goodenough found the test to be successful in sorting out children who were ahead, normal, or backward for their age in school work. She also found a limited relationship between scores on the test and primary-school teachers' ratings of the children's brightness. Owing to the fact that it does not require that the child have a normal American middle-class background or even much in the way of verbal proficiency, the Draw-a-Man test is particularly useful in cross-cultural work and in schools with children of various language stocks.

The use of a scale of points to measure *mental age* originated with the intelligence test developed in France by Alfred Binet. In 1904 the Paris Minister of Education commissioned Binet to come up with an objective way of identifying mentally retarded children in the public schools, so that they might be given special instruction. Until then, personal opinions of teachers and clinicians had been relied on, but it had become increasingly apparent that opinion alone was unreliable and easily influenced by factors other than intellectual potential.

To develop his test, Binet and his collaborator Theophile Simon, looked into a multitude of possible predictors of intelligence, ranging from handwriting analysis and palmistry to the more promising ones of memory, calculating ability, and common knowledge. They eventually collected a set of 30 tasks which spanned a wide range of difficulty and dealt mostly with the kinds of problems a child faces in everyday life, such as naming household objects or remembering numbers. They then tested many children of different ages. On the basis of the information obtained, they arranged the tasks into a graded scale by grouping them according to the earliest age at which a majority of children could pass them. Any individual child's *mental age score* was then determined by referring to the scale. If the child, for instance, performed on the tasks to the standard of most six-year-olds, his mental age was said to be six. If his age in years happened also to be six, he was considered average in intelligence; if it was four, he was considered intellectually advanced; if it was eight, he was considered backward. (The intelligence quotient, or IQ, computed by the formula [Mental age ÷ chronological age] x 100, would be 100 for the first child, 150 for the second, and 75 for the third).

The Binet test was adapted for American children by Lewis Terman at Stanford in 1916 and became known as the Stanford-Binet test. Terman had to replace some of Binet's tasks which, while quite familiar to the ordinary French child of a particular age, were not part of the standard knowledge of an American child of the same age, or sometimes, even one much older. For a similar reason, the Stanford-Binet is periodically brought up to date (once in 1937 and again in 1960), removing antiquated items such as identification of a picture of a wooden washboard or a wood-burning stove.

Some typical tasks on the Stanford-Binet include stringing beads, building a tower of blocks, and copying a circle at age 3; tracing a maze, defining words, counting blocks, and naming the difference between two objects, (such as an apple and an orange) at 6; and, at age 14, solving a mystery and deducing a rule for how many holes will appear when a folded paper is cut. The test is considered a fairly good predictor of a child's academic success in that it correlates well with school grades, teacher's ratings, and college achievement.

A test which was patterned in part after the Stanford-Binet, called the Weschler Intelligence Scale for Children (WISC), includes two subtests, one measuring verbal and the other primarily nonverbal ability. The verbal subtest includes tasks such as word definition, arithmetic, reasoning, and measures of general knowledge. The performance subtest includes tasks such as puzzles, picture completion, copying designs, and picture recognition. Since the WISC yields two separate IQ scores, it is useful when a child's verbal ability underestimates his general intelligence, for example, if he has only a limited knowledge of the language in which he is being tested.

A test that goes even further toward minimizing verbal factors is the Progressive Matrices Test developed in England by J.C. Raven [1956] to measure what he described as abstract reasoning ability. Each item in this test consists of an orderly arrangement of geometrical patterns with one piece missing. The person being tested has to select the missing piece from a number of alternatives (for example, a sample item might be a design resembling a tic-tac-toe board with the lower right intersection of lines cut out, and the choices might consist of, a cross, an X, a vertical line, and a horizontal line). Again, items are arranged in order of increased difficulty to form a graded scale for determining a given child's standing in relation to others of the same age.

All of the tests considered so far are individual and require that one child at a time be tested by a trained examiner. This procedure has certain advantages: the skilled tester can ascertain whether an individual child is in a fit condition to take the test, can make sure he understands and follows the instructions properly, and can, when necessary, take time out to put the child more at his ease or to motivate him to do his best. The disadvantage is that the individual test is impractical in certain situations such as the public schools, where a large number of children must be tested in a relatively short time. Group tests such as the Lorge-Thorndike Intelligence Tests, the California Test of Mental Maturity, the Otis-Lennon Mental Ability Tests, and the Kuhlmann-Anderson Intelligence Tests were devised to meet this need. Some typical items from the Lorge-Thorndike are vocabulary, sentence completion, arithmetic, verbal analogy, picture classification, and numerical relations.

As noted, the issue of intelligence testing is currently a controversial one. At the hub of the controversy is the problem that the word *intelligence* tends to imply more to most people than a score earned on an IQ test and more even than the potential for success in school, which IQ tests have been found to measure adequately, though not perfectly. Just what the more is is hard to define, though some psychologists have attempted to. Piaget, for example, equates intelligence with the superior forms of mental organization that result from the developmental interplay of the processes of assimilation and accommodation. J.P. Guilford [1967] presents a three-dimensional, cube-like model in which the dimensions of (1) *content* (letters, numbers, words, and behavioral descriptions), and (2) *product* (units, classes, relations, systems, transformations, and implications) define the 120 separate intellectual abilities which combine, in his view, to make up intelligence. It is not surprising that a test such as the Binet (or the others described in this chapter, which are in one way or another derived from it), constructed for the avowed purpose of sorting out school children in terms of their ability to profit from traditional classroom instruction, should be found inadequate as a measure of either of these theoretical notions of intelligence. According to Guilford, no single IQ test score ever can be adequate, since "there are no one unitary ability called intelligence and no unitary ability to learn" [p. 464].

The struggle in psychology to define and measure intelligence is paralleled in many ways by the struggle to define and devise a test for creativity. It is held that although creativity is at least as valuable an asset as intelligence, both for the individual possessing it and for society, tests of intelligence do not adequately identify creative children. In fact, by assuming that each question has a single best answer, intelligence tests may penalize the creative child whose thought, according to most definitions, is original and unusual.

Michael Wallach [1970] based his conception of what creativity is on the reported introspection of famous creative writers, artists, and scientists; for example, the poet Dryden's description of his mental process as "a confused mass of thoughts tumbling over one another in the dark." Wallach concluded that creative thinking requires an abundant store of unusual ideas, plus a rather playful mental attitude.

In devising a test to measure creativity in children, Wallach and Kogan [1965] used three verbal and two pictorial measures. The verbal procedures consisted of: (1) an *instances* task, in which the child was asked to name all the things he could think of that had a certain property such as moving on wheels; (2) an *alternate uses* task, in which the child had to think of as many ways as he could to use a given object such as a newspaper; and (3) a *similarities* task, in which the child had to name common properties of pairs of things such as a cat and a mouse. The pictorial procedures involved showing the child abstract line patterns and asking him to say what they looked like.

The child's responses on each of the five measures were scored in terms of uniqueness, or how many of a given child's answers were made by no other child tested, and in terms of quantity, or the total number of ideas offered in response to each question. Wallach and Kogan found that quantity was strongly correlated to uniqueness, both within and across tasks, and that the tasks themselves correlated well with one another. They therefore defined creativity jointly as high productivity and high originality on each of the five task measures. Wallach reports that scores on this test bear essentially no relationship to intelligence test scores, confirming his belief that what he calls *creativity* must be measured independently of the traditional IQ test. He also reports little relationship between creativity scores and school achievement. This is clarified somewhat by the results of an experiment (Walker [1962]) which used a different creativity test and showed that highly creative high school boys have more varied report-card grades than boys low in creativity. In other words, the creative boys seem to devote special effort, and earn high grades, in courses that interest them while letting their other courses slide.

Kornei Chukovsky [1963], a Russian poet and observer of children, found evidence of creativity in young children's spontaneous speech. He was impressed by what the diarist called a child's "aptness and originality in choice of words." Chukovsky gave many examples: A little girl who murmured in her sleep, *Mom, cover my hind leg!* Or another who exclaimed, *Daddy, look how your pants are sulking!* And still another: *Oh Mommy! How balloony your legs are!* One little girl was fond of flowers. She drew a picture of some and then drew several dozen dots. Someone asked, *What are those? Flies?* She replied, *No! They are the fragrance of the flowers.*

At four and a half, Candida spoke of the fragrance of flowers in a way which illustrated Chukovsky's notion of creativity in choice of words: "She smelled one of the asters and said, *It doesn't have a very deep smell.*" Earlier, when Candida was 2 years and 10 months old, the diarist recorded: "I was running the power sander on some wood. *That's a cold sound,* said Candy. *I'm shivering!*"

Chukovsky recognized that some of the child's neologisms were due to ignorance. An obvious mistake in choice of words was recorded when Candida was two and a half: "She said yesterday, *I won't play with Pogue because I'm so angry to eat. You mean anxious. Yes, I'm so anxious to eat.* But Chukovsky felt that most childish metaphors were genuine metaphors, deliberate alterations of the usual meaning of a word, in order to give it a new connotation.

Heinz Werner [1948], an influential theorist in developmental psychology, disagrees with this view: "I do not believe that many of the so-called metaphors so common to children . . . are actually metaphors springing from an inadequacy of exact verbal expression. It is quite reasonable to assume that they are often rooted in an actual undifferentiated experience of sensation" [p. 88].

According to Werner, Candida used the adjective *deep* to refer to an odor, not for lack of a better word, but because she was as yet unable to differentiate clearly between her sense of sight and her

Four and a Half

sense of smell. Similarly, he would argue that her use of *cold* to refer to a sound, derived from a lack of differentiation between sound and temperature sensations, intensified by the fact that they both caused her to shiver. Werner cited some related examples. A three-year-old child smelled a pellargonia leaf and said, *The leaf smells green.* while after smelling the purple pellargonia flower, he remarked, *That smells red* and of the lilac, *That smells awfully nice and yellow.*

Werner called the inability to distinguish between sensations on the basis of the modality they arise from, *synaesthesia.* He found evidence of synaesthesia among primitive peoples (the Zuni Indians, according to Werner, associate a color with each direction of the compass), the mentally ill (Werner quoted a schizophrenic patient as saying, *Man has not five senses but only one*), and in reports from users of hallucinogenic drugs such as mescalin.

According to Werner, the phenomenon of synaesthesia is one instance of a more general principle which he called *orthogenesis* and which states that development—and here he meant cultural as well as individual development—consists of a steady progress from an initially global or undifferentiated state through a state of differentiation to an eventual hierarchic integration in which differentiated parts are reunited as separate elements of the whole. In the example of synaesthesia, the global state occurs in the young child who cannot distinguish between the inputs of his various sense organs; differentiation occurs, and synaesthesia disappears, when he learns to treat his senses as separate processes; finally, with hierarchic integration, synaesthesia reappears in the form of cross-model metaphor, as when the adult calls a kind of music *blues* or uses the adjective *cold* to refer to a tone of voice.

Chukovsky studied children's poetic creativity as well as their creative use of words. He noted that when children begin to compose verse, around the age of three, rhythm and movement are essential features. He felt that the child of this age had to move some part of his body while composing or reciting poetry; most of the poems were made up in the course of vigorous running about during a climax of emotion. As an example, he cited a rhyme by his four-year-old won who was chasing his sister around the garden on a broomstick: *I'm a big, big rider–you're smaller than a spider.*

Chukovsky observed several distinctive qualities of poems by three-year-olds: repetitiveness (a single line is often reiterated over and over), a regular beat, frequent rhyme, and an almost invariably joyful theme. These qualities are illustrated in a poem Candida composed when she was three:

> *Book, book*
> *Tra la la*
> *Nice book*
> *You're a nice book*
> *Tra la la*
> *Book, book.*

Chukovsky found that preschoolers value these qualities just as much in the verse of others. He felt this was due to the integral connection they see between poetry, physical movement, and music.

According to Chukovsky, the urge of the child under six to compose poetry is as inevitable as his urge to draw and paint, and all but the very sad or sickly make up short rhymes. They are also prone to make up lists of rhyming words, like Candida did when she was five and a half. Chukovsky once heard children in a Moscow nursery school take turns adding one rhyming nonsense word to another: *trunk, nunk, lunk* laughing at each new addition.

Like Goodenough, who found that most children give up drawing during the early years in elementary school, Chukovsky found that all but a few cease composing poetry, and the poems of those children who do continue, take on a new quality. In comparison to the verse of preschoolers, he describes poems of 6 and 7-year-olds as more literary and intellectual. Free verse is common, "since clapping and chanting are now replaced by thought and introspection." Finally, around age 9 there is another change, and child poets begin to use the metric forms of adult verse. Thus by age 9, Candida was using iambic meter when she composed this:

> *The sky is covered with a pink light*
> *A light so beautiful and bright*
> *A light that changes day to night.*

14
Five
Years
Old

MARCH 22: Christmas and New Year's have come and gone
with no comment in this journal, but I mustn't overlook
Candy's fifth birthday. The party was last Friday, was
scheduled to terminate at 5:30, but was still proceeding
boisterously when I got home at 6:00. There were eight
children present. Though she still does little visiting
herself except at Merry's house, others have been over
to play with her, and these were her guests. They
included another Candy (Candace), Karen, Frederick

(soon to move next door), and Karen's younger brother Timmy. All are in school or kindergarten. Thus her circle is gradually widening and her handicap of being in a one-child family is being surmounted.

In health, too, she was fortunate last winter. Except for a couple of accidents and bruises, her only ill health was a week-long bout of indigestion. Her rash is less troublesome.

Drawing and coloring with crayons are still her favorite pastimes, and she also enjoys being read to, especially from comic books. She prints and recognizes all capitals and some lower case letters, most numerals from 1 to 9, and some of the others. She can count to 12 and perhaps higher, knows the days of the week, and can tell the hour by the clock ("nearly" or "past"). She knows that hours are longer than minutes and dollars are bigger than pennies, nickels, dimes, and quarters. She is learning left from right.

For about a year she has received 25 cents a week as an allowance and, with no special encouragement, she saved most of it to buy herself a walkie doll for Christmas. After Christmas, in anticipation of her birthday party, she decided to save the remainder in order to buy chocolate Easter eggs for her guests.

Flowers are her one great passion and none of her birthday presents pleased her more than the packages of flower seeds she received. She can recognize and name more flowers than I can, including several weeds and wild flowers. Her latest acquisitions of toy animals and dolls have been given names like Anemone, Camellia, Carnation, and especially Rose. She actually danced for joy at Christmas time when a gift of poinsettia arrived, from one of my business contacts.

Her new walkie doll, which she named Candy, displaced Sleepytime Pogue in her affections—a thing I thought could never happen. Sleepy, in her third incarnation and scheduled for a fourth that apparently won't be necessary, languishes in the bottom of the toy box. Candy has rayon hair that can be combed and curled; but now a small air-filled plastic bunny has even taken Candy's place, though it is not a new toy. When the doll Candy got a bride's dress for the birthday party, the girl Candy was envious and wept because she didn't get one!

Five Years Old

I have a scribbled notation on a discussion of the expression "Believe you me" the radio and TV commentators seem currently in love with, and Candy's observation: "Maybe they figure . . . that that's the believest one . . . that lots of people will believe it."

APRIL 14: When Candy said she hadn't heard something, I reminded her that she was present when it was said. "Maybe," she answered, "I was listening to my thoughts."

MAY 3: "Snowflake, snow flake
In the meadow.
You are not a breakfast flake.
You are only a snow flake."
So goes one of the songs she has made up. Similarly, after she had answered "because" when I asked her the why of something, "Because is not why," I protested. "Tell me why." "All right," she said. "Why." Privilege has become her most jealously guarded possession: privilege or the right to a thing more than the thing itself. Being read to before going to bed, for example. Nothing, the lateness of the hour, staying up for television, or home movies, must stand in its way. To the question, "Which would you rather do, see another reel or be read to?" the answer is, "Both. Just read me one square." It isn't what she reads that counts; simply her established right to reading at bedtime. So it is on other occasions, like taking Bop for his morning walk. She doesn't always want to go with him, seldom to the extent of hurrying with her dressing. But if her mother goes off without her, just because she is not dressed, she sets up a loud wail.

Insistence on hollow privilege is generally looked upon as a childish trait. With Candy, however, it seems to be growing as she grows. Later on in life, she may not actually cry when her rights or privileges are taken away, but will her sense of outrage be less? Is privilege, in other words, something we acquire as part of the process of asserting our individuality?

AUGUST 14: There are a couple of high wooded dunes near our camp here on Lake Michigan. Peg and Candy are busy climbing them right now, taking Bop for his morning walk. Now they are back. "Wouldn't you like to do that again, Mommy? It seems like it was shorter than last time. When are we going to do it again?"

"Well, first we have to put our bathing suits on and go to the beach."

Candy pouts, her lower lip reaching out as far as it will go. It is an exaggerated pout, largely for dramatic effect, and goes quickly when she hears she can climb the dunes again this afternoon. She likes the water and especially likes making cookies and cakes of wet sand. Here she returns again and crying. She stubbed her toe while off with Mom on some errand. Now she is getting the cut washed and is quite a baby about it.

AUGUST 15: We drove to the beach again yesterday morning, to the same place we had been by the roadside and down the steep bluff. The water was rather rough. Candy got her nose full when a wave dashed over and was leery about going back in. But she did after awhile, holding her mother's hands and jumping up and down with the waves.

AUGUST 16: She has a fever, an apparent recurrence of her tonsillitis. She had tonsillitis early this summer and received penicillin treatment for it. Then a few weeks later, it flared up again and the doctor put her on a regular course of penicillin: two half-teaspoons a day. She went back for a check-up and he ordered the course continued; so she has been getting penicillin even as the fever broke out. I should like Peggy to have the doctor explain that.

AUGUST 17: Except for Candi's illness (yes, I'm spelling her name the way she now spells it) this has been a very nice vacation. Even though the temperature is fairly high (80 degrees or so), it is comfortable inside the trailer, and it was never so in Florida last May.

About the spelling of her name: she has a small chair with the word "Scandi" printed on it. It means "people" in one of the Scandinavian tongues. I suggested one day that if the "s" were taken away, it would spell her name, that ending in "i" was just as good as "y" and less confusing with the candy you eat. She took to it immediately and discovered, incidentally, how much

185

Five Years Old

easier it is to print "i" than "y." "I can leave the tails off," she said.

She draws the vertical first in a capital Y and then the upper V, which she calls the tails. For good measure she learned to write her last name and, on the strength of being able to write her full name without help, she obtained a Detroit library card.

OCTOBER 26: Asked what I had to do before I could play with her, I named a couple of things, adding "and Lord knows what else." Candi said, "When will you ask the Lord what else?"

I marvel at how grown up she is. She is tall and weighs 50 pounds. We just got her some blue jeans, size 6X from Sears, where clothes are generally oversize. They are too small for her. But more than her size, her behavior makes her seem grown up. She likes, first of all, to feel she is grown up, which is true, no doubt, of most little girls of $5\frac{1}{2}$ years. The easiest way to discourage her from doing something is to tell her it is too childish (like screaming, for instance--though now that I think of it, she continues to scream); and to encourage her is to tell her big girls do it (like wearing blue jeans or eating peas). The thing she wants most for Christmas is a beauty set with real lipstick and rouge. Perhaps she is not grown up so much as that she would like to be grown up.

She is in kindergarten for two hours every afternoon--the most Livonia schools can give--will do almost anything to get to school. Too bad we'll be taking her out to go to California. We put off leaving till after the school Hallowe'en party and promised to return in time for the Christmas party. That seemed to be all she required and she says she wants to go--but I can't really tell.

OCTOBER 30: We couldn't have ordered a better day to start the trip. After Wednesday's rain and cold and gloom, I thought our sunny days were gone for the winter. But today's skies were cloudless and it was cool enough for comfortable driving. The country is beautiful. Many of the trees are bare, but many others are in color. The willows are still green. Farmers are husking and hauling corn. The fields seem unusually full of sheep, hogs, and cows. And the road seemed less cluttered with trucks than usual.

OCTOBER 31: Candi napped again this afternoon. She is up playing with a visiting kitten. We thought there might be another Hallowe'en party but this trailer park is much quieter than the one in Marion. Last night's party was a dud. The kids arrived in their masks and sat around waiting for something to happen or refreshments to arrive. They were still waiting when Peg went to fetch Candi, not at all sorry to leave.

NOVEMBER 5: Candi is a cheerful traveller. She plays or sews with her mother in the morning while I drive, and she sings and talks. After lunch she naps while Peggy drives. Here in the rain she is coloring and pasting at the table as contented as you please. Bop, for a change, is also in the trailer with us on account of the miserable weather. And Candi generally has something to say about him.

NOVEMBER 8: Our tenth day out and we are in Deming, New Mexico. Candi drew a page full of pictures and then made up a story about them. She told the story without pause or hesitation. It was rather inventive, too, about two good bunnies named Judy and Andrew and a bad bunny named Awful Heart. After telling this story, she moved to another set of pictures and told a story about them. Now she is practicing handwriting.

NOVEMBER 11: Travelling as we have been, with only a few daylight hours at each stop, she has had to learn to make friends quickly. A little boy at Ponca City, Oklahoma taught her one sure-fire method by presenting her with half a bagful of candy the minute he arrived. Here at Calexico, California, there is a little girl of school age. Without delay when she saw her last evening, Candi gave her a lollipop and now this morning they are playing like old friends. Candi seems to do most of the talking, telling about her various dolls and who gave them to her, about the Ewens whom we are to visit, her cousins, her friend Merry. Every anecdote is precisely annotated with full names and circumstances. She certainly has an excellent memory for details.

NOVEMBER 14: She had a fine time at the San Diego trailer park playing Supergirl. This involved wearing her coat like a cape and running to make it fly while she hollered "Supergirl!" She was delighted with the flowers growing at every patio. Here at Carpinteria there are no flowers, but the park is very nice all the same. We are on a grassy lawn beside an outdoor gas cooker and a table. We can hear the steady roar of the surf just over a low hill and can walk to the beach a few hundred feet away.

NOVEMBER 21: She asked what people used to eat potatoes with before silverware was invented. I told her there was a saying that "fingers were invented before forks." She said, "Why sure! Fingers were invented when people were invented; before people even. Animals' paws are their fingers." But what gave her the idea that animals came before people?

After taking the trailer to the gas station for service, I brought Candi back to the trailer park to play with a new friend Cathy and to give her the package of Japanese toys she had bought for her. But though it was after ten, Cathy didn't come out and Candi was too shy to knock on her trailer door. The park owner's daughter, a four-year-old named Jean, came over, but Candi wouldn't play. All her thoughts were on Cathy and the toys they would open up together.

NOVEMBER 22: The park here at Pismo Beach has flowers and a little boy going on 5 named Pony. He is very friendly and came to our car asking, "Do you have any little boy or little girl I can play with?" Candi piped up that she would be out as soon as her shoe was buckled and they played on Pony's swing while he kept up a running fire of chatter.

NOVEMBER 25: She has a loose front tooth, one of the lower ones. A new tooth has been pushing up behind it. I tried to pull the loose one out with thread but I couldn't, which was a disappointment. She wants to put it under her pillow and make a wish. She is in bed now and has just asked for a drink. After her first swallow she said, "I'm

188

pretending that I'm in dreamland and I'm eating supper."
That was what she wanted the drink for.

NOVEMBER 29: At the last minute, after we had called
them, Candi decided she didn't want to visit the Ewens,
not until tomorrow. I reminded her how much fun she had
had with young John two years ago and this seemed only to
stiffen her resistance. So we agreed to call them back
after supper and beg off. They came while we were eating,
however. We went back with them for another supper, and
she and John hit it off immediately. He was playing shy
when we arrived, hiding in his room. He had refused to
believe she was any but the tiny child he remembered or
that she could have grown to near his own size. He is a
year older than she. I asked her this morning what she and
John did. She answered enthusiastically, "We did sword
fighting." She even wants to wear blue jeans instead of a
dress today (an unheard-of decision) in order to play
with Johnny. Leaving L.A. is going to be difficult.

NOVEMBER 30: Her tooth came out this morning. She pulled
it out herself. She plans to wish for a bride doll.

DECEMBER 1: She got the bride doll she wished for. She
didn't seem surprised. Either she had supreme faith in
the lost tooth or she guessed what her mother was up to
when we visited the toy store.

DECEMBER 3: In the car this morning she counted on her
fingers up to ten, then announced, "Five and five are
ten." She had figured it out for herself. She followed
with, "One and one are two, two and two are four." "How
much is three and three?" I asked. "Just a minute and I'll
tell." She counted on her fingers. "Six!"

DECEMBER 11: Candi got mad at me last evening and besides
saying she hated me she threatened to make something for
Mom but not for me. This morning I asked her if she would
make me something after all. She happily agreed to make
me a drum. I supposed she meant to draw me one instead she
actually made it out of paper, and a very ingenious
product it turned out to be. With her mother's help she
wrote the numbers 1 to 1,000, and now she is trying to tie
a bow on Sleepy. She was delighted to hear the trailer

Five Years Old

park owner call his dog Boppie. She and I had thought
there was no other dog but ours with that name.

It is easy to appreciate a parent saying, as the diarist did, "No
doubt about it, the development of a four-year-old is less spectacular and noteworthy than that of an infant or a child of two or three."
Apart from the changes in weight, height, shape of the figure, skill
with the hands, and participation in adult recreations such as arranging flowers, which the diarist remarked on, there are few obviously
noticeable new physical, social, emotional, or linguistic developments during the late preschool and early elementary school years.
This is, however, a time of truly remarkable intellectual development.

In a summary of research on children's learning and cognition,
Sheldon White [1965] reported that 21 major changes occur during
the years from five to seven, and concluded: "This is an extremely
interesting convergence in a developmental literature not given to
major convergences" [p. 196]. Seven of the changes were in the
area of learning, including the Kendlers' finding of increasing ease
of the reversal shift. Six dealt with perception and orientation,
among them the child's learning to tell his left hand from his right.
Two dealt with intelligence-testing, one being the greater accuracy
of tests given after age five in predicting what the adult IQ will be.
The remaining six changes were miscellaneous, including
Vygotsky's finding of the emergence of the planning function of
speech.

The diarist also remarked on some of Candida's intellectual
achievements when he wrote on her fifth birthday: "She prints and
recognizes all capitals and some lower case letters, most numerals
from 1 to 9, and some of the others. She can count to 12 and perhaps
higher, knows the days of the week, and can tell the hour by the
clock (*nearly* or *past*). She knows that hours are longer than minutes
and dollars are bigger than pennies, nickels, dimes, and quarters.
She is learning left from right."

From some of these examples, such as her ability to count, it
would appear that Candida has achieved a basic understanding of
numbers; others, such as her recognition that hours are longer than
minutes, reveal a basic understanding of quantity. However, according to Piaget, the child's understanding of number and quantity is

incomplete without a concept of *conservation*. As he defined it, conservation is the notion that certain properties of things, (number, length, weight, etc.) remain unchanged after certain transformations, or changes in their appearance (moving the things, breaking them into pieces, changing their shape, etc.).

While the list of Candida's accomplishments could be proudly displayed by her father, had she been subjected to one of Piaget's tests for conservation, she might well have failed it, along with the overwhelming majority of children her age. If Candida had been tested in Piaget's laboratory for conservation of liquid amount, she would probably have been shown two identical glasses of lemonade, filled to exactly the same level. Piaget would have asked her if there was the same amount to drink in each glass and, if she said there was, he would have emptied one of them into a taller but narrower glass and asked the same question. Now, if she held to the pattern of most four-to-six-year-olds, she would have answered that the amount in the two glasses was no longer equal, claiming either that the tall glass had more in it because the level of lemonade was higher or that there was more in the short glass because it was wider. According to Piaget, children of this age fail to recognize that simply changing the shape of a container cannot change the amount of liquid in it (provided none is spilled or added). In other words, they do not *conserve* amount when visual appearances change.

To see if this also applied to number, Piaget showed children two evenly spaced rows of seven pennies, each six inches long, and asked if there were the same number of pennies in each row. Those who thought there were, then watched Piaget lengthen one row by spreading the pennies apart. When questioned again, most children under six thought there were more pennies in the longer row. Surprisingly enough, this was even true of children who counted the pennies in each row and came up with the correct totals of seven.

In addition to conservation of liquid amount and number, Piaget specified at least eight other conservations, among them conservation of mass, weight, and volume. These he studied, using two round balls of clay which the child initially judged as equal. For conservation of mass, he rolled one ball into a sausage and asked if it still contained as much clay as the ball. Most nonconservers said it contained more because it was longer. For conservation of weight, he asked if the ball and sausage would weigh the same when placed on a scale; and for volume, he asked if they would move the water level up by an equal amount when submerged in identical basins.

Five Years Old

Piaget found that conservation of mass developed around age seven and weight around age nine, while conservation of volume was infrequent under the age of 12.

In all of the conservation tasks, Piaget found a series of three stages—an initial one of no conservation, in which quantity was judged simply by appearances; a stage of *on and off* conservation, in which the child seemed to waver between perception and conservation (for example, he might conserve number when the objects in one row were flowers and in the other, vases; but not conserve it when both rows contained pennies); and a final stage of "complete" conservation, in which the child backed up his conservational judgments with appropriate explanations such as *You didn't add any so they must be the same* or *You can tell they are the same if you pour back the lemonade (press the row of pennies together, roll the clay back into a ball).* In the last stage, also, the children were frequently surprised or even scornful that the examiner would ask such an obvious question.

Before a child can develop conservation of number, several other numerical abilities must develop, and these too have been shown to follow a regular series of stages. Typically, the first one a child masters is rote counting, and Candida had partly done so by 18 months when the diarist wrote: "She counts from one to six, omitting two and four in the process."

After the child learns to recite the number series up to 10 correctly, he is likely still to be unable to count things. He may, for example, run his finger quickly over a row of five checkers, counting, *one, two, three.* Or if his finger is slower and his reciting is faster, he may reach a total of eight. The child is as yet unaware of the function of number as either denoting a quantity or to be paired with the objects being counted. By the time Candida was 2 years and 10 months old, her accuracy in counting things showed she had become aware of these functions: "We have a new game called playing store. She sells me things, I sell her things, and we count out the money in each other's hand. She counts up to six with no trouble and yesterday discovered with some slight surprise that she has five fingers on each hand, five toes on each foot, two eyes, cheeks, ears, and hands, and one nose, chin, and forehead."

Even after the child learns to count things, he has difficulty matching sets of things by number. Long and Welch [1941] tested counting by asking children to select a specified number of marbles from a larger collection, and tested matching by asking them to pick out as many marbles as there were in a set already selected by the experimenter. The counting task was mastered by age 3½, while the matching task was not mastered until age 7.

Continuing in the search for an order of development of numerical aptitudes, J.F. Wohlwill [1960] gave a card-matching test to 77 children between the ages of 4 and 7. There were eight parts to the test, and in each part the child had to pick a choice card which contained as many dots as were represented on a sample card. The sample card contained arrangements of dots, arrangements of geometrical shapes, partitioned rectangles, groups of dots to which new dots were added, and so on, in the various parts of the test.

Wohlwill interpreted his results as indicating three stages in number development. During the first, the child failed all the tests except the simplest, in which dots were matched to other dots and there were less than five dots on each card. He concluded that at this stage, the child judged number by rough perceptual estimation rather than by counting. In the second stage the children, though still limited to numbers under five, passed tests of number abstraction (matching dots to colored squares or triangles according to number), eliminated perceptual cues (matching partitioned rectangles to dots), and memory (delay between viewing the sample and making a choice). Wohlwill concluded that children at this stage could abstract numbers from other perceptual cues, but that they had no notion of relating individual numbers to one another. The latter ability developed in the third stage, when the child's now sophisticated number concept was evidenced by his ability to deal with higher-order relationships such as number conservation, matching numbers over five, addition, and subtraction.

Contrary to his expectation, Wohlwill found that addition developed before number conservation. This is in line with the diarist's observation that Candida discovered addition spontaneously at the age of five and a half: "In the car this morning she counted on her fingers up to ten, then announced, *Five and five are ten*. She had figured it out for herself. She followed with, *One and one are two, two and two are four. How much is three and three?* I asked. *Just a minute and I'll tell*. She counted on her fingers. *Six!*."

Still another ability the child must develop according to Piaget, before attaining mathematical concept of number is the ability to construct a series, for example, by arranging a set of sticks of graded lengths in order from longest to shortest. Piaget found that five-year-olds tended to make minor errors in this task and had difficulty inserting new sticks once the original series had been completed. He inferred that they used a pictorial approach and simply tried to make the whole thing look right. Seven-year-olds, on the other hand, constructed series and inserted new sticks with ease. Piaget concluded that they used a relational approach, being aware that any given stick was shorter than certain sticks while it was longer than others, these two facts jointly determining its position in the series.

By the same token, Piaget saw a relational approach as being necessary for the development of more complex notions of left and right. Though the diarist reported of five-year-old Candida, "She is learning left from right," Piaget's data suggest that at this age, she would be aware of these terms only as they applied to her own body and that she would have had difficulty in identifying the left hand of a person facing her or in saying of three objects on a table which was to the left of which. The latter tasks were typically not accomplished by Piaget's subjects until age 8, and he inferred that by this age they had come to view left and right as relational terms which depend on a particular vantage point being taken.

The studies so far considered—on conservation, mathematics, and relational concepts, as well as those reviewed by White [1965]—testify that the diarist was wrong in contending that child psychologists had devoted little attention to *brain* development—or, at any rate, that he had been reading the wrong books: "I wondered why, amidst all the studies of child development, I have read, none has been given to brain development. The brain is, after all, much like any muscle: it needs exercise in order to grow . . . Lord knows there is enough in print about child nutrition, training to be a polite and considerate person, psychological (which is to say, emotional) development, and muscle-building. Why not give some thought to helping young children to a full realization of the capacities of the human mind. Or have I simply missed seeing it?"

The work of Piaget alone spans many volumes and is devoted almost entirely to mental development. In fact, Piaget [1931] even probed children's own concept of their mental process. He asked five and six-year-olds what people think with. They replied, *We think with our mouths* or in some way equated thinking with speaking. Candida seems to have done this implicitly when she was five, since she referred to thought as something to be listened to: "When Candy

194

said she hadn't heard something, I reminded her that she was present when it was said. *Maybe* she answered, *I was listening to my thoughts.''*

Piaget's five-year-olds contended that not only could thought be heard, it could be seen as *wind making the trees and grasses wave.* Some of them made an exception for animals which, being unable to speak, thought with their ears instead of their mouths. Piaget sensed that, at a slightly older age, between 7 and 10, children were confused between their own spontaneous belief that thought was a voice and the influence of adults telling them that thought was in the head. He found that they resolved the confusion by describing thinking as *a little voice inside our heads* or *what we hear inside our heads.* It was not until age 11 that children came to view thought as something inner, psychological, and distinct from material activity.

Interestingly enough, these three stages in children's descriptions of the thought process parallel Vygotsky's three stages in the merging of speech and thought—from *external* to *egocentric* to *inner* speech. The responses Piaget obtained from children are thus surprisingly accurate descriptions of what Vygotsky theorized their thinking to be.

Piaget explained the development of conservation, relational concepts, and the notion that thought is insubstantial and subjective as being due in large measure to the child's social interchange with his peers. He especially favored children's engaging in arguments with one another, since in the course of an argument the child is often forced to see someone else's viewpoint. For example, if two children argue about who has the most lemonade and decide to resolve it by trading glasses, the child who initially judged quantity exclusively by the height of the column of lemonade may suddenly notice width when he himself receives the taller but much narrower glass. According to Piaget, such forced alterations of viewpoint lead eventually to simultaneous consideration of the two dimensions and thence to conservation.

The value of argument for conservation was affirmed in an experiment by Frank Murray [1972]. He tested 6-year-olds' conservation ability individually and divided them into groups of three (generally one nonconserver and two conservers). Each group then had to reach a consensus on the answers to some new conservation problems. The nonconserver was always questioned first. When there was disagreement, the experimenter directed the children to discuss the

Five Years Old

problem and explain their answers to one another. One week later, each child was tested again individually. In comparison with their scores on the pretest and with a control group who did not participate in the group judgments, all the children, and especially the nonconservers, made significant gains in conservational judgments and in the explanations with which they supported them.

Also in keeping with the view that these rapid strides in intellectual development are due in part to peer social interaction is the fact that between the ages of 5 and 7, when the child enters school, his social circle typically widens markedly. The diarist noted this in describing Candida's fifth birthday party: "There were eight children present. Though she still does little visiting herself except at Merry's house, others have been over to play with her, and these were her guests. They included another Candy (Candace), Karen, Frederick (soon to move next door), and Karen's younger brother Timmy. All are in school or kindergarten. Thus her circle is gradually widening and her handicap of being in a one-child family is being surmounted."

As well as stimulating intellectual functioning, the kindergartener's and elementary schooler's widening social contact with peers is responsible for the development of two important social behaviors: conformity and competition.

As the term *conformity* is used in psychology, it refers to a person's tendency to change his own judgment or viewpoint to make it agree with that of others, even in the face of evidence that the other people are objectively wrong. A procedure for studying it was developed by Solomon Asch and first used with children by Ruth Berenda [1950]. From the point of view of her child subjects, the task simply involved deciding which one of a set of lines was equal in length to a standard line. However, the subject was always asked to give his judgment last, either after eight of the brightest children in his class or after his teacher. Actually the eight other children and the teacher were *stooges* of the experimenter: they had been primed beforehand to give unanimously false judgments on some of the lines. Conformity was indicated when a child gave the false judgment of the majority. There was little likelihood of this being a genuine error, since all subjects had shown high accuracy in a pretest, when they answered alone.

Berenda found a great deal of conformity to both peers and teacher among all the children he studied. However, the

7-to-10-year-olds conformed more than the 11-to-13-year-olds, and peers were conformed to more than the teacher.

Constanzo and Shaw [1966] conducted a study similar to Berenda's using subjects ranging from 7 to 21 years old. These subjects also made line judgments after witnessing the false judgments of three simulated stooges (the experimenter lit up the lines they supposedly chose). Conformity was least among 7-to-9-year-olds and greatest among 11-to-13-year-olds. It began to decline at age 15, and among college students it was almost as low as among second and third graders. The early adolescents, who conformed the most, tended also to place the blame for lack of agreement on themselves (for example, *I must be going blind*). At the younger and older ages, subjects blamed the stooges (*I think the others guys were crazy*).

Two studies with preschool children—one involving 10 kindergarteners (Hunt and Synnerdahl [1959]) and the other, a larger number of 3-to-6-year-olds (Starkweather [1964])—found essentially no conformity to peer-group pressure. However, the diarist described a case of conformity in Candida when he wrote on her fourth birthday: "She leans heavily on her closest friend Merry, even refusing certain foods she normally likes when Merry does."

Age differences are similarly found in children's competitiveness toward one another. C. Leuba [1933] engaged children in a peg-board task either alone or side by side. The performance of 2-year-olds was generally unaffected by the presence of the other child. Three-and 4-year-olds did worse when the other child was present, which Leuba attributed to distraction produced by rivalry. Five-year-olds did better when working side by side; Leuba concluded they also felt competitive, but in their case, rivalry served as a spur toward better performance.

In a similar vein, P.J. Greenberg [1932] found that the amount of rivalry produced by competition-inducing instructions increased greatly between the ages of 2 and 7. The diarist remarked of 5-year-old Candida: "She will not push forward in competition with other children. Yesterday Karen, Timmy, and Fred were over playing with her toys. She stood off on one side not joining them and resenting their invasion." In addition to her age, Candida's backwardness in competition might be partly explained by her sex. Maller [1929] found that in a series of schoolroom contests, boys were more competitive than girls.

Whether or not competition harms children's friendships for one another was a question studied by Muzafer and Carolyn Sherif [1953] in the setting of a boys' summer camp. They left the boys alone for three days while budding friendships formed. Then they

Five Years Old

split up pairs of friends by separating them into two groups and isolating the groups for five days. During this period new friendships formed within each group. The third phase of the experiment involved strenuous competition in team contests between the two groups. The abilities of the two teams were found to be unequally matched: one consistently won the contests, while the other consistently lost. Within the losing group, friends turned hostile toward one another. In addition, boys from both groups showed hostility toward the former friends who were now their opponents on the other team. The experimenters' efforts to reunify friendships by involving the boys in cooperative projects had achieved only partial success by the time the camp ended.

Although this study indicates that competition damages friendship, a later study by the Sherifs [1961], in which the teams' abilities were more evenly matched, found increased solidarity within groups as a result of competition.

15
Five
and a Half

DECEMBER 13 : As we approached Greenville she saw the
sign and said, "It's something ville ."

DECEMBER 16 : She got a thistle spine under her little
fingernail yesterday. She began complaining about it in
the car, but when we parked she had so much fun playing in
the snow that she forgot about it . Then in the trailer it
bothered her again . I sterilized a needle to pull it out

Five and a Half

and this made her miserable. She cried more from fear of
the needle than she had from the nettle. But after supper
she was a little braver and quite happy when the spine was
out.

DECEMBER 19: It was a wonderful trip when I look back on
it. Just about perfect even to the homecoming. Candi
went back to school yesterday. Her Christmas party is
next Wednesday. And she grew during the trip. She
herself remarked that she could reach the trapeze coming
back through Marion, whereas she couldn't on our way
out. She is now taller than Karen; I matched them back to
back before we left and they were the same height. But big
as she is—bigger she says than the others in
kindergarten—she is still rather babyish. She will not
push forward in competition with other children.
Yesterday Karen, Timmy, and Fred were over playing with
her toys. She stood off on one side not joining them and
resenting their invasion.

DECEMBER 23: She announced yesterday, "Santa Claus
isn't really Santa Claus. He's your mother and father."
This heresy was openly proclaimed on the school bus when
the driver warned the children Santa wouldn't come if
the broke a window. Merry piped up that there was no
Santa Claus and Candi chimed in; but I got the impression
that skepticism among the five-year-olds was pretty
general.

DECEMBER 26: Yesterday was her fifth Christmas and
probably her best. She participated in giving as well as
receiving and was more adult in looking and marvelling
at what others received than many adults. She took over
the distribution of presents from under the tree. There
were not many. She was first out of bed and saw her vanity
table and toy refrigerator, both unwrapped, and played
with them; and after breakfast was impatient for
Grandma to arrive so she could open the others. The best
was a toy cash register which she most wanted. It
provides lots of action when a key is punched: the figure
goes up in a window, a drawer pops out, and a bell rings.
She knows her numbers well enough now, including the
tens, to punch the right keys. She had made us each a

present at school: a pair of hand outlines shaded by brush flocking and a pencil holder of clay. In the afternoon she went with Mom to take Grandma home and was still talking all evening about how nice Christmas was. This morning Merry's mother telephoned, Candi answered, conversed with her, and accepted an invitation to come over. Then she dialed her back to say when she would be there. She almost always is the one to answer the phone when it rings.

DECEMBER 28: She will probably like poetry if it isn't spoiled for her as it is for so many school children. She already has a certain knack for rhyme, notices rhymes that come accidentally and recites lists of rhyming words that she thinks of deliberately. Now she is beginning to reveal a slight sense of rhythm, though not to the point of beating time to music. Occasionally she will say things in a rhythmic way and this evening she enjoyed having me read Milne's "Now We Are Six." But she got her biggest bang last evening reading one of the Winnie the Pooh stories where Pooh gets caught in the doorway of the rabbit's home. She laughed almost uncontrollably over it, something she has not done before.

JANUARY 12: Discipline has never been a problem with Candi. We have never hit her even after being hit. To the question, "How would you like me to do that to you?" she has usually answered, "Go ahead, I'd like it." And perhaps she would, but neither Peggy nor I could do it. I can't recall even punishing her in the accepted sense of the word except to deprive her of something for being destructive with it. This, too, she often looked upon as a game and, while happy to get it back, was not visibly upset over losing it temporarily. Disapproval is the worst treatment she has ever had for wrongdoing. "I'm sorry!" she cries. Or removal of an object such as a book she might be hitting someone with. I don't mean the we—especially I—never get angry and do something unpleasant to her, like the time I threw the bag of candy out the car window. That wasn't punishment, however.

Yet with all this indulgence, if it is indulgence, she is not a troublesome or spoiled child; nor do I think

Five and a Half

there is something in her character which other children
don't have. I frankly doubt that any young children need
forceful discipline: I suspect such discipline fosters
the very behavior it is supposed to correct. It starts
with slapping the baby's hand for reaching to some
forbidden thing and the blows get heavier as the infant
gets bigger, all with the aim of compelling obedience.

With Candi encouragement has always been more
effective than compulsion. To get her to blow her nose
properly, for instance, I tell her what a good blow that
was, how she didn't blow through her mouth. And even when
she is, in a sense, compelled to do something—such as
get to bed on time—the secret is to explain why and, if
possible, offer an alternative. The reason is that she
needs enough sleep for good health so, if she wants to
stay up late to do something special, she must take an
afternoon nap. If she misses her nap she goes to bed
early. Now, nearly 6, she rarely naps and will probably
soon be unable to. But she lies quietly, nevertheless,
for she understands that the alternative is having to
lie down for a longer period. In eating, if she wants
dessert, she cleans her plate. But she is not required to
clean her plate—unless she wants dessert.

JANUARY 14: Her current interest is learning how to
spell—phonetically. I seem to recall reading that this
is wrong, that children should learn first to recognize
whole words. It may well be, but Candi is curious about
the spelling of words and how the different letters
relate to their sounds. They don't always relate,
goodness knows, but the initial consonants often do. You
can usually tell by the sound that a word starts with b,
or with d, f, or h; or with j (sometimes), or k (also
somtimes), or l, m, p, or r; or with s (sometimes), or with
t, v, w, or z. These are the guesses she is making now.
"Teach," she says; "t-e-e-itch."

Apart from learning ease, which seems to be the
primary goal of modern schooling, I wonder why a child
should not learn the logic of words, how they are put
together, and why. The picture reading method is a form
of learning by rote, like learning geometry by
memorizing the proofs. Candi, in trying to read, has
never seemed to cotton on the word-picture idea. No
doubt she will end up reading whole words and even whole

202

groups of words as single pictures but now, for good or
ill, she sees them as arrangements of letters, and those
letters—even in our imperfect phonetics—do often
have names that to some extent reproduce their sound.
Whereas the words, seen as pictures, don't look the
least bit like the things they symbolize, they often do
reproduce the consonants that compose them and
sometimes the vowels. There are exceptions, and these
are what she is learning now as she spells her way to
reading skill. Similarly, she is learning to add and
subtract by counting on her fingers.

A schoolmate called her on the telephone this
afternoon. They talked for ten minutes and it seemed
like Candi did most of the talking.

JANUARY 15: "I'm learning to sew," she sings,
        But I already know.
        So why am I learning
        How to sew?"
She asks her mother, "Isn't that a funny song?"
    "Yes, it sure is."
    "Did you get the rhyme part?"
    Then she fixes up a little doll in a basket and brings
it in to me. "See Jesus?"
    "Oh yes! You've got him in a basket."
    "I'm going to pray beside him."
    "Good."
    Into her room she goes, flops on her knees, and makes
up a scarcely audible prayer.

FEBRUARY 12: At breakfast this morning, after Candi had
eaten most of her egg, I asked if she'd like Mom to scrape
up the last of the yolk for her. She answered something
that sounded like: "Why have her scrape up the yolk? I'd
have to see her first." That making little sense, I asked
her to repeat it, then myself repeated what I thought she
said. "No!" she protested. "You don't know how to talk.
You're understandless." However, she agreed to say it
once more and did so in a shy, mumbling way. I repeated it
as well as I could, substituting yolkum for yolk.
Encouraged, she agreed to say it again, and this was the
statement: "Why should I have her scrape up the Mammy
Yokum? I'd have to see her first."

Her second kindergarten report card again spoke of

203

Five and a Half

her wide vocabulary and she was rated "outstanding" in the use of crayons. However, her teacher said she lacks self-confidence, participates in discussions reluctantly, and plays self-consciously with her hair and clothes while talking. She had a very difficult time when it was at last her turn to play the phonograph. (She had been looking forward to it for weeks.) Despite repeated explanations, she could not get the hang of it and seemed miserable playing it.

Yesterday when I offered to let her play our phonograph, she watched me go through the motions once and caught on immediately. Her problem at school was being in the limelight; she had stage fright. This could also be the reason she is so backward in the discussions. I suggested to Peg that her insistence on Candi being so prim and prissy away from home may be at the base of her trouble. "What," she asks, though not, to be sure, in so many words, "will people think of me if you behave so?" Only yesterday, telling her to fill some cupcake papers evenly, she said something like, "Then they'll look better at school." The cakes had to be right not for their own sake but for the sake of people's opinions of the one who baked them. She also criticized her rather severely for telling some woman who brought cookies to a school party, "We don't like those kinds of cookies." This was an honest statement and reflected the opinion of the group, but Peg's concern was over the hurt to the woman's feelings. I told her a prim and prissy youngster was quite the thing 50 years ago, but today, when kids are all pushy and self-assertive, a child overly respectful of others' feelings is completely out of step. Anyhow, most people learn consideration for others late in life or not at all. We don't want Candi to become grandmotherly at the age of 6.

Today she has her Valentine party at school and is taking cupcakes and valentines to exchange with the other children. All of the preparations are keeping Candi and her mother pretty busy.

MARCH 2: She continues to be interested in art. She spends much of her time drawing, painting, and coloring with crayons. Sometimes she does representations of real things which she can describe fully and in detail, indicating how true her representations are in her own eyes. This morning in her "scrapbook" we looked at some drawings she had made before Christmas. Without hesitation, she was able to tell me about each one, just as though she were looking out the window and describing what she saw. Sometimes when I ask her about a picture, she says it is just a "design." Occasionally there is evidence that a "design" is a realistic representation that went wrong. Other times it would appear that she aimed at an abstract design in the first place.

At Merry's house the other day she saw somebody on TV draw a squirrel. It was one of those chalk-talk drawings where lines curve around neatly to form a conventional stereotype image. I have no idea how much or how little drilling there was on the drawing, but this morning Candi duplicated it. Every line was exactly right, as though she were tracing it on the television screen. She made the picture a couple of times, and I suggested she do it for her teacher this afternoon. She agreed, but taking the crayon again, went to work on another squirrel. The chalk-talk one evidently didn't measure up to her standards, didn't look real enough perhaps. After a couple of tries she made her own, far less slick and polished but more to her and—incidentally—my liking. I doubt that she'll make another like she saw on television.

The other day when she did something—hit her mother I believe—she excused herself on the plea that her mother had done something wrong to her. "Two wrongs don't make a right," I said, wondering if that might not be too abstract or perhaps I should say too abstruse a thought for her to grasp. Evidently not. Today at lunch she apologized for failing to put out a special coffee spoon in setting the table—one that I use to measure out the soluble coffee. Knowing how much pride she takes in remembering that particular spoon (her mother always forgets it), I said, "That's all right. Mom forgot the coffee anyhow." "Two forgets don't make a remember," said Candi.

One opinion concerning the effect of punishment on learning is contained in the often-quoted piece of advice to parents: *Spare the*

205

Five and a Half

rod and spoil the child. In his writings about 70 years ago, Edward L. Thorndike was among the psychologists who concurred with this advice in viewing punishment as the simple opposite of reinforcement. His *law of effect* [1911] stated that satisfaction or reward following an act strengthens it and makes it likely to be repeated, while punishment or annoyance following an act weakens it and eventually eliminates it. In other words, reward was seen to build up habits and punishment was seen to break them down.

The diarist disputed this view: "I frankly doubt that any children need forceful discipline: I suspect such discipline fosters the very behavior it is supposed to correct. It starts with slapping the baby's hand for reaching to some forbidden thing and the blows get heavier as the infant gets bigger, all with the aim of compelling obedience."

Support for the diarist comes from an experiment by William K. Estes [1944] using a Skinner box, which is a device used frequently in learning experiments with animals, consisting of a small metal chamber about the size of a rat's cage, with a lever in one end that releases food pellets when it is pressed. In Estes' experiment, two groups of rats were trained to press the lever until they reached a consistently high rate of response. Then the rats in one group were punished by being given an electric shock every time they pressed the lever. Finally, both groups were placed in extinction: they no longer received either food or shock for lever-pressing.

Estes contended that if punishment weakened the lever-pressing habit, the punished animals should press it less often than the ones not punished. Actually he found that both groups pressed equally often. The rate of pressing by the punished rats went down while they were peing punished, but it went up again during extinction.

This increase in responding following the termination of punishment has been found reliable in animal experiments (for example, Azrin and Holz [1966]) leading to the view that punishment temporarily suppresses behavior, rather than permanently weakening it. In other words, the individual usually stops doing the activity that brings punishment *while he is being punished.* But if conditions change—for example, if some time elapses or if the one who administered the punishment leaves the scene—he is quite likely to begin doing it again.

In animal experiments, it has also been found that the stronger the punishment, the longer the suppression. In one animal study (Azrin [1960]) the suppression that followed an extremely intense electric shock was seen to be complete; there was no recovery of response for six days after the punishment had been discontinued.

Perhaps because equivalently severe punishments have not been used, these relationships have not been confirmed for human subjects. Azrin [1958] was unable to produce complete suppression in adults, using a loud noise as the punishing stimulus. Experiments with children do not reveal a consistent relationship between intensity and efficacy of punishment.

For example, in a discriminative learning study (Nelson, Reid, and Travers [1965]) which involved three groups of children, one group heard a tone, one group heard the word *wrong*, and one group received an electric shock after each error. In spite of the fact that the shock was so strong it brought tears to the eyes of some children, it produced neither more nor less rapid learning than the tone or the word. As far as these children's learning was concerned, the only effect of the shock seemed to be to convey the information that an error had been made. Though the results of this experiment are interesting, the experiment raises certain ethical questions which should be clear to the reader.

Parke and Walters [1965] punished children for touching a *forbidden* toy by either a mildly or an intensely unpleasant noise, both coupled with a verbal rebuke. Those who had the intense noise were slower to touch the toy, and touched it slightly less often than the mildly punished children when left alone with it after the punishment period. However, J.L. Freedman [1965] found that children who had been threatened with mild punishment were less likely to play with a forbidden toy when tested three weeks later with the threat lifted than were those who had been threatened with severe punishment. In addition, Martin Hoffman [1970] summarized several observational studies of parent and child behavior, and reported a negative relationship between the intensity of punishment used by parents and their children's resistance to temptation.

The diarist's suspicion that punishment "fosters the very behavior it is supposed to correct" has also been confirmed in some instances of child behavior. A hypothetical case suggested by Azrin and Holz [1966] is that of a boy who plays truant from school and on his return to school the following day is rather harshly punished. Such punishment should strengthen the boy's desire to escape from the punishing school environment and should therefore foster his penchant for truancy.

Five and a Half

There is theoretical as well as empirical support for the view that aggression is fostered by physical punishment. A parent who inflicts physical punishment, such as a slap or a spanking, is himself behaving aggressively and is thereby serving as a model of aggression in the child who emulates him. In addition, since punishment is frustrating, an increase in aggression following punishment is predicted by the frustration-aggression hypothesis. Bandura and Walters [1959] report that parents of delinquent children *do* make more use of physical punishment than do parents of nondelinquents. Parents of aggressive third grade children were found in another study to use physical punishment for aggression more often than the parents of nonaggressive third graders (Eron, Walder, Toigo, and Lefkowitz [1963]).

The diarist reports that Candida's parents made virtually no use of physical punishment: "We have never hit her even after being hit. To the question, *how would you like me to do that to you?* she has usually answered, *Go ahead. I'd like it.* And perhaps she would, but neither Peggy nor I could do it. I can't recall ever punishing her in the accepted sense of the word except to deprive her of something for being destructive with it. This, too, she often looked upon as a game and, while happy to get it back, was not visibly upset over losing it temporarily. Disapproval is the worst treatment she has ever had for wrongdoing. *I'm sorry!* she cries. Or removal of an object such as a book she might be hitting someone with. I don't mean that we —especially I—never get angry and do something unpleasant to her, like the time I threw the bag of candy out the car window. That wasn't punishment, however."

This places them in a very small minority. Sears, Maccoby, and Levin [1957] reported that 99 percent of the 379 New England mothers they surveyed made at least occasional use of physical punishment, but older mothers and mothers of girls used it less often than the others.

Martin Hoffman [1970] classified parental punishment techniques into three categories: (1) power assertion, which included physical punishment, as well as the technique Candida's parents used of depriving her of objects she was destructive with; (2) love-withdrawal, including Candida's parents' disapproval, as well as such stronger measures as threats to leave the child or to send him away; and (3) induction or reasoning, such as when Candida's parents asked, after being hit, how she would like it if they hit her back. Hoffman found that induction—and in particular, a type he called *other-oriented* induction, which consisted of explaining to the child how his behavior would affect other people (for example, *If you throw snow on their walk, they will have to clean it up all over again; He's afraid of the dark, so please turn the light back on; Don't yell at him, he was only trying to help*)—was more conducive than the other punishment methods in promoting a child's good behavior, as measured by his resistance to temptation, his tendency to confess, his feeling of guilt after wrongdoing, and his reliance on internal moral standards.

Taking a somewhat different approach, Piaget [1948] sought to determine how children themselves view the punishment that is meted out to them and what their attitude is toward punishment in general. He told his 6-to-12-year-old subjects a pair of stories, each about a boy who stole paper from his father's desk. In one case, the father gave the boy a sound whipping; in the other, he explained that taking the paper wasn't nice and that the boy wouldn't like it if the father took his toys while he was in school. Piaget asked the children which of the two fathers was fairest. Those under 8 declared almost unanimously that the one who gave the whipping was the fairest, while over half of those over 8 favored the one who used reasoning.

Piaget continued the stories by asking his subjects to imagine that a few days later, the two boys—the punished one and the one reasoned with—were playing in their respective yards and found their fathers' lost pens. He asked the children to guess which boy returned the pen to his father and which boy kept it. Again, almost all of those under 8 thought that the punished boy would be more likely to return the pen, out of fear of further punishment, while a majority of those over 8 thought that the one who was reasoned with would return it because he understood better or because he wanted to please his father.

On the basis of this and other questioning, Piaget concluded that children under the age of 8 tend to view punishment as a kind of necessary revenge for disobedience and that they advocate severe punishment, provided it is in proportion to the fault committed. Older children, on the other hand, are not convinced that punishment is necessary at all—explanation to the child of the consequences of his action may be more effective in many cases. Where punishment is used, they see it merely as a means of preventing future wrongdoing.

One of the undesirable side-effects of the use of punishment is the state of fear it produces in its recipient. In the case of a parent's punishment of his child, such fear may interfere with their mutual social relationships outside the punishment situation. In the case of its use as a learning procedure, the fear produced by punishment may interfere with the subject's attention to that which is to be learned, or it may immobilize him to the point where he is unable to do whatever is necessary to show what he has learned.

The effect of fear on Candida's ability to perform a simple task in kindergarten was reported by the diarist: "She had a very difficult time when it was at last her turn to play the phonograph. (She had been looking forward to it for weeks.) Despite repeated explanations, she could not get the hang of it and seemed miserable playing it. Yesterday, when I offered to let her play our phonograph, she watched me go through the motions once and caught on immediately. Her problem at school was being in the limelight; she had stage fright."

The diarist attributes Candida's fright to a lack of self-assertion: "I suggested to Peg that her insistence on Candi being so prim and prissy away from home may be at the base of her trouble. . . . I told her a prim and prissy youngster was quite the thing 50 years ago, but today, when kids are all pushy and self-assertive, a child overly respectful of others' feelings is completely out of step." As such, his showing her how to use the phonograph at home was a proper method of dealing with it. L.M. Jack [1934] showed experimentally that training in technical skills can increase the self-assertion of initially submissive youngsters.

She first observed preschoolers during a five-minute play period in the sandbox and selected a group of children who showed their submissiveness during this period by yielding to the direction of more dominant children or submitting to their interference. She then gave the submissive subjects a series of individual training sessions in which they learned to master difficult tasks (putting together puzzles, working with mosaics, etc.). After this training, she paired them with highly dominant, but untrained, peers to do the same tasks. The initially submissive children now became dominant, as shown by their telling the other children what to do, demonstrating to them how to use materials, and so on. Furthermore, when she observed all of the children 10 weeks later in the sandbox, the formerly submissive children still reflected the effects of their training in being more dominant than previously.

Five and a Half

A few months before her episode of stage fright, the diarist reported another of Candida's fears: "She got a thistle spine under her little fingernail yesterday. She began complaining about it in the car, but when we parked she had so much fun playing in the snow that she forgot about it. Then in the trailer it bothered her again. I sterilized a needle to pull it out and this made her miserable. She cried more from fear of the needle than she had from the nettle. But after supper she was a little braver and quite happy when the spine was out."

Arthur Jersild [1954] collected data on children's fears from several sources: direct questioning of 400 elementary school children, reminiscences of 300 adults, and three-week observational records kept by parents, teachers, and nurses about their charges. From this data he concluded that fears grow as the child does at least up to adolescence. By contrast with an older child, the infant is relatively immune to fears, the few he has revolving around events in his immediate environment. As experience and memory increase, so does fear, but, according to Jersild, fears based on past experience form only a small fraction of the fears of the child over two, whose imagination has opened the doors of the future, the unrealistically possible, and the supernatural.

Candida's fear of the needle was irrational, at least in its intensity, since it caused her more anguish than the actual pain did. Jersild found that many of the fears of preschool and school-age children are similarly irrational: they occur when there is no real danger or they are out of proportion to the danger that does exist. This was shown clearly when Jersild asked children to tell about their worst fear and to describe the worst thing that had ever happened to them. Fears of animals were seven times as frequent as actual bad experiences with animals, and impossible situations (ghosts, etc.) comprised 20 percent of the fears. On the other hand, bodily injury and accidents were included more often among the *worst happenings* than among the fears. In another study Jersild found that 53 percent of children in a particular school were afraid they might not be promoted, while the actual policies of the school were such that only 1 percent would be held back.

Jersild noted that stage fright developed during the late preschool years, he related it to the phenomenon of stranger fear in infancy. He also charted the developmental course of several other specific causes of fear over the period from birth to age six. The fears that declined over this age span were noise, falling, strangers, and pain. Those that increased were imaginary creatures, animals, darkness, personal injury, dreams, and signs of fear in others.

Writing in 1969, J.W. Croake noted that no studies of children's fear had been made during the preceding 11 years and therefore proposed to repeat Jersild's procedure on a more modern sample of children. He administered a questionnaire to 213 pupils from 12 elementary and junior high schools and conducted personal interviews with a smaller number. His most striking departure from Jersild's results concerned political fear (war, *communists taking over,* etc.), which Croake found to be the most frequent of all fears among sixth and ninth graders and the most frequently anticipated fear of third graders when he asked them to project themselves three years into the future. Croake remarked that while previous studies had noted the existence of political fears, no other had accorded it such a position of importance.

As well as raising the question of how effective punishment was for learning, the diarist questioned what he took to be the prevailing viewpoint about how reading should be taught: "Her current interest is learning to spell—phonetically. I seem to recall reading that this is wrong, that children should learn first to recognize whole words. It may well be, but Candi is curious about the spelling of words and how different letters relate to their sounds. They don't always relate, goodness knows, but the initial consonants often do . . . . Apart from learning ease, which seems to be the primary goal of modern schooling, I wonder why a child should not learn the *logic* of words, how they are put together, and why. The picture reading method is a form of learning by rote, like learning geometry by memorizing the proofs. Candi, in learning to read, has never seemed to cotton to the word-picture idea. No doubt she will end up by reading whole words and even whole groups of words as single pictures but now, for good or ill, she sees them as arrangements of letters, and those letters—even in our imperfect phonetics—do often have names that to some extent reproduce their sound."

The two approaches which the diarist mentions, learning how individual letters relate to sounds and learning to recognize whole words, have been called, respectively, the *phonics* and the *look-say* methods. Arthur Heilman [1968] reported that the issue of which method is best was the source of a long debate in the field of reading instruction. He noted that the prevailing opinion of educators in the late 1940's and early 50's, when the diarist raised the question, was that a beginning reader should learn at least 100 words by the look-say method before being introduced to phonics. Heilman's own view was that the two methods should be combined from the beginning, with look-say for phonetically irregular words and phonics for words whose sound agreed with their spelling.

This controversy attracted the attention of psychologists. Reese and Lipsitt [1970] suggested that a possible rationale for the look-say approach is Heinz Werner's orthogenetic theory of perception, which holds that details such as letters are not readily abstracted by the young child from global wholes such as words. They found, however, that the results of experiments designed to test this aspect of Werner's theory were contradictory. Most of the studies which used Rorschach ink blots as stimuli lent it support by finding that children under age 6 tended to interpret the whole blot, while older children tended to limit their interpretations to small details. But when drawings of real objects were used, the emphasis of the drawing on inner detail versus contour appeared to be far more important than the child's age in determining whether parts or wholes would be perceived.

Two psychological experiments were addressed directly at a comparison of look-say with phonics as methods of teaching reading. In the first, by Carol Bishop [1964], the subjects were college students. Their task was to learn to read eight Arabic words. The letter-training (or phonics) group were initially given training in associating the correct sounds with each of the 12 Arabic letters from which the eight test words were composed. The word-training (or look-say) group were trained initially to pronounce eight different Arabic words, also made up of the same 12 letters. Then both groups were taught to read the test words. The phonics group learned this faster than the look-say group. In fact, the only subjects in the latter group to show positive transfer were those who had spontaneously analyzed the words given during initial training into letter-sound components.

Jeffrey and Samuels [1967] repeated Bishop's procedure, using kindergarten subjects and English words. They found that only the phonics/letter-training resulted in positive transfer; the subjects in the look-say/word training group did no better than a control group of children who were given no initial training. These results suggest

Five and a Half

that phonics training has more value than look-say training for reading instruction. Their limitation is that in the words used in both studies, there was a perfect correspondence between letters and sounds, and, as the diarist notes, this is not always true of English spelling.

16
Six
Years
Old

JUNE 1: Candi's sixth birthday has come and gone and I
have been so distracted with leaving Michigan after a
lifetime of residence that I failed to record even her
birthday party. Our house is up for sale. As soon as it is
sold, we'll be off for California. A couple of times it
looked as though buyers would take the house immediately
and both times I found myself resisting it, reluctant to
leave old friends and associations. Candi, with friends

of far shorter acquaintance, does not disguise her
reluctance. She'd like nothing better than to hear we've
decided to stay.

I feel sure she'll make new friends, although she is
anything but a glad-hander. She is shyer than most
children, lacks their self-assertiveness when away
from home. Her dolls and playthings form a large part of
her life, especially when she rediscovers one.

Not long ago the rediscovery was an air-filled
plastic bunny, and this absorbed her. She had to have it
with her every minute. Then it was a hand-puppet she had
bought in St. Louis last fall. When the puppet's monkey
head broke I substituted the head of a plastic rabbit,
and this became her inseparable companion. Now it is a
rubber cow named Bessie that she has owned since
infancy. It languished in the attic a year or so until she
discovered it again and brought it down. She holds it
almost constantly, sleeps with it under her pillow,
dresses it in fancy clothes, and sucks its nose when she
feels hungry or forlorn.

Next to playing with her cuddly toys, she likes best
to draw and make things--cards, stamp albums, books of
various kinds. She likes to write her name, address, and
such other words as she may know or can have spelled for
her. She likes to add and subtract, using her fingers as a
calculator. She likes television and she especially
likes being read to. She also likes to cut out and paste
up pictures from magazines.

Yes, and she likes making puns and rhymes, and
catching people--at home or on television--who make
mistakes in speech. Yesterday one of the hucksters was
peddling some sort of toy that has goggles with one-way
vision. "I can see you but you can't see me," he boasted.
"No you can't see me," she hollered back. "You're on
television and I'm not!"

JUNE 23: She seems somehow to have matured in the last
few days. I don't mean that she has grown up, rather that
she has moved from babyhood into childhood. Perhaps I
should say completely into childhood, for of course she
has been losing babyish traits over the years. Watching
her yesterday outdoors gave me that feeling. She
displayed such independence, no longer exclusively
conscious of herself as part of a family but seeing

herself for the first time as an individual separate and distinct. Or perhaps I was merely reading all this into her gestures.

She is lovely now, too beautiful I sometimes fear. She is extremely self-conscious in the presence of outsiders, especially strangers; won't answer questions except in an undertone and plays with her dress. I should like to help her be more comfortable with others but I haven't figured out how. I can only hope she'll work out of it herself as her range of experience widens.

Little by little she is teaching herself to read. Short words like "dog," "fan," "house," and "bite," whose phonetics agree with their spelling, are her first step, with sometimes a little help on the phonetics. So far she has made no obvious attempt (since she first mastered "Candy," "Mom," "Dot," and "Bop") to learn familiar words by their shape and size, although she may have to come to it when phonetics fail. I think, on the whole, she'd rather reason her reading out in the same way that she has already reasoned out simple addition and subtraction.

JUNE 27: She showed me a book she made and titled, "The Issue of Your Life." It tells the story of a fairy who discovered a fire and put it out with her wand, and that brought her a baby. That is how fairies get fairy babies: by discovering and putting out fires. I asked how they discovered the fires and she said by the smell: the smoke. She said that all fairies want fairy babies. Then she showed pictures she had made of the fire, of the fairy putting it out with her wand, of the fairy holding the fairy baby and patting its head. The book is a paste-up with crayon drawings.

JULY 19: We have been visiting Ted and Ellen Houseman in Chicago on our way to the Coast. We left them fairly late yesterday and the traffic out of town was heavy. It was nearly dark when we reached our overnight camp and quite dark by the time Peg had the beds made and the trailer ready for occupancy. When Candi entered, the first thing she demanded was her box of knick-knacks that had been on the bed. Mom, having put it away to make the bed, told her not to pull it from where it had been stowed. When she did so, nevertheless, I added my warning that if she spilled the box, everything that fell on the floor would be thrown away. (Empty threat no. 4,379.) In her weariness and frustration, Candi got mad and began to cry. ""I wish I didn't have you for mother and father. You both cause me too much unfun!"

Ellen was apparently quite impressed by her thoughtfulness toward others. I said I had not especially noticed this trait in her, but Ellen thought it was outstanding.

JULY 22: We were to have left Chicago today after having said goodbye to the Housemans' last evening. But this morning Candi discovered that her rubber cow Bessie was lost. Peggy called the Housemans and they promised to mail it if they found it, but [Candi] would not be consoled. She went into the car and cried as if her heart would break all the while we were hitching up the trailer. It was as if she had lost her dearest friend. So--I offered her a deal. We would go back to the Housemans and hunt for Bessie and so lose a day of travel. In return, she would have to give up any idea of shopping during the whole trip. I reminded her that she often went to stores on our trips and quite often had things bought for her without spending her own money. I felt sure she would decide to wait for Bessie to arrive in the mail, especially when I reminded her that she would probably find another and newer Bessie in one of the stores we visited. But no. She understood the terms and accepted them. She still preferred to go back for Bessie.

So we went. In town we telephoned again and learned that Bessie had not been found. We would come anyway. The deal went whether Candi found Bessie or not, but she must be allowed to hunt for herself. When we got to the Housemans they proudly brought out Bessie; she had been found. Candi was happy. We had baths and stayed for supper, and now at 8:30 are preparing for bed in hopes of an early start tomorrow.

AUGUST 3: California and Carpinteria again at last. Candi quickly made friends with a 2½-year-old girl in the trailer next door and adopted the role of big sister, patiently waiting on her hand and foot, picking up her toys as she threw them down, watching her throw them again and picking them up, time after time after time. She went walking with the family and then we all got to bed for a long night's sleep. We needed it after our exhausting trip.

AUGUST 7: The best thing about living in a trailer park is that Candi has an opportunity to learn how to make friends with different children as families come and go. Carpinteria, being on the ocean, is a summer refuge from the blistering heat of California's interior valleys. Now that two-year-old Karen has left, she has begun playing with two boys nicknamed Nick and Tuck, 6 and 8, who live in the trailer across the way. She played well when Tuck was showing her a game of his, but in this morning's rough and tumble she fell and skinned herself in several places. That made her cry at first and left her cranky afterward, so that she was repeatedly complaining about the boys' actions, how they were taking away her seashells and how they were taking Bop for walks without her permission. I said she would either have to stop complaining or stay in the trailer and play by herself. She decided to stop complaining. She still has much learning to do about other children before she starts school next month.

AUGUST 9: Her new friend Stephanie is something of a prodigy. Though only $4\frac{1}{2}$, she is nearly as big as Candi, looks older and even acts older. Like nearly all other children, she is more independent. It was she who sought Candi out; not the other way around. Stephanie escorted her to the swings and they played happily together for an hour or so. Candi came back without her, not knowing where she'd gone, but Stephanie was over again later and has been here most of the time ever since. She's a very self-possessed child, aroused my sympathy by saying she wished she had a daddy; hers was dead. Then yesterday when a male voice called her from somewhere I asked, "Who is that?" "My daddy." "You told me your daddy was dead." She laughed. "I was only kidding." When she was gone, Candi asked, "Do you think Stephanie really has a horse?" "She might. Did she say she did?" Yes, she had and she had boasted of many other things, too, even that she owned the trailer park and all the trailers on it. I argued reasonably that she couldn't own our trailer since we owned it, but that left unanswered the question of whether Stephanie owned a horse.

219

Six Years Old

One of the items besides a big batch of rare 78 rpm phonograph records in our trailer's excess cargo is a smaller batch of "Omnibooks" of 1940-1942 vintage. They had been in storage all the years since and I still hated to throw them away. The last few days before we left Michigan I tried devouring them but they were too much and so, over Peggy's protests, I loaded them in the trailer. I'm glad I did. Never in recent years have I had so much free reading time. And the best part is that I've been reading aloud not simply to Peggy but to Candi. Candi enjoys it. So far I have read three abridged novels: ""Letter of Credit" by Jerome Weidman, "Before Breakfast" by Angela Thirkell, and "The Unvanquished" by Howard Fast; and am in the midst of a fourth, "The New Hope" by Joseph C. and Freeman Lincoln. Candi listens intently and makes many concessions--like undressing rapidly and lying quietly in bed with her eyes closed--just to have them read. They don't put her to sleep but she usually drops off as soon as I've finished.

Stephanie listened with her yesterday afternoon and enjoyed it just as much, which raises the interesting question of whether books need to be written down to children after infancy. They comprehend adult conversation and television shows; and Candi I'm sure would rather have such a book read to her than see most television shows.

AUGUST 16: Still very laggard about making friends. While other children are playing together in various quarters of the trailer park, she is generally to be found on her own patio playing by herself. She will never join others who are already at play. If one comes over to play with her, she makes him welcome but away from our trailer, she won't make the first move, even when she finds another child alone.

I thought this might be because she is an only child with no brothers or sisters to initiate her into the rough and tumble of childhood play. But yesterday I talked with another couple whose daughter, 11, is an only child. They have moved around a lot and claimed it was good for the child. She gets better marks than when she stays for a whole year at the same school. "But does she make friends easily?" "Oh sure. I've seen her walk right up to a group of strange kids the moment she arrived and join in with them."

Of course there is a lot to be said for Candi's ability to play by herself, talking to and for her dolls. She is rarely afflicted with boredom. At the same time, I'd like her to learn to live more with other people, to join the give and take of casual social contact. Her feelings are too easily hurt, by name-calling, by having a toy snatched and run away with. She is still too much her mother's girl, going with her to empty the garbage, or to take Bop, and requiring her to come with her when she goes to the rest room.

AUGUST 21: Life in the trailer park is both lazy and varied. New people are constantly replacing others who go out, leaving a relatively small core of "permanent" residents, ourselves included. Candi has had to make and break friendships quite rapidly; but now fortunately she has a new friend Janie, age 6, who lives just across the drive and who will stay until school opens. The youngsters all play outdoors until dark, Candi also when she has had a nap. Then they go to bed and most adults also go to bed then or shortly after. Saturday night may produce a party and cars are apt to drive close beside your window at any time of the night, but noise is rarely troublesome. Mornings especially are quiet. Few people get up and out before 9:00.

AUGUST 29: Besides Janie and Ellie across the drive, she has made friends with a four-year-old named Cooky who lives in San Fernando and will be leaving today. At the moment Cooky is in church and Janie and Ellie are at the beach, but after a few minutes of playing by herself, Candi went out and picked up another little girl, also I should judge about 4. We visited the Santa Barbara Library on Friday at the time of the regular weekly story hour, and Candi drew some pictures. When I looked in, she was standing by herself twisting her dress in her hands but after she was given a table and materials she set happily to work.

AUGUST 30: She still enjoys answering back to radio and TV commercials. This evening a cigarette called

Six Years Old

Cavaliers made some such claim as being the product of
"over two years" of something or other. "Maybe," said
Candi, "they were slow working." "That's a thought,"
said I. "Maybe," she continued, "they first took a year
and half vacation, and then didn't work very long
hours."

SEPTEMBER 7: Candi went to school this morning, entering
the first grade. Her teacher is Miss Solari. Peggy went
with her to register and left her when the school bell
rang, a trifle unhappy with all the strangeness around
her but bravely fighting back the tears. She has been
looking forward eagerly to school again, especially to
the romance and prestige of the first grade. No longer is
she a "kindergarten baby" but a real first grader. She
will buy her lunch at school. Her hours are from 9:00 to
2:30.

OCTOBER 14: It is interesting to watch her learning to
read in school. The class began identifying objects and
colors, then associating the name of each color with the
same color as they produced it with crayons. They can now
read: red, blue, green, yellow, orange, purple, black,
and brown. Brown still gives Candi a little trouble.
From colors they progressed to other words associated
with pictures: Dick, look, June, run, see, oh, Jane,
Spot, Puff, and to the numbers associated with different
groups of pictures. Candi learns fast but works slowly,
so that many of the pages she brings home from school are
unfinished. However, when I test her on the unfinished
ones she invariably knows them. I suspect her slowness
is due in part to extra pains with the drawing and
coloring, in part to her extreme fear of making a
mistake.

OCTOBER 16: She will attend a birthday party this
afternoon in honor of Frances, a first-grade friend of
hers with Mexican parents. She had to buy the present in
Santa Barbara so we drove there after school and spent a
bit of time in the library as well.

OCTOBER 20: I've been meaning to remark if I haven't
already on Candi's progress in reading. She is in the top

third of the class and reads the names of colors, a few
names of persons like Dick and Jane, and words like run,
oh, and come. But the thing I marvel most at is her
ability in drawing. She has taken to drawing pictures
here at home, full—scale productions like those of any
landscape painter. She discovered the mountains are
purple and drew them. Her trees are surprisingly
realistic. She does pictures of the beach and ocean, and
one that she drew last evening of a sailing battleship
(her own version) with flags (stripes against the pole and
stars to the outside edge) and cannons. The cannons (two)
are shooting big cannon balls straight out from the
ship. The sea under the ship is a regular succession of
waves, and the sky overhead has pink clouds and a white
moon. At my suggestion she drew a setting sun on the
horizon, but that became almost obscured by the cannon
balls. In this picture there are no human figures, but
she is not at all afraid of them and inserts them whenever
she thinks they'll do some good.

OCTOBER 30: We went to the Hallowe'en parade at school.
There were perhaps 50 spectators, a couple hundred
pupils, and a dozen teachers. The grass on the
playground had been marked in a large white circle and
the children in their costumes paraded on the white
line. But the teachers had no clear idea of a plan for the
march and so, while some of the classes went around two or
three times, others including Candi's class failed to
complete a single circuit. Many of the costumes were
quite elaborate; others were no more than paper bags
with holes to see out of. Candi, dressed as a fairy in her
nylon nightgown, with crown, wand, and shoes I made her
out of aluminum foil, looked as pretty as any. Coming out
of her classroom she was, characteristically, the very
last in line.

After the parade Peggy and I visited her class where
the children were having a party. She sits near the end of
one table almost entirely surrounded by boys: one other
girl is in the group. I supposed they were grouped by
their progress in reading and learned from Candi that
this was partly true but that two of the boys are not in
her advanced reading group. None of the group is
Mexican.

Six Years Old

NOVEMBER 21: She continues to make progress in reading, spends a great deal of her free time at it and at drawing, coloring, and cutting out paper dolls of her own design. She does remarkably well with the human figure and shows considerable talent and imagination in her other drawing, especially landscapes.

We watched a star rise over the mountains one evening and she made a picture of that. The evenings here are especially beautiful, first looking toward the mountains until they fade into shadow and then over the sea. The ocean is too bright for comfort during the day when the sun shines directly in your eyes but at twilight and early evening it surpasses even the mountains.

DECEMBER 4: Yesterday Miss Solari told Peggy she might like to borrow books from the library for Candi to read. She has been bringing school readers home at the rate of three or four a week and reading them aloud to me (50 or more pages) before taking them back. Yesterday it was a hard-cover primer that she read in class in two days and will doubtless read again over the weekend. Peggy told Miss Solari about her shyness and how she wanted to ask her questions but was afraid. So to break down her reserve Miss Solari called her up to her desk the following day and Candi came, her mouth quivering and two big tears about to fall. Miss Solari said, "Why don't you smile like your mother does?" and Candi essayed a weak smile, forcing her mouth up at the corners. When I think of something like that, I feel like crying myself, wanting so much to help her overcome her fears.

DECEMBER 25: An odd Christmas this, though not really much odder than many we have spent. I recall how after our first trailer trip we got home in deep snow, our pipes were frozen, and we spent Christmas without water. Still I do believe we had a tree. This year we have none. Candi had a choice: a tree or an extra present with the money the tree would have cost. She chose the extra present, naturally. Anyhow, we should have to have mounted the tree in our half-finished house, and if it had rained (which it didn't), we should scarcely have enjoyed sitting around it. As it was, we huddled in the trailer. Candi

opened a number of her presents and left five more to be
opened, one each day in the week to come. She reads better
and better all the time and continues to draw and color
well. Her outstanding deficiency is musical. She seems
to have no sense of tune whatever. Neither has her
mother.

FEBRUARY 4: We moved in last Monday. Rather I should say
we moved our trailer into the carport, the only part of
our new house that is finished. Meanwhile Candi is
becoming established in the community with three
favorite playmates: Jill and Butch, brother and sister
next door, and Melissa who lives just down the hill. She
nearly always has someone to play with, even though she
still won't call on her friends; they must come to her.

MARCH 4: Nearing her seventh birthday, she is learning
to read very rapidly, and largely on her own. Road signs,
advertising circulars, comics are all grist to her mill.
She sets to work at figuring them out no matter how
difficult they may appear. Usually she does figure them
out herself, words like "Ambassador," "Bermuda," and
such that often mean nothing to her as useful words but
that reveal themselves phonetically. Sometimes she
asks, "What word is this?" but if I tell her to guess she
will usually guess right. Occasionally I help her with
the phonetics by breaking a word apart and having her
sound each syllable; on other occasions I show her the
similarity between the word in question and one she
already knows. But this is becoming less and less
necessary as she does it on her own initiative.

She loves school, and the worst thing that can happen
to her is to have to stay home on account of illness.
We've planned to go down to L.A. the latter part of this
month, but because that will take her out of school a few
days Candi vigorously opposes the trip. She has, I
think, definitely made the break from Livonia to
Carpinteria, and now even Merry, who for so long she
described as her "best friend," has become little more
than a nostalgic symbol. She still misses Merry as she
misses snow, but she is quite able to get along without
them.

She practices faithfully on her bike, an admittedly

difficult task since she has so little to show for it.
Other kids have learned to ride in far less time, but
Candi still needs outrigger wheels and is only now able
to pedal up the hill in front of the house. Yet, tiresome
as it must be, she regularly gets the bike out and goes to
work--unless, to be sure, she has other children to play
with or something else more interesting to do.

Infants are dependent on their parents, for food, warmth, protection, and their very survival. Dependency is not entirely outgrown as the child learns to do more and more things for himself. While the infant's passive, helpless dependency declines, at least two new dependencies—emotional and instrumental—arise to take its place.Instrumental dependency is manifested when the child seeks help in reaching a material goal, and the response of the person the child is dependent on is seen as a means rather than an end in itself. Candida's instrumental dependency was evident at age 2 when her father gave her a toy nut and bolt:"I showed her how and let her try, but she always wanted to pull the nut off the bolt rather than turn it. When it would not budge, she got mad and insisted I take it off for her."

In emotional dependency, responses of other people are the end goals. Some responses typically sought are comfort, physical contact, praise, approval, reassurance, and proximity. The diarist described emotional dependency in 6-year-old Candida when he wrote: "She is still too much her mother's girl, going with her to empty the garbage, or take Bop, and requiring her to come with her when she goes to the rest room."

In observing emotional dependency in nursery school, Glen Heathers [1955] noted a change with age. Two-year-olds directed most of their dependency strivings toward teachers. The kinds of dependent behavior they engaged in included clinging, hugging, trying to be near, and bids for *negative* attention (where the child does something disruptive such as interfering in another's play, with the aim of provoking a response, albeit an angry one, from the teacher). Among 5-year-olds, however, these unabashed physical manifestations had abated somewhat. Children more often sought verbal attention, praise, or approval, and they more often directed their dependency bids toward peers.

Six Years Old

The shift from adult-oriented to peer-oriented emotional dependency continues into elementary school. Thus we see dependency on her mother while Candida is in nursery school, and the diarist writes: "At nearly four and a half Candy is still rather tightly tied to her mother's apron strings. She is still shy with other children, except Merry when Merry is alone, refuses to play with them and no longer plays by herself as she used to. We took a short trip to Glen Haven with the trailer a few weeks ago. Merry's parents were vacationing at the State park up there, and we thought it might be nice for Candy if we should join them. Candy did too and for once was eager to start on a trip. All the way up she talked of seeing and playing with Merry. But when we got there and Merry and her sister Kim came to play with her, Candy would not leave her mother."

Three years later, in connection with Haloween trick-or-treating, the diarist remarked on Candida's dependency on her closest friend, Melissa: "The two girls covered most of the tract and got home about 7:30. Last year she wouldn't go out without her mother. But she does lean heavily on Melissa or rather, on Melissa's readiness to come and call for her. Yesterday afternoon without her, she was at loose ends but couldn't bring herself to go next door and ask for Jill. Instead, she stood around in our yard hoping Jill would catch sight of her, which she eventually did."

In another experiment Heathers [1953] sought to determine how parental practices reflect on children's emotional dependency. Each of his 56 6-to-12-year-old subjects was blindfolded and asked to walk to the end of a six-foot, bouncy plank which was suspended eight inches above the floor and wobbled both up and down and sideways. As the child started, Heathers took his hand and offered to walk beside him. Those children who accepted help were taken as being emotionally dependent. Upon later examining the records of home observations of each child's interactions with his mother, Heathers noted that many of the children who were emotionally dependent in his task had what he called *child-centered* families, where the parents were prone to make large sacrifices for the child. Those who were emotionally independent, on the other hand, tended to have *accelerating* parents who encouraged the child to develop and use skills appropriate for his age.

Dependency is usually considered a sex-typed behavior, in that it is theoretically discouraged in small boys and permitted or even encouraged in girls. However, there are less clear-cut sex differences in young children's dependency than there were in the other sex-

Six Years Old

typed behavior, aggression. R.M Oetzel [1966] summarized 14 observational studies of nursery school children, of which six reported no difference between the sexes, four more dependency in girls, and four more in boys. Among 12 behavior ratings, seven found girls more dependent, two boys, and three found no sex difference. The clearest evidence that dependency is a feminine trait came from five studies employing self-report questionnaires with teens and adults. All five found women more dependent.

A child's dependency on adults has been found to detract from his popularity with his peers (McCandless and Marshall [1957]). At the same time, popular children are seen to be more dependent on their peers than are the unpopular (Campbell and Yarrow [1958]). The measure of popularity in these studies is called a *sociometric.* It is a simple procedure in which each child in a group names the two or three other children in the group whom he likes best and/or least.

The *popular* child is defined as one who receives many *likes best* votes, while the *socially isolated* child is one who receives few votes in this category. The *socially rejected* child receives many votes in the *likes least* category. Other variants of the sociometric measure children's ability to get along in work relationships with peers (*With whom would you rather plan a class party?*) and sex-role stereotyping (Who is always in the middle of the tough games?). Sociometric rankings are found to remain stable for up to a year among preschoolers and even lónger among older children.

Friendliness, as seen in such behavior as sociability, cheerfulness, sensitivity to the feelings of others, and nurturance, has been found highly correlated with popularity in children. Generosity also tends to go along with popularity. Hartup [1970] reports that a child's sociometric popularity can be increased experimentally by having him share rewards with others. This was also noted by the diarist when Candida was 5: "Travelling as we have been, with only a few daylight hours at each stop, she has had to learn to make friends quickly. A little boy at Ponca City, Oklahoma taught her one sure-fire method by presenting her with half a bagful of candy the minute he arrived. Here at Calexico, California, there is a little girl of school age. Without delay when she saw her last evening, Candi gave her a lollipop and now this morning they are playing like old friends."

The child's body build is seen to have a bearing on his popularity. In his description of Candida on her fourth birthday—"She is taller by three inches than most four-year-olds, huskier too, though in play with other children she has not learned to take advantage of her strength"—the diarist saw her physique as providing the potential for self-assertion. However, the feelings and expectations which a child's body build arouse in the minds of other children are at least equally important influences on his potential social relations.

In a study aimed at determining what these expectations were, J.R. Staffieri [1967] had elementary school children rate child silhouettes which depicted the three body builds W.H. Sheldon proposed as stereotypes of adult physique: the mesomorph (lithe, muscular), the ectomorph (thin, wiry), and the endomorph (fat, stocky). The mesomorphic silhouette received the highest ratings by the children and was ascribed traits such as leadership, good sport, popular, etc. The ectomorph was rated slightly less favorably and was seen as being nervous, withdrawn, and submissive. The lowest ratings were given to the endomorphic silhouette, which was seen by the children as being that of a bully, a poor sport, and a generally poorly socialized individual—in striking contradiction to the fabled *jolly, fat child* so often depicted in children's literature.

Another study (Walker [1964]) demonstrated that these expectations are generally accurate by measuring nursery school children's typical patterns of interaction with their peers (as rated by their teachers) in relation to their body build (as rated by other judges from nude photographs). Mesomorphic boys were seen to be energetic, fearless, and assertive; ectomorphic boys were quiet and cooperative; and endomorphic boys were unsociably aggressive. Mesomorphic girls were also seen as active and assertive, but endomorphic girls were docile and cooperative, while ectomorphic girls were cranky, tense, and unfriendly.

Popularity is also found to bear a relationship to the amount of time a child spends watching television. A large-scale investigation in England matched 1,854 10-and 13-year-old television viewers with an equal number of children of the same age, intelligence and social class, who did not have access to television. The viewers were divided into three, equal subgroups on the basis of the amount of time they spent watching TV, and those who spent the longest—an average of half the hours between school and bedtime—were labelled *addicts* (Himmeleweit, Oppenheim, and Vince]1958]). It was found that the addicts, more often than any of the other children, were described by their mothers as *hardly ever visits, hardly ever entertains friends,* and *does not want to bring friends home to watch TV.* In addition, the investigators reported, "We found, contrary to expectations, that it was not the only child or the child whose mother goes out to work who was a heavy viewer, but the insecure child, in particular the child who had difficulty making friends with other children. The addict, more often than other viewers, was described by his teacher as a follower, not a leader, as submissive, shy and retiring" [p. 388].

Although in this kind of research it is often difficult to decide which factor is the cause and which is the effect—is a child unpopular because he watches a lot of television or does he watch TV as a means of escape from a social environment where he finds himself rejected?—the investigators drew the inference from the fact that no apparent differences in popularity appeared between light and moderate viewers and nonviewers, that the second alternative was more nearly accurate.

A study of third grades in the United States showed that shy, nonaggressive boys spent more time watching TV than did aggressive boys, but the latter watched more violent programs (Eron [1963]). The suggestion from this study, that violent television promotes violent behavior, was further investigated by Aletha Stein and her colleagues [1973] who divided nursery schoolers into two groups, one that watched an aggressive and the other a prosocial TV program. Pairs from each group then interacted with a mildly frustrating toy designed for older children. Boys' aggressive behavior increased after viewing aggressive television, and prosocial behavior increased following prosocial television. As in the earlier study, there was no significant relationship for girls.

These studies support a modeling theory: that children (boys at least) emulate the aggression engaged in by the actors on the screen. However, another recent study (Feshbach [1970]) supports a *drainage* hypothesis—that aggressive feelings which build up in real life can be harmlessly released by watching aggressive television. In this study boys in institutions (private boarding schools and homes for the impoverished) were given a six-week diet of predominantly aggressive or predominantly nonaggressive TV programs. Daily records of their behavior, including aggressive incidents, were kept by their cottage supervisors. Verbal and physical aggression were consistently higher in the group exposed to the nonaggressive programs. The difference was statistically significant for the boys' homes but not for the private schools.

The contradiction over the influence of aggressive television is matched only by the question of what, if any, educational value television may have. As one group of researchers has put it, "Whereas there has been worry lest the child not learn *enough* in school, there has been a corresponding fear that he might learn *too much* and the wrong kind of thing from television" (Schramm, Lyle, and Parker [1961]). They set about testing what and how much children do learn from TV, both by comparing light and heavy viewers in the U.S. and by comparing the children in two small Canadian towns which were comparable in most respects, except that one had television reception and the other did not.

Three main conclusions emerged from their study: (1) television is of more intellectual benefit to first graders than to sixth graders; (2) it is of more benefit to bright and dull children than to the intellectually average; (3) among older children, heavy viewers have more knowledge in the specific areas of entertainment and fantasy (for example, names of popular singers), while light viewers have more knowledge of literature and public affairs (for example, names of writers, statesmen). Schramm, Lyle and Parker explained these results on the premise that for the young child, television is new, interesting, and seems real, while for older children—who tended to watch mainly entertainment programs—little new information is provided outside the limited areas of fantasy and music.

An additional explanation is suggested by the diarist's observation of how much 6-year-old Candida and her 4-year-old friend enjoyed having adult novels read to them: "Stephanie listened with her . . . and enjoyed it just as much, which raises the interesting question of whether books need to be written down to children after infancy." If the alternative to television for most children is children's books, the superiority of television for the intellectual development of young children may be partly due to the greater complexity of the dialogue and plot of the television program.

Earlier we read of Stephanie: "She's a very self-possessed child, aroused by my sympathy by saying she wished she had a daddy; hers was dead. Then yesterday when a male voice called her from somewhere I asked, *Who is that? My daddy. You told me your daddy was dead.* She laughed. *I was only kidding.* When she was gone, Candi asked, *Do you think Stephanie really has a horse? She might. Did she say she did?* Yes, and she had boasted of many other things, too, even that she owned the trailer park and all the trailers on it. I argued reasonably that she couldn't own our trailer since we owned it, but that left unanswered the question of whether Stephanie owned a horse."

Six Years Old

William Stern called such spontaneous distortions of the truth *pseudo-lies*. Their prevalence in children under 7 prompted him to advise that children's testimony be regarded as expressions of their feelings or wishes rather than as truthful propositions.

Intrigued by Stern's observations, Piaget [1948] questioned children themselves about lying, asking them what a lie was and probing their views on the morality of lying. The youngest children he interviewed, between 5 and 6 years old, defined lies as *naughty words* and made no distinction between untruthful statements and swear words or indecent expressions. This is the age of the pseudo-lie when the child, according to Piaget, feels no inner obstacle to the practice of lying, but notices that after saying certain things which his parents regard as untrue, a negative reaction ensues and that the same reaction occurs when he uses certain expressive words which they regard as improper. The child, therefore, concludes that a lie is something which would have been better left unsaid.

At some time between the ages of 6 and 10 children arrive at a more advanced definition of the lie as any statement which is factually untrue. Swearing is thus excluded, but the concept of the lie is still broader than an adult's, since the child includes mistakes and jokes along with deliberate deceptions. Piaget noted this when he asked the children to guess his age. They were invariably off by at least a year and when he informed them of their error they felt they had told a lie. The eventual definition of a lie as an *intentional* distortion of the truth was observed by Piaget among 10- and 11-year-olds.

To study their evaluations of the morality of lying, Piaget told the children two stories. The first dealt with a boy who was frightened by a dog and came home to his mother reporting he had seen a dog as big as a horse. The second was about a boy who returned from school and told his mother that the teacher had given him good marks when she had actually given him no marks at all, good or bad. Then Piaget asked which lie was naughtier.

Most children under 8 thought the first one was because it was *bigger* (there are no dogs as big as horses, whereas children do sometimes get good marks in school) or because the mother would see immediately that it was a lie, while she might believe the second one. Older children, by contrast, found the second lie naughtier precisely because the mother might be taken in by it. In their view, the lie's purpose to deceive made it bad, since deliberate deception jeopardized people's ability to trust one another.

As a side note, Piaget observed that the younger children felt better about lying to peers than to adults because the adult was more likely to discover the truth or, as one 8-year-old put it; *Because a grown-up is worth more than a child.* Older children, on the contrary, felt that lying to another child was worse. Piaget quotes a 12-year-old as saying, *Sometimes you almost have to tell lies to a grown-up, but it's lousy to do it to another kid.*

17
Seven
Years
Old

APRIL 1: Another birthday unrecorded, this time the
seventh. We are anticipating the Easter school holiday
by trailering down to Los Angeles. This morning we went
shopping in Glendale for Candi's benefit, this being the
inducement that reconciled her to being taken out of
school early. We found a nice Oriental import store
having a clearance sale and a most pleasant
proprietress. We talked about our daughter and hers, age

10, and ended up buying slippers for ours and a paper
knife for me. Then, when the lady made it easy for her by
knocking a quarter off the price, Candi spent a dollar of
her own money on a box of colorful china birds. She is a
very careful shopper. Though she had six dollars saved
of her regular spending money, she turned down dozens
of things there and in other shops because she didn't
consider them a good value.

APRIL 4: We had lunch in Glendale and after lunch went to
visit the Ewens, intending to stay only a short time and
come back early to the trailer park. But they felt like a
Sunday drive, so we all crowded into our Pontiac and
drove to the observatory in Griffith Park. Young Johnny
was ready with jokes and riddles including one "easy"
one having to do with an apple and banana that visited
the Empire State Building. The apple jumped off, but the
banana didn't. Why? I couldn't think of an answer and
neither could Peg, but Candi thought awhile and said,
"Because it's yellow." I still find it hard to believe
she hadn't heard the riddle before, but evidently she
hadn't.

APRIL 11: Candi has asked me several times whether I
believe in God. Usually the form of her question is, "I
believe in God; do you, Dot?" Well, I do, and tell her so.
But the interesting thing to me is that the question of
belief or disbelief should rise in her mind. In our last
discussion, on the Los Angeles trip, she inquired
whether some people hate God. "No," I said, "nobody
hates God."

    "But some people don't believe in God."

    "True. But if they don't believe in Him, obviously
they don't hate Him. You can't hate what you don't think
exists. For instance, I don't believe in ghosts but I
don't hate ghosts either."

    "I hate ghosts."

    "Do you believe they exist?"

    "No."

    "Then how can you hate them?"

    "I don't know. I just do. They make me scared."

    I suggested that maybe she hated the way people look
when they dress up as ghosts. But that is neither here nor
there. Candi at 7 has to make up her mind whether God

Seven Years Old

exists. I at 7, and others of my age 40 years ago, never gave the matter a second's thought. It was as natural for us to believe in God as in ourselves.

APRIL 14: More than any other child I know, Candi puts life into her dolls. To other children here and in Livonia dolls are simply toys. Often they have given their dolls no names before meeting Candi. They apparently get the idea from her.

Candi's dolls are almost real people. She talks to them and tells of what they say and do, greets them in the morning, neglects them when they fall out of favor, and restores them to her good graces.

Shortly before Christmas she took up with Sleepy again and had to have new clothes for her. Then a new doll that she named Mary claimed nearly all of her love and has held it since. Day before yesterday she was playing with Melissa and came home crying her heart out. Melissa had torn off Mary's arm. It wasn't "my doll's" arm. Candi rarely breaks her own toys, yet she sheds no tears when other children break them as they frequently do. But Mary was a person and needed that arm. Peggy went back to Melissa's house with her and Melissa's mother, by some magic I was unable to conjure when Sleepy lost her arm, got Mary's arm back on.

Because Candi gives so much personality to her dolls, they have also come to have a personality to her mother and me. I felt almost as bad as she did when Mary lost her arm and I made no attempt to convince her that Mary was only a doll. I knew better.

JUNE 10: School is out and Candi has completed the first grade with good marks, all "excellent" except one "satisfactory" in "completion of work." Toward the end of the school year she began looking forward to vacation, then changed again at the last day and wished classes would go on.

JUNE 13: Coming back yesterday from a short holiday in Antelope Valley, we played an arithmetic game. We would ask each other sums like 9 and 6 or 12 take away 5 or 2 times 9. She would attempt to answer correctly, but I might be wrong or right. If wrong, she would correct me and give the right answer. Another game we've played is to name, each in turn, words beginning with a particular letter. Candi likes both games and does rather well at them.

JUNE 28: Well, we got her off this morning for a ride around the neighborhood on her bike. She has had the bike since Christmas and tried hard at first to master it but, finding she lacked the skill to keep up with the other kids, she lost the incentive to practice. So it is with other activities that require physical aptitude. She likes to dance, but when she took dancing lessons she refused to practice and finally reached the stage where the lessons themselves were unattractive because of her backwardness in the class.

Intellectual problems seem to provide their own incentive for her; manual problems need something extra. So today when she returned from her bike ride I made a proposition. If she does the same seven days straight I'll give her a dollar. Then I plan to offer her two more dollars when she succeeds in riding without training wheels. After that, I think she may find she enjoys bike riding.

AUGUST 4: The bike plan in working. Candi now rides around the tract at least once a day and her allowance has been raised to 50 cents a week. Last Sunday we took the outrigger wheels off and she rode with little trouble, and is in a fair way to earn her two dollars. She finds her bike easier and more pleasant to ride without the wheels but, like nearly all the kids of her age around here, she seldom finds the bike of use in her play. The kids would rather wander off on foot to their various hideouts—and they have several, she and Jill and Butchie. Lately she has been coming home late to her meals, but we think the venturesome spirit she is acquiring is worth delaying a meal for.

AUGUST 20: Melissa has been away much of the summer, and while she was gone, Candi played with Jill and Butch; but as soon as Melissa came back she again became Candi's favorite. They spend most of the day together in quiet play with dolls, whereas with Jill and Butch the play is more vigorous, off to adventure in remote parts of the tract.

Seven Years Old

Candi still rides her bike, however, and Melissa usually rides with her. Yesterday, too, they practiced roller skating. Neither girl is very good at it, but when Candi inquired what new thing she could do for extra money—after earning her two dollars for riding her bike without training wheels—I thought of the roller skates and offered a half dollar when she learns to use them well. She doesn't really want the money, but winning a reward appeals to her.

Thus after a long vacation from reading, she discovered a Tom Sawyer reading club at the Santa Barbara Library with the chance to whitewash a fence picket after reading four books and to win a certificate after reading ten. So Candi, whose other vacation interests had taken place of reading, set to work on the ten books and earned her certificate. She reads conscientiously, perhaps too much so, skipping the little words to tackle the big ones and so sometimes losing the meaning. When this happens, she complains, "This doesn't make sense," and wants to throw the book up in disgust. But I see she brought four more books home yesterday although the certificate was already hers.

SEPTEMBER 3: School is just around the corner again. Candi is happy to be going, but quietly happy, not as excited as last year when she entered first grade. Her teacher will be the very one she did not want, but I'll wager she'll like her after getting to know her better. "She yells at you," Candi complains. "Once when the bell rang and Jill and I were playing, she yelled at us to hurry up."

SEPTEMBER 23: School, I'm afraid, has become something of a bore. There has been no new instruction since it started three weeks ago. Everything has been simply a review of first grade work; and while this may be of value to some of the children, it is dull as dishwater to Candi.

Next year perhaps we'll take our vacation the first few weeks of school and let Candi miss the reviewing. Its sole effect this year has been to make everything connected with schoolwork, even books, distasteful to her.

This is what comes of grouping the children according to their abilities. It looked good in the first grade, with the fast learners allowed to set their own pace unhampered by the slow. But it breaks down now when, in order to keep all the groups together in the same class, the fast learners are made to sit all day marking time while the slow learners catch up.

In the old days the advance children would skip a grade or half grade. But half grades have been done away with and a whole grade might well be too much to skip this early in school.

OCTOBER 27: Candi has returned to books again after having been off them along with schoolwork in general. She borrows books from school and reads for an hour after supper as she is doing now. She reads for entertainment rather than instruction and usually brings home a thick rather than thin book because the thick books have more interesting stories. She brought one of the easy ones home on another child's recommendation and it bored her to actual tears. She was almost too angry to finish it and did so only because she had to in order to get credit for it.

As I compare her now with a year ago, I find a great development both physically and socially. She is an expert bike rider and roller skater and enjoys them both as much as playing house. She frequently goes off for hours with her bike and our problem is to find her before sundown when it gets quite chilly. Time and again, Peg has to hunt her up to give her a sweater. Socially she is still slow at making friends and reluctant to join her friends when strange children are with them, but she seems to have numerous friends and is quite popular. At school she plays with a half dozen or so; at home, usually with Melissa, but mainly because Melissa is first on hand to claim her.

NOVEMBER 1: Last evening she went out in her Hallowe'en costume calling at neighbors' doors on "Trick or Treat" by herself at first and then teamed up with Melissa. The two girls covered most of the tract and got home about 7:30. Last year she wouldn't go out without her mother. But she does lean heavily on Melissa or rather, on

Seven Years Old

Melissa's readiness to come and call for her. Yesterday afternoon without her, she was at loose ends but couldn't bring herself to go next door and ask for Jill. Instead, she stood around in our yard hoping Jill would catch sight of her, which she eventually did.,

This morning she asked to be allowed to wear her best shoes to school again, after having lost the privilege until she should learn to take better care of her clothes. I told her she was learning and improving all the time, but I'd still like to see further improvement. "I already put them in my closet," she protested. "Where do you want me to put them? In--in God's mouth?"

DECEMBER 18: Just one week till Christmas and I'll say, as I probably said last year, it doesn't seem like Christmas here in California. It isn't the snow we miss because we seldom had much snow in southern Michigan before Christmas. It must be the frosty weather and dim, crowded streets.

JANUARY 28: I have been reading to Candi, morning and evening, some old favorites of my own childhood. She enjoyed Mark Twain until we read The American Claimant. She also like the Penrod but it was Little Women that took her heart. She set her dolls in a tableau to represent the family.

Beth was her favorite--the "good one" that I perceived very early was marked for death in accordance with the literary conventions of the period. When we reached the place of Beth's near-fatal illness, she insisted on knowing whether Beth would recover before she'd read further. So we read one of the Anne of Green Gables series instead--not as good as I remembered, unfortunately. But ultimately her interest in the outcome of Little Women grew too strong and we finished it, to enjoy Beth's recovery--that time. Checking ahead in the second volume, I found my suspicions confirmed, that Beth would die, die one of those inexplicable deaths that come to the "good" in books; so I read Hans Brinker instead.

Here, too, we ran into difficulties because of the troubles of the Brinkers and Candi not wanting to hear about them before going to sleep. They were too "scary." So we shifted to The Story of a Bad Boy, a real old

favorite of mine, but one about which I began to have
serious doubts after glancing through it. But I needn't
have. Candi enjoys it, if not as much as Little Women,
certainly more than Hans Brinker. Part of its appeal is
its lack of suspense. It isn't scary as even most movies
are, which is why she doesn't particularly care to
attend movies. They spoiled The Wizard of Oz for her by
making a thriller out of it.

MARCH 11: The reading goes on, nearly every morning and
evening, and a pleasant habit it is, I enjoy the books as
much as Candi: Heidi, Black Beauty, Gulliver's Travels,
Uncle Remus. And Candi, after another hiatus, has taken
up reading on her own. Home with the flu last weekend she
read a story from "Pooh" and another in a collection of
fairy tales.

That was part of her "schoolwork away from school;"
the rest was drawing. She and I would look at a picture
and then try to draw it from memory. Although not as
skilled as I am, she can generally remember details
better; and if our drawings disagree, hers is the more
apt to be right.

A week from tomorrow is her eighth birthday and she
will receive, at her own wish, a mail-order course in
painting, complete with oil paints and brushes. It is
interesting to compare the guest list for her party this
year and last. Last year it was about evenly divided
between boys and girls: this year only one boy, our next
door neighbor Butchie. All the girls but one this year
are from our immediate neighborhood; last year they were
all from school.

I'm delighted with a story she has just written and
with the workmanlike way she set about writing it.
Providing herself with a large sheet of drawing paper
folded into eight pages 10" by 16", she sat down at the
dining table and went to work. It tells the story of a
girl named Jean who "is selfish like all six year olds"
but who nevertheless "is a nice little girl" and "has
lots of friends." She goes shopping with her mother and
sister Jane and her friend May, she and May go to the dime
store where they each spend ten pennies on a tiny doll,
and Jane and mother to the food store where for five
pennies Jane buys a jump rope and Mother buys food for
lunch.

Seven Years Old

"Mother said may can eat lunch with us if she wants to oh yes said May I'll ask my mother may's mother said it was all right so may ate lunch with Jane and Jean and May and Jean played together till Dinner time they went for a walk. on the way they saw some flowers and some trees. Jean met some more of her friends. May an Jean went on they came to a creek with watter in it. and then, they came to some trees with poison ivy on them and then to a hill with soft green grass on it

"after the walk may said Good—by to Jean and went home Jean went in side and ate supper and went to Bed the next morning she and May played together and ate lunch together. And the next day they went to school together. their teacher was Mrs. Gill

they Did reading writing an arithmetic and then they ate lunch it costs

god

in 25 cents we

1956

trust

to buy your lunch. after lunch the children have recess and then play a game and then go home"

When the last page was filled, the story was finished, complete with illustrations. She has promised to give it to me as soon as she makes a copy, and I'll bind it with these notes: Candi's first story.

One of the surprising things about developmental psychology, considering how much laughter children engage in, is how little attention has been devoted to what they think is funny. An exception is a study of children's humor by Zigler, Levine, and Gould [1966] who showed wordless cartoons dealing with a variety of emotional situations and child-adult relationships to 64 children in the second through the fifth grades. Each child went through the set of cartoons twice, first to see if he laughed or smiled, and next, to see if he could explain the jokes. The ability to understand the cartoons increased steadily across the four grades tested. There was an increase in expressions of mirth through the fourth grade, followed by a drop at grade five down to the level of the second graders.

The investigators' explanation of their results was that the funniest jokes are those a child can understand with effort. This was supported by their finding of a strong relationship at each grade between understanding a particular cartoon and laughing at it. The drop in mirth at grade five was clarified when they ranked the jokes from easy to difficult according to the proportion of children who could explain them. Fifth graders were found to have laughed most at the most difficult jokes.

In other words, the investigators reasoned, the set of cartoons they had happened to select were in keeping with the cognitive abilities of second through fourth graders; each joke these children managed to understand was enough of a challenge to seem funny. On the other hand, many of the cartoons were too easily understood by fifth graders to be humorous. Additional support for this view comes from an older study by Kenderline [1931] who found that bright preschoolers laugh more than their peers of average intelligence.

Brian Sutton-Smith [1973] advanced a cognitive-developmental explanation for children's enjoyment of riddles compatible with Zigler's theory of children's humor. He found that 80 percent of the riddles recommended to him by 8-year-olds involved the cognitive process of classification. An example of such a riddle is recorded in the diary: "Young Johnny was ready with jokes and riddles including one 'easy' one having to do with an apple and a banana that visited the Empire State Building. The apple jumped off, but the banana didn't. Why? I couldn't think of the answer and neither could Peg, but Candi thought awhile and said, *Because it's yellow.* I still find it hard to believe she hadn't heard the riddle before, but evidently she hadn't." Here the problem was to reclassify the banana from the category of fruit to the category of something yellow, in addition to noting the double meaning of *yellow*.

Piaget [1970] studied the cognitive operation of classification in school-aged children and found that the ability to classify an object in two ways simultaneously, as required in the above riddle, did not develop until age eight. When, for example, he showed children under 8 a collection of wooden beads, 15 red and 5 blue, and asked: *Are there more red beads or more wooden ones?* they responded: *More red ones.* Though they had agreed with him that all the beads were wooden before he posed the question, once their attention had been drawn to color, they seemed unable to classify the beads also by what they were made of.

Seven Years Old

Sutton-Smith felt it was no coincidence that the classificatory riddle was the favorite joke of children who, according to Piaget's data, had just developed the ability to classify on multiple dimensions. He found that older children, for whom multiple classification was presumably old hat, preferred jokes that focused on behavior irregularities, while children under 8, who, according to Piaget, were not yet familiar with classification, preferred what Sutton-Smith called the *preriddle*: an ambiguous question with a strictly arbitrary answer, for example, *Why did the man chop down the chimney? He needed the bricks*. Sutton-Smith felt that pleasure of the preriddle derived from its mimicry of adult questions and explanations which, in the eyes of the child under 8, may be equally arbitrary and ambiguous.

The diarist reported that after hearing Johnny's riddle, "Candi thought awhile" before giving her answer. It has been observed that when children are faced with cognitive problems, some, like Candida, spend a lot of time pondering before advancing a solution, while others respond very fast, seeming content to give the first answer that comes into their heads. The ones who pause and reflect on the quality of their cognitive product are said to have a *reflective cognitive tempo;* the tempo of the ones who respond immediately is said to be *impulsive*.

On certain problems such as the Matching Familiar Figures Test, which is used frequently to measure cognitive tempo and requires the child to pick a given drawing out of a set of six similar ones, impulsive children are found to make more errors than reflective children, presumably because they do not allow themselves sufficient time to examine all the alternatives. Impulsivity has also been found to decline with age (for example Kagan and Kogan [1970]). However, at any given age, from as early as age 2, some individuals score higher in impulsivity than others. These individual differences tend to remain stable as dimensions of the personality during one's entire life. Thus when a highly impulsive 2-year-old reaches age 10, he will probably be more impulsive than the average 10-year-old, even though his overall level of impulsivity will have declined.

Other evidence besides Candida's reaction to the riddle indicated that she had a reflective tempo. In describing her first report card, the diarist wrote: "School is out and Candy has completed the first grade with good marks, all excellent except one satisfactory in *completion of work*. Earlier he suggested a reason for her relatively slow tempo:

244

"Candi learns fast but works slowly, so that many of the pages she brings home from school are unfinished. However, when I test her on the unfinished ones she invariably knows them. I suspect her slowness is due in part to extra pains with the drawing and coloring, in part to her extreme fear of making a mistake."

Kagan and Kogan [1970] propose that individual differences in cognitive tempo might be explained simply by the theory that this "fear of making a mistake" is stronger in some children than in others. Those with a large dose of it, like Candida, respond cautiously and therefore reflectively; those without it have no reason to inhibit the first response to come to mind.

As an alternative theory, Kagan and Kogan suggest that reflectivity and impulsivity may be the result of two different kinds of anxiety, each stemming from a different mode of child-rearing. The fear that worries the reflective child, according to this view, is that if he makes a mistake he will be judged imcompetent by the social environment. This fear is thought to be due to the parents placing a heavy emphasis on the *inhibition of inappropriate behavior*—for example, scolding the child for breaking something or for hitting someone. The diarist felt this to be Candida's mother's approach to child-rearing: "I suggested to Peg that her insistence that Candy be so prim and prissy away from home may be at the base of her trouble. *What,* she asks, though not in so many words, *will people think of me if you behave so?* . . . She also criticized her rather severely for telling some woman who brought cookies to a school party, *We don't like those kinds of cookies.*"

By contrast, the impulsive child's fear is thought to be that people will judge him incompetent if he responds slowly. This is due, presumably, to parents who are less concerned than those of the reflective child with inhibiting and more concerned with exhibiting, thus placing heavy emphasis on achievement in areas such as walking, climbing, and talking.

In some cases, solving a problem brings with it a material reward, such as when Candida at 13 months figured out how to open cupboard doors and thereby gained access to the interesting things inside. In other cases, no reward is apparent except the knowledge that the problem has been solved: adults do crossword puzzles with only this incentive, and even infants have been found to learn complex sequences of head turns for the simple reward of a flash of light informing them when they are correct (Papousek [1967]). The diarist

Seven Years Old

wrote of 7-year-old Candida: "Intellectual problems seem to provide their own incentive for her; manual problems need something extra."

D.E. Berlyne [1965] proposes that the motivation to solve otherwise unrewarding intellectual problems is *curiosity*. He defined curiosity as *a state of high drive induced by conflict traceable to disharmonious symbolic processes*. According to Berlyne, the conflict, could stem from at least six sources: (1) *doubt*—when a tendency to believe something is opposed by a tendency to disbelieve it; (2) *perplexity*—an inclination toward two mutually exclusive beliefs; (3) *contradiction*—inclination to believe that a given statement is both true and untrue; (4) *incongruity*—an inclination toward a pair of beliefs which seem incompatible on the basis of one's experience; (5) *confusion*—when no clear solutions emerge from the information given; and (6) *irrelevance*—the tendency to pursue solutions which are unrelated to the problem at hand. He inferred that since the tension produced by cognitive conflict is unpleasant, the person experiencing it seeks to relieve it by solving the problem. If he solves it, the reduction in tension serves as a reward and may incline him toward future problem-solving.

Berlyne adduced support for this theory from the reported effectiveness of "discovery" methods of teaching which attempt to make the pupil aware of a problem before providing information that will solve it. For example, he reports that a class of Russian junior high school students who were introduced to latitude and longitude by means of a story about a boy faced with the practical problem of finding his location, understood better and were more interested than a *control* class given a traditional lesson outlining the bare facts of polar coordinates. He explained the superiority of the story lesson as due to cognitive conflict aroused by the hero's uncertainty.

Berlyne reports further that in the library of the same school, the books in heavy demand were those that raised questions before answering them; those in light demand simply purveyed information. He also notes that discovery methods have been found superior to traditional methods in American classrooms, citing as an example a physics lesson (Suchman [1961]) which began with a film demonstrating perplexing physical phenomena (a brass ball expanding when heated, an empty varnish can collapsing when cooled, etc.).

Although Candida required more than the knowlege of results that sufficed for her mastery of intellectual problems as an incentive for mastering motor skills, with the help of monetary rewards she eventually learned to ride a bike and roller skate: "Candi still rides her bike, however, and Melissa usually rides with her. Yesterday, too, they practiced roller skating. Neither girl is very good at it but when Candi inquired what new thing she could do for extra money—after earning her two dollars for riding her bike without training wheels—I thought of the roller skates and offered a half dollar when she learns to use them well."

The mastery of motor skills is of importance not only for the child's physical health, but for his social development and emotional well-being as well. For boys, at least, sociometric popularity correlates with strength and athletic skill (Hartup [1970]). In addition, the child's opportunities for social interaction are largely conditioned by the skills he possesses. When teams are chosen for sports such as softball or dodge ball, the child who is clumsy with a ball may very likely find himself excluded, and the child who does not know how to ride a bicycle runs the danger of being left out whenever his playmates decide to go somewhere on their bikes. The diarist noted, however, that the latter danger was fairly remote in the peer group Candida belonged to at age 7: "She finds her bike easier and more pleasant to ride without the [outrigger] wheels but, like nearly all the kids of her age around here, she seldom finds the bike of use in her play. The kids would rather wander off on foot to their various hideouts—and they have several, she and Jill and Butchie."

In addition to missing opportunities for social interaction, the physically awkward child may suffer the emotional difficulties accompanying loss of self-esteem. The child's everyday play provides countless opportunities for evaluation of his own athletic prowess relative to that of his peers. Thus Candi quickly learned her inferior status in bike-riding: "She has had the bike since Christmas . . . but, finding she lacked the skill to keep up with the other kids, she lost the incentive to practice." The child who continually finds himself at a disadvantage in such contests may well suffer a weakening of self-esteem and, since low self-esteem is itself found to be correlated with unpopularity in children (Reese [1961]), this can set up a vicious circle which further limits the awkward child's opportunities to develop skills.

Erik Erikson [1963] saw the development of motor skills as being centrally important to the growth of a healthy personality. In his view, the child of school age goes through a crisis comparable to that which

Seven Years Old

Freud postulated in the infant being weaned or the toddler being toilet-trained. For the school child, the crisis surrounds the task of learning the physical, social, and intellectual skills, that are necessary for normal participation in society. The child who learns them well acquires heightened cultural status and a sense of the pleasure to be found in achievement. But according to Erikson, the child who fails to acquire them experiences a sense of inferiority which jeopardizes his ability to cope with subsequent developmental crises (for example, that over a sense of identity during adolescence or that over productivity and sense of worth during middle age).

Mary Gutteridge [1939] devised a four-step scale to measure the development of motor skill. The first step denoted lack of skill: the child either withdrew from opportunities to engage in the activity or remained passive. The second step began when the child attempted to perform the skill with someone else's help and ended when he was seen to practice it by himself. During the third step, the child acquired coordination, accuracy, and poise and came to express satisfaction with his own performance. At the fourth step, the skill itself having already been fully mastered, the child tested it by adding difficulties or taking risks, competed with others, and incorporated it into larger projects such as dramatic play.

Gutteridge used the scale with preschoolers, kindergarteners, and first graders, to measure skills including hopping, skipping, galloping, jumping, climbing, sliding, tricycling, and bouncing, throwing, and catching balls. She confirmed the common observation that children of any given age differ greatly in their proficiency at a particular skill. For instance, one boy of 3½ was at step four in the skill of climbing; another of the same age was at step one. She also found that some of the skills were generally more difficult than others. The easiest—sliding—was mastered by the average child of 2 or 2½, while the average age for mastering galloping, catching, and throwing balls was nearly 6.

Although Gutteridge found a certain degree of consistency in a given child's pattern of motor behavior, she also noted that proficiency in one skill was no guarantee of proficiency in others. A 3-year-old named Alison, for example, was described as an expert tricycler but still needed help in climbing in the jungle gym. Inconsistency held even for skills as similar as sweeping and painting: Alison was clumsy with a broom yet dexterous with a paint brush.

Aileen Carpenter [1941] further investigated the question of

248

whether a child who does well at one skill is likely to do better than average at most others. After observing the performance of 253 6-to-10-year-olds in 14 separate skills, she concluded that two general factors, speed and strength, were individual traits that showed transfer over a wide range of activities, but that they were not highly related to one another. Thus a child skilled at chin-ups should also be good at a strength task such as weight-lifting but need not be as adept as his peers in speed tasks such as sprinting.

Stemming from a longitudinal study of motor abilities in twin boys, Myrtle McGraw [1951] reported four other factors that influence the acquisition and performance of skills: the amount of practice the child has had at the skill in question, the child's timidity over the possibility of mishaps, his physical state (including muscle tone, neural maturity, and relative proportion of parts of his body), and his motivation to master this particular skill, balanced against his distraction from other interests. The diarist remarked on the importance of practice for 7-year-old Candida's motor development: "She likes to dance, but when she took dancing lessons she refused to practice and finally reached the stage where the lessons themselves were unattractive to her because of her backwardness in the class."

In McGraw's study the twins spent a 40-hour week in the laboratory from shortly after birth until age 2. During this time, one boy, Johnny, was given extensive training in motor activities, including swimming, jumping, roller skating, and riding a tricycle. Jimmy received no special training until two months before his second birthday, when he embarked on a program like Johnny's but with lengthier practice periods. At age 6 both boys returned to the lab for a follow-up examination.

By comparing the two boys' relative ease of acquisition of the skills initially and by assessing how much their performance deteriorated during the four years without training, McGraw was able to infer the operation of the factors listed above. For example, Johnny had become a proficient roller skater at 16 months, while Jimmy never gained full proficiency. McGraw attributed this to the extra practice Johnny had had, to Jimmy's greater timidity about falling when his training was begun at nearly 2—the bumps and scrapes of learning to walk being by then well in the background—and to Jimmy's weakened motivation as a result of conflicting interests. She found that by age 6 both boys had lost most of what skating skill they had had, and attributed this to a change in body configuration which had

Seven Years Old

been produced by the disproportionate growth of their legs and which made balancing a new problem.

She found, on the other hand, almost no deterioration in Johnny's ability to jump from pedestals over the four-year period, although Jimmy's—which had not been up to the same standard initially—did deteriorate. She explained this by a difference in attitude, reasoning that Johnny had learned to jump when he was still too young to have a firm fear of heights and his boldness had persisted, while Jimmy's fear of jumping, which first showed itself when his training began at 22 months, had become more intense during his four years away from the laboratory.

18
Summary

In these pages we have watched a child grow up from birth through age 7. Candida's first year transformed her from a helpless bundle of reflexes, simple wants, and sleep into an alert, independently mobile, and socially responsive person. Her progress toward self-sufficiency continued during her second year, most notably through her acquisition of language, as she began first naming objects, then expressing complex meanings by single words, and finally combining words to form original *pivot* and *telegraphic* sentences. She also began expressing her growing independence in social situations, along with a wide repertoire of other feelings, ranging from affection to rage.

Summary

With entry into nursery school during her third year, her social horizons broadened to include peers, and her contact with them stimulated the growth of social skills as diverse as aggression, generosity, and cooperation. Her fourth year saw significant developments of her personality and imagination, while her fifth and sixth witnessed marked intellectual strides in areas such as learning, reasoning, and numerical and logical concepts. She began school in her seventh year and took to it eagerly, benefiting as much from the extracurricular opportunities it provided for the formation of friendships and for emotional and moral growth as from its tuition of reading and motor skill. By her eighth birthday she bore few resemblances to the Candida the diary began with. Although much time and many developments still separated her from adulthood, the changes during her first eight years were without a doubt the most remarkable.

In the course of tracing Candida's first eight years of development, we examined several different theories about child behavior and the developmental process. Alfred Baldwin [1968] compares these theories to a patchwork quilt: each has its own insulated domain of study and though theories occasionally share a border, they rarely overlap with one another. Thus the most important requirement for the formulation of a unified theory of child development is missing, since theories must overlap—in the sense of either confronting one another with different predictions about the same situation or concurring in their explanations of a particular phenomenon—in order that they may be tested against one another and the best of each of them preserved. Instead, each major theory deals with a single slice of the problem and ignores the very issues the next theory regards as fundamental. Freud concentrates on personality, Piaget on cognition, Gestalt theory on perception, and stimulus-response theory on learning. While each is concerned in its own way with the child and with development, the points of view they take on these issues are so different that it is difficult for them even to argue effectively.

In the light of this, points where the theories do converge seem noteworthy, and their mutual assertions seem all the more compelling, holding the promise that they may one day be the building blocks from which a unified theory will be constructed. One such point of convergence is in the impulsivity of the preschooler. Kagan observed that preschool children tend to respond rapidly and make more errors than do older children in problem-solving tasks, while

Summary

Freud noted that infants and preschoolers tend to demand immediate gratification of their impulses—which he ascribed to the predominance of the id in their personalities. Another convergence is between Freudian theory and social-learning theory on the importance for socialization (including development of a conscience and a sex role) of certain features in the early environment such as the emotional tone of the family and the methods of child-rearing employed. However, while both theories concur in their estimates of the importance of variables such as the mother's warmth and the father's dominance, the models by which they explain their influence differ completely—resolution of conflict on one hand, and direct and observational learning on the other.

Perhaps the clearest convergence between theories occurs in their respective treatments of intellectual development. Piaget outlines a progression from direct sensorimotor functioning to an increased skill in dealing with the world symbolically, first through loosely organized *preconcepts* and later in terms of coordinated conceptual systems. Vygotsky concurs in postulating that the child's first *concepts* are complexes that evolve with age into hierarchical classifications, while Werner's theory that intellectual development consists of the gradual differentiation of an initial state of globality is in keeping with the organic unity in Piaget's sensorimotor stage between knowing the world and acting upon it. The Kendlers' theory of conceptual development parallels Piaget's in postulating the predominance of a nonmediated, single-link stimulus-response mode of processing in the 2-year-old and the increasing use of a conceptually mediated mode as the child grows older. White postulates that a simple, associative learning process is laid down early in development and that a cognitive process capable of inhibiting it develops by about age 7. Even Freud, whose major work was in the field of personality, distinguishes the id-controlled thinking of the very young child from the ego-controlled thinking of his elders, postulating that the former is controlled by desire and the latter by reason.

Noting these parallels, Baldwin concludes: "there seems to be a fair consistency among theories that there is a primitive noncognitive functioning which is gradually superseded and controlled by a more advanced cognitively mediated logical process" [p. 592]. White's theory, that the transition from the former to the latter climaxes between the ages of 5 and 7, reinforces the view . . . we leave Candida at age 8 closer, at least in intellectual functioning, to the adult she will become than to the infant she has been.

References

Aldrich, C.A. 1928 A new test for hearing in the new-born: the conditioned reflex. *American Journal of Diseases in Children* 35:36-37.

Altus, W.D. 1966 Birth order and its sequelae. *Science* 7:44-49.

Anastasi, A. 1958. Heredity, environment, and the question "How?" *Psychological Review* 65:197-208.

Azrin, N. 1958. Some effects of noise on human behavior. *Journal of the Experimental Analysis of Behavior* 1:183-200.

————. 1960. Sequential effects of punishment. *Science* 131:605-606.

Azrin, N.H., and Holz, W.C. 1966. Punishment. In *Operant behavior a review of research and application*, ed. W.K. Honig. New York: Appleton.

References

Bandura, A., and Huston, A.C. 1961. Identification as a process of incidental learning. *Journal of Abnormal and Social Psychology* 63:311-18.

Bandura, A.; Ross, D.; and Ross, S.A. 1961. Transmission of aggression through imitation of aggressive models. *Journal of Abnormal and Social Psychology* 63:575-82.

Bandura, A., and Walters, R.H. 1959. *Adolescent aggression*. New York: Ronald Press.

Barker, R.G.; Dembo, T.; and Lewin, K. 1941. Studies in topological and vector psychology, II: frustration and regression: an experiment with young children. *University of Iowa Studies in Child Welfare* 18:1.

Berenda, R.W. 1950. *The influence of the group on the judgments of children*. New York: King's Crown.

Berlyne, D.E. 1965. *Structure and direction in thinking*. New York: Wiley.

Birch, H.G. 1945. The relation of previous experience to insightful problem-solving. *Journal of Comparative and Physiological Psychology* 38:367-83.

Bisett, B.M., and Rieber, M. 1966. The effects of age and incentive value on discrimination learning. *Journal of Experimental Child Psychology* 3:199-206.

Bishop, C.H. 1964. Transfer effects of word and letter training in reading. *Journal of Verbal Learning and Verbal Behavior* 3:215-21.

Boring, E.G. 1952. *A history of psychology in autobiography*. New York: Russell and Russell, pp. 237-56.

Bower, T.G.R. 1964. Discrimination of depth in premotor infants. *Psychonomic Science* 1:368.

Bowlby, J. 1969. *Attachment*. New York: Basic Books.

Brackbill, Y., and Jack, D. 1958. Discrimination learning in children as a function of reinforcement value. *Child Development* 29:185-90.

Braine, M.D.S. 1963. The ontogeny of English phrase structure: the first phase. *Language* 39:1-13.

————. 1970. The acquisition of language in the infant and child. In *The learning of language*, ed. C. Reed. New York: Appleton-Century-Crofts.

Bridges, K.M.B. 1932. A genetic theory of the emotions. *Child Development* 2:214-341.

Brown, D.G. 1958. Sex-role development in a changing culture. *Psychological Bulletin* 55:232-42.

Brown, R. 1958. How shall a thing be called? *Psychological Review* 65:14-21.

————. 1965. *Social psychology*. New York: Free Press of Glencoe.

————. 1970. *Psycholinguistics*. New York: Free Press of Glencoe.

Brown, R., and Bellugi, U. 1964. Three processes in the child's acquisition of syntax. *Harvard Educational Review* 34:133-51.

Bruner, J.S.; Olver, R.; and Greenfield, P.M. 1966. *Studies in cognitive growth*. New York: Wiley.

Bryan, J.H. 1969. How adults teach hypocrisy. *Psychology Today* 3:7:50-53.

Buhler, C. 1930. *The first year of life*. New York: Day.

————. 1931. The social behavior of children. In *Handbook of child psychology*, ed. C. Murchison. Worcester, Mass.: Clark Univ. Press.

Burtt, H.E. 1941. An experimental study of early childhood memory: final report. *Journal of Genetic Psychology* 58:435-39.

Campbell, J.D., and Yarrow, M.R. 1958. Personal and situational variables in adaptation to change. *Journal of Social Issues* 14:29-46.

Carpenter, A. 1941. The differential measurement of speed in primary school children. *Child Development* 12:1-7.

Cazden, C. 1965. Environmental assistance to the child's acquisition of grammar. Unpublished doctoral dissertation, Graduate School of Education, Harvard University.

Chamberlain, A.F., and Chamberlain, I.C. 1904. Studies of a child. *Pedagogical Seminary,* vol. eleven.

Charlesworth, R., and Hartup, W.W. 1967. Positive social reinforcement in the nursery school peer group. *Child Development* 38:993-1002.

Carmichael, L.; Hogan, H.P.; and Walter, A.A. 1932. An experimental study of the effects of language on the representation of visually perceived form. *Journal of Experimental Psychology* 15:73-86.

Chomsky, N. 1967. The formal nature of language. In *Biological foundations of language,* ed. E.H. Lenneberg. New York: Wiley.

Chukovsky, K. 1963. *From two to five.* Berkeley: Univ. of California Press.

Clark, B.S. 1965. The acquisition and extinction of peer imitation in children. *Psychonomic Science* 2: 147-48.

Constanzo, P., and Shaw, M. 1966. Conformity as a function of age level. *Child Development* 37:967-75.

Croake, J.W. 1969. Fears of children. *Human Development* 12:239-47.

Darwin, C. 1877. A biographical sketch of an infant. *Mind* 11:286-94.

Davitz, J.R. 1952. The effects of previous training on postfrustration behavior. *Journal of Abnormal and Social Psychology* 47:309-15.

De Laguna, G. 1927. *Speech: its functions and development.* Bloomington: Indiana Univ. Press.

Dennis, W. 1941. Infant development under conditions of restricted practice and of minimal social stimulation. *Genetic Psychology* 23:143-91.

————. 1960. Cause of retardation among institutionalized children: Iran. *Journal of Genetic Psychology* 96:47-59.

Dennis, W., and Dennis, M. 1941. Infant development under conditions of restricted practice and minimum social stimulation. *Genetic Psychology Monographs* 23:147, 149-55.

————. 1940. The effect of cradling practices upon the onset of walking in Hopi children. *Journal of Genetic Psychology* 56:77-86.

Dinitz, S.; Dynes, R.; and Clarke, A. 1954. Preferences for male or female children: traditional or affectional? *Marriage and Family Living* 16:128-30.

Dollard, J.; Doob, L.W.; Miller, N.; Mowrer, O.; and Sears, R.R. 1939. *Frustration and aggression.* New Haven: Yale Univ. Press.

Ellis, H. 1926. *A study of British genius.* Boston: Houghton Mifflin.

Erikson, E.H. 1963. *Childhood and society.* New York: Norton.

Eron, L.D. 1963. Relationship of TV viewing habits and aggression behavior in children. *Journal of Abnormal and Social Psychology* 67:193-96.

Eron, L.; Walder, L.; Toigo, R.; and Lefkowitz, M. 1963. Social class, parental punishment for aggression, and child aggression. *Child Development* 34:849-67.

Ervin, S.M. 1964. Imitation and structural change in children's language. In *New directions in the study of language,* ed. E.H. Lenneberg. Cambridge: M.I.T. Press.

Estes, W.K. 1944. An experimental study of punishment. *Psychological Monographs* 57:263.

References

Ferguson, C.A. 1964. Baby talk in six languages. *American Anthropology* 66:103-14.

Feshbach, S. 1970. Aggression. In *Carmichael's manual of child psychology*, ed. P.H. Mussen, Vol. 2. New York: Wiley.

Flavell, J.; Beach, D.; and Chinsky, J. 1966. Spontaneous verbal rehearsal in a memory task as a function of age. *Child Development* 37:283-99.

Forer, L.K. 1969. *Birth order and life roles*. Springfield, Ill.: Thomas.

Freedman, J.L. 1965. Long-term behavior effects of cognitive dissonance. *Journal of Experimental Social Psychology* 1:145-55.

Freud, S. 1935. *An autobiographical study*. London: Hogarth.

Furth, H. G. 1964. Research with the deaf: implications for language and cognition. *Psychological Bulletin* 62:145-64.

————. 1971. Linguistic deficiency in thinking: research with deaf subjects, 1964-1969. *Psychological Bulletin* 76:58-72.

Gardener, R.A., and Gardener, B.T. 1969. Teaching sign language to a chimpanzee. *Science* 165:664-72.

Geber, M., and Dean, R.F. 1964. Le developpement psychomoteur et somatique des jeunes enfants Africains en Ouganda. *Courrier* 14:426-33.

Gibson, E.J. 1969. *Principles of perceptual learning and development*. New York: Appleton-Century-Crofts.

Goodenough, F.L. 1926. *Measurement of intelligence by drawings*. Yonkers, N.Y.: World.

————. 1931. *Anger in young children*. Minneapolis: Univ. of Minnesota Press.

Greenberg, P.J. 1932. Competition in children. *American Journal of Psychology* 44:221-48.

Groos, K. 1901. *The play of man*. New York: Appleton.

Guilford, R.B., and Worcester, D.A. 1930. A comparative study of the only and non-only child. *Journal of Genetic Psychology* 38:411-26.

Gutteridge, M.V. 1939. A study of motor achievements of young children. *Archives of Psychology*, no. 244.

Hall, G.S. 1904. *Adolescence*. New York: Appleton.

Harlow, H. 1959. Learning set and error factor theory. In *Psychology: a study of a science*, ed. S. Koch, vol. 2. New York: McGraw-Hill.

Harlow, H.F., and Harlow, M.K. 1965. The affection systems. In *Behavior of nonhuman primates*, ed. A.M. Schrier, H.F. Harlow, and F. Stollnitz, vol. II. New York: Academic Press.

————. 1967. The young monkeys. *Psychology Today* 1:5:40-48.

Harris, D.B. 1957. *The concept of development*. Minneapolis: Univ. of Minnesota Press.

Hartup, W.W. 1964. Friendship status and effectiveness of peers as reinforcing agents. *Journal of Experimental Child Psychology* 1:154-62.

————. 1970. Peer interaction and social organization. In *Carmichael's manual of child psychology*, ed. P.H. Mussen, vol. 2. New York: Wiley.

Hartup, W.W., and Coates, B. 1967. Imitation of a peer as a function of reinforcement from the peer group and rewardingness of the model. *Child Development* 38:1000-16.

Heathers, G. 1953. Emotional dependence and independence in a physical threat situation. *Child Development* 24:169-79.

————. 1955. Emotional dependence and independence in nursery school play. *Journal of Genetic Psychology* 87:37-57.

References

Heilman, A. 1968. *Phonics in proper perspective.* Columbus, Ohio: Charles Merrill.

Helmreich, R.L., and Collins, B.E. 1967. Situational determinants of affiliative preference under stress. *Journal of Personality and Social Psychology* 6:79-85.

Heroard, J. 1868. *Journal de Jean Heroard sur l'enfance et la jeunesse de Louis XIII.* Paris: Firmin Didot.

Hicks, D.J. 1965. Imitation and retention of film-mediated aggressive peer and adult models. *Journal of Personality and Social Psychology* 2:97-100.

Himmelweit, H.; Oppenheim, A.N.; and Vince, P. 1958. *Television and the child.* London: Oxford Univ. Press.

Hindley, C.B.; Filliozat, A.M.; Klackenberg, G.; Nicolet-Meister, P.; and Sand, E.A. 1966. Differences in age of walking in five European longitudinal samples. *Human Biology* 38:364-79.

Hochberg, J., and Brooks, V. 1962. Pictorial recognition as an unlearned ability: a study of one child's performance. *American Journal of Psychology* 75:624-28.

Hoffman, M.L. 1970. Moral development. In *Carmichael's manual of child psychology,* ed. P.H. Mussen, vol. 2 New York: Wiley.

Horowitz, F.D. 1967. Social reinforcement effects on child behavior. In *The Young child,* ed. W.W. Hartup and N.L. Smotherg. Washington, D.C.: National Association for the Education of Young Children.

Hudson, W. 1960. Pictorial depth perception in sub-cultural groups in Africa. *Journal of Social Psychology* 52:183-208.

Hunt, R.G., and Synnerdahl, V. 1959. Social influence among kindergarten children. *Sociology and Social Research* 43:171-74.

Ingram, D. 1971. Transitivity in child language. *Language* 47:888-910.

Jack, L.M. 1934. An experimental study of ascendant behavior in preschool children. In *Behavior in the preschool child,* ed. L.M. Jack, E.M. Maxwell, I.G. Mengert. *University of Iowa Studies in Child Welfare* 3:7-65.

Jakobson, R. 1968. *Child Language, aphasia, and general sound laws.* (German, 1941.) The Hague: Mouton.

Jeffrey, W., and Samuels, S.J. 1967. Effect of method of reading training on initial learning and transfer. *Journal of Verbal Learning and Verbal Behavior* 6:354-58.

Jensen, K. 1932. Differential reactions to taste and temperature in the newborn infant. *Genetic Psychology Monographs* 12:361-479.

Jersild, A. 1954. Emotional development. In *Manual of child psychology,* ed. L. Carmichael, 2d ed. New York: Wiley.

Jones, H. E. 1954. The environment and mental development. In *Manual of child psychology,* ed. L. Carmichael. New York: Wiley.

Kagan, J. 1970. Determinations of infant attention. *American Scientist* 58:298-376.

—————. 1971. *Change and continuity in infancy.* New York: Wiley.

Kagan, J., Kogan, N. 1970. Individual variation in cognitive processes. In *Carmichael's manual of child psychology,* ed. P.H. Mussen, vol. 1. New York: Wiley.

Katz, D. 1950. *Gestalt psychology: its nature and significance.* New York: Ronald.

References

Kelleher, R.T. 1956. Discrimination learning as a function of reversal and nonreversal shifts. *Journal of Experimental Psychology* 51:379-84.

Kellogg, R. 1967. Understanding children's art. In *Readings in developmental psychology today*, ed. P. Cramer. Del Mar, Cal.: CRM Books.

Kendler, H.H., and D'Amato, M.F. 1955. A comparison of reversal shifts and nonreversal shifts in human concept formation problems. *Journal of Experimental Psychology* 49:165-74.

Kendler, T.S. 1961. Concept formation. *Annual Review of Psychology* 12:447-72.

Kendler, T.S., and Kendler, H.H. 1959. Reversal and nonreversal shifts in kindergarten children. *Journal of Experimental Psychology* 58:56-60.

Kendler, T.S.; Kendler, H.H.; and Wells, D. 1960. Reversal and nonreversal shifts in nursery school children. *Journal of Comparative and Physiological Psychology* 53:83-87.

Kendler, H.H., and Kendler, T.S. 1962. Vertical and horizontal processes in problem-solving *Psychology Review* 69:1-16.

Kendler, T.S., and Kendler, H.H. 1967. Experimental analysis of inferential behavior. In *Advances in child development and behavior,* ed. L.P. Lipsitt and C.C. Spiker, vol. 3. New York: Academic Press.

Kenderline, M. 1931. Laughter in the preschool child. *Child Development* 2:228-30.

Kessen, W. 1962. *The child.* New York: Wiley.

————. 1962. "Stage" and "structure" in the study of children. *Monographs of the Society for Research in Child Development* 27:2.

Klima, E., and Bellugi, U. 1966. Syntactic regularities in the speech of children. In *Psycholinguistic Papers,* ed. J. Lyons and R. Wales. Chicago: Aldine Press.

Koch, H. 1955. Some personality correlates of sex, sibling position, and sex of sibling among five and six-year-old children. *Genetic Psychology Monographs* 52:3-50.

Koffka, K. 1935. *Principles of Gestalt Psychology.* New York: Harcourt, Brace.

Kohlberg, L. 1966. A cognitive-developmental analysis of children's sex-role concepts and attitudes. In *The development of sex differences,* ed. E.E. Maccoby. Stanford: Stanford Univ. Press.

Kohler, W. 1925. *The mentality of apes.* New York: Harcourt, Brace.

Kraus, R., and Sendak, M. 1952. *A hole is to dig.* New York: Harper.

Laosa, L.M., and Brophy, J.E. 1970. Sex and birth order interaction in measures of sex typing and affiliation in kindergarten children. *American Psychological Association Proceedings* 5:363-64.

Lenneberg, E.H. 1969. On explaining language. *Science* 164:635-43.

Leuba, C. 1931. A preliminary experiment to quantify incentive and its effects. *Journal of Abnormal and Social Psychology* 25:275-88.

Levine, M. 1963. A model of hypothesis behavior in discrimination learning set. *Psychology Review* 70:254-76.

Levinson, B., and Reese, H.W. 1967. Patterns of discrimination learning in preschool children, fifth graders, college freshmen, and the aged. *Monographs of the Society for Reasearch in Child Development* 32:7.

Lewis, M.M. 1936. *Infant speech.* New York: Harcourt, Brace.

Lewis, M., and Brooks-Gunn, J. 1972. Self, other and fear: the reaction of infants to people. Paper presented at the Eastern Psychology Association.

References

Lipsitt, L.P.; Engen, T.; and Kaye, H. 1963. Developmental changes in the olfactory threshold of the neonate. *Child Development* 34:371-76.

Long, I., and Welch, L. 1941. The development of the ability to discriminate and match numbers. *Journal of Genetic Psychology* 59:377-87.

Luquet, G. H. 1927. *Le dessin infantin*. Paris: Alcan.

Luria, A.R. 1961. The role of speech in the regulation of normal and abnormal behavior. New York: Liveright.

Maller, J.B. 1929. Cooperation and competition; an experimental study in motivation. *Teacher's College Contributions to Education* #384.

Maudry, M., and Nekula, M. 1939. Social relations between children of the same age during the first two years of life. *Journal of Genetic Psychology* 54:193-215.

McCarthy, D. 1954. Language development in children. In *Manual of child psychology*, ed. L. Carmichael. New York: Wiley.

McCandless, B.R., and Marshall, H.R. 1957. A picture sociometric technique for preschool children and its relation to teacher judgments of friendship. *Child Development* 28:139-47.

McGraw, M. 1951. Later development of children specially trained in infancy. In *Readings in child psychology*, ed. W. Dennis. New York: Prentice-Hall.

McNeill, D.P. 1970. The development of language. In *Carmichael's manual of child psychology*, ed. P.H. Mussen, vol. 1. New York: Wiley.

Merrill, B.A. 1946. Measurement of mother-child interaction. *Journal of Abnormal and Social Psychology* 41:37-49.

Miller, L.B., and Estes, B.W. 1961. Monetary reward and motivation in discrimination learning. *Journal of Experimental Psychology* 61:501-504.

Mischel, W.A. 1966. A social-learning view of sex differences in behavior. In *The development of sex differences*, ed. E.E. Maccoby. Stanford: Stanford Univ. Press.

Moss, H.A. 1967. Sex, age and state as determinants of mother-infant interaction. *Merrill-Palmer Quarterly* 13:19-36.

Murray, F. 1972. Acquisition of conservation through social interaction. *Developmental Psychology* 6:1-6.

Nagel, E. 1957. Determinism and development. In *The concept of development*, ed. D.B. Harris. Minneapolis: Univ. of Minnesota Press.

Nelson, K.E.; Carskaddon, G.; and Bonvillian, J. 1973. Syntax acquisition: impact of experimental variation in adult verbal interaction with the child. Paper presented at the Society for Research in Child Development meeting.

Nelson, R.; Reid, I.; and Travers,R. 1965. Effect of electric shock as a reinforcer of the behavior of children. *Psychological Reports* 16:123-26.

Oetzel, R.M. 1966. Annotated bibliography. In *The development of sex differences*, ed. E.E. Maccoby. Stanford: Stanford Univ. Press.

Papousek, H. 1967. Conditioning during early postnatal development. In *Behavior in infancy and early childhood*, ed. Y. Brackbill and S.G. Thompson. New York: Free Press.

Parke, R.D., and Walters, R.H. 1967. Some factors influencing the efficacy of punishment for inducing response inhibition. *Monographs of the*

References

Society for Research in Child Development 32:1.

Parten, M. 1932. Social play among preschool children. *Journal of Abnormal and Social Psychology* 27:430-40.

Patterson, G.R.; Littman, R.A.; and Bricker, W. 1967. Assertive behavior in children: a step toward a theory of aggression. *Monographs of the Society for Research in Child Development* 32:113.

Pavlov, I. 1927. *Conditioned reflexes.* London: Oxford Univ. Press.

Peterson, C. 1973. Preference for sex of offspring as a measure of change in sex attitudes. *Psychology* 10:3-5.

Piaget, J. 1926. *The language and thought of the child.* New York: Harcourt, Brace.

————. 1930. *The child's conception of physical causality.* London: Kegan Paul.

————. 1931. Children's philosophies. In *Handbook of child psychology,* ed. C. Murchison. Worcester, Mass.: Clark Univ. Press.

————. 1948. *The moral judgment of the child.* Glencoe, Ill.: Free Press.

————. 1952. *The origins of intelligence in children.* New York: International Universities Press.

————. 1962. *Play, dreams and imitation in childhood.* New York: Norton.

————. 1970. Piaget's theory. In *Carmichael's manual of child psychology,* ed. P.H. Mussen, vol. 1. New York: Wiley.

Piaget, J., and Inhelder, B. 1969. *The psychology of the child.* New York: Basic Books.

Pick, A. 1965. Improvement of visual and tactual information. *Journal of Experimental Psychology* 69:331-39.

Preyer, W. 1888. *The mind of the child.* New York: Appleton.

Raven, J.C. 1956. *Guide to using progressive matrices.* London: Lewis.

Reese, H.W. 1961. Relationship between self-acceptance and sociometric choice. *Journal of Abnormal and Social Psychology* 62:472-74.

Reese, H.W., and Lipsitt, L.P. 1970. *Experimental child psychology.* New York: Academic Press.

Reynolds, M.M. 1963. Negativism of preschool children. In *Readings in child psychology,* ed. W. Dennis. Englewood Cliffs: Prentice-Hall.

Richards, T.W., and Nelson, V.L. 1938. Studies of mental development. *Journal of Genetic Psychology* 52:327-31.

Robbins, L.C. 1963. The accuracy of parental recall of aspects of child development and child rearing. *Journal of Abnormal and Social Psychology* 66:261-70.

Rosenhan, D.L. 1966. Effects of social class and race responsiveness to approval and disapproval. *Journal of Personality and Social Psychology* 4:253-59.

Rosenow, C., and Whyte, A. 1931. The ordinal position of problem children. *American Journal of Orthopsychiatry* 1:430-34.

Rutherford, E., and Mussen, P.H. 1968. Generosity in nursery school boys. *Child Development* 39:755-65.

Sameroff, A.J. 1971. Can conditioned responses be established in the newborn infant? *Developmental Psychology* 5:1-12.

Schaffer, H.R. 1966. The onset of fear of strangers and the incongruity hypothesis. *Journal of Child Psychology and Psychiatry* 7:95-106.

References

Schramm, W.; Lyle, J.; and Parker, E.B. 1961. *Television in the lives of our children*. Stanford: Stanford Univ. Press.

Schwarz, J.C., and Wynn, R. 1971. The effect of mothers' presence and previsits on children's emotional reaction to starting nursery school. *Child Development* 42:871-81.

Sears, R.R. 1963. Dependency motivation. In *Nebraska symposium on motivation*, ed. M. Jones. Lincoln: Univ. of Nebraska Press.

Sears, R.R.; Maccoby, E.E.; and Levin, H. 1957. *Patterns of child rearing*. Evanston, Ill.: Row, Peterson.

Shepard, O. 1938. *The journals of Bronson Alcott*. Port Washington, N.Y.: Kennikat Press, p. 28.

Sherif, M.; Harvey, O.; White, B.; Hood, W.; and Sherif, C. 1961. Intergroup conflict and cooperation: the robbers' cave experiment. Norman: Univ. of Oklahoma Press.

Sherif, M., and Sherif, C.W. 1953. Groups in harmony and tension. New York: Harper.

Sherman, M. 1927. The differentiation of emotional responses in infants. I. Judgments of emotional responses from motion picture views and from actual observations. *Journal of Comparative Psychology* 7:265-84.

Shirley, M.M. 1931. *The first two years: a study of twenty-five babies*. Minneapolis: Univ. Of Minnesota Press.

Snow, C. 1972. Mothers' speech to children learning language. *Child Development* 43:549-65.

Sontag, L.W. 1966. Implications of fetal behavior and environment for adult personalities. *Annals of the New York Academy of Sciences* 134:782-86.

Spelt, D. 1948. The conditioning of the human fetus in utero. *Journal of Experimental Psychology* 38:338-46.

Spiker, C.C. 1956. Stimulus pretraining and subsequent performance in the delayed reaction experiment. *Journal of Experimental Psychology* 52:107-11.

————. 1960. Associative transfer in verbal paired-associate learning. *Child Development* 31:73-88.

————. 1966. The concept of development: relevant and irrelevant issues. *Monographs of the Society for Research in Child Development* 31:5.

Spitz, R. 1950. Anxiety in infancy. *International Journal of Psychoanalysis* 31:138-43.

Staffieri, J.R. 1967. A study of social stereotypes of body image in children. *Journal of Personality and Social Psychology* 7:101-103.

Starr, A.S. 1923. The diagnostic value of the audito-vocal digit memory span. *Psychologia Clinica* 15:61-84.

Starkweather, E.K. 1964. Conformity and non-conformity as indicators of creativity in preschool children. Cooperative Research Project #1967, U.S. Office of Education.

Stein, A.H.; Friedrich, L.K.; and Deutsch, F. 1973. The effects of aggressive and prosocial television on the social interaction of preschool children. Paper presented at Midwestern Psychological Association.

Stevenson, H.W.; Weir, M.W.; and Zigler, E.F. 1959. Discrimination learning in children as a function of motive incentive conditions. *Psychological Reports* 5:95-98.

Stott, D.H. 1961. An empirical approach to motivation based on the behavior

263

References

of a young child. *Journal of Child Psychology and Psychiatry* 2:97-117.

Suchman, J.R. 1961. Inquiry training: building skills for autonomous discovery. *Merrill-Palmer Quarterly.*

Sutton-Smith, B. 1973. A developmental structural account of riddles. Paper presented at Society for Research in Child Development meeting.

Taine, H.M. 1877. Taine on the acquisition of language by children. *Mind* 2:252-59.

Terrell, G.; Durkin, K.; and Wiesley, M. 1959. Social class and the nature of the incentive in discrimination learning. *Journal of Abnormal and Social Psychology* 59:270-72.

Terrell, G., and Kennedy, W.A. 1957. Discrimination learning and transposition in children as a function of the nature of the reward. *Journal of Experimental Psychology* 52:257-60.

Thomas, A.; Chess, S.; Birch, H.; Hertzig, M.; and Korn,S. 1963. *Behavioral individuality in early childhood.* New York: New York Univ. Press.

Thorndike, E.L. 1911. *Animal intelligence.* New York: Macmillan.

Titkin, S., and Hartup, W.W. 1965. Sociometric status and the reinforcing effectiveness of children's peers. *Journal of Experimental Child Psychology* 2:306-15.

Toman, W. 1969 . *Family constellation.* New York: Springer.

Uddenberg, N.; Almgren, P.; and Nilsson, A. 1971. Preference for sex of the child among pregnant women. *Journal of Biosocial Science* 3:267-80.

Vygotsky, L.S. 1962. *Thought and language.* Cambridge: M.I.T. Press.

Walker, R.N. 1962. Body build and behavior in young children: I. body and nursery school teachers' ratings. *Monographs of the Society for Research in Child Development* 27:1-94.

Wallach, M.A. 1970. Creativity. In *Carmichael's manual of child psychology,* ed. P.H. Mussen. New York: Wiley.

Wallach, M.A., and Kogan, N. 1965. *Modes of thinking in young children: a study of the creativity-intelligence distinction.* New York: Rinehart and Winston.

Walters, J.; Pearce, D.; and Dahms, L. 1957. Affectional and aggressive behavior of preschool children. *Child Development* 28:15-26.

Watson, J.B. 1928. *The psychological care of infant and child.* New York: Norton.

Watson, J.B., and Morgan, J.J.B. 1917. Emotional reactions and psychological experimentation. *American Journal of Psychology* 28:163-74.

Watson, J.B., and Raynor, R. 1920. Conditioned emotional reactions. *Journal of Experimental Psychology* 3:1-4.

Weir, R. 1962. *Language in the crib.* The Hague: Mouton.

Werner, H. 1948. *Comparative psychology of mental development.* New York: International Universities Press.

—————. 1957. The concept of development from a comparative and organismic point of view. In *The concept of development,* ed. D.B. Harris. Minneapolis: Univ. of Minnesota Press.

White, B. 1971. *Human infants.* Englewood Cliffs, N.J.: Prentice-Hall.

White, S. 1965. Evidence for a hierarchical arrangement of the learning processes. In *Advances in child development and behavior,* ed. L.P. Lipsitt and C.C. Spiker, vol. 2. New York: Academic Press.

References

Whiting, J., and Child, I. 1953. *Child training and personality.* New Haven: Yale Univ. Press.

Williams, C.D. 1959. The elimination of tantrum behavior by extinction procedures. *Journal of Abnormal and Social Psychology* 59:269.

Wohlwill, J. 1960. A study of the development of the number concept by scalogram analysis. *Journal of Genetic Psychology* 97:345-77.

Yarrow, L.J. 1973. Child development research: interface of theory and application. *Society for Research in Child Development Newsletter* pp. 1-5.

Zaporozhets, A.V., and Elkonin, D.B. 1971. *The psychology of the preschool child.* Trans. J. Shybut and S. Simon. Cambridge: M.I.T. Press.

Zigler, E.; Levine, J.; and Gould, L. 1966. Cognitive processes in the development of children's appreciation of humor. *Child Development* 37:507-18.

Glossary

accomodation—The modification of a schema in order to adjust to new inputs.

adultomorphism—Erroneous interpretation of child behavior in terms of rules which explain the behavior of adults.

assimilation—The incorporation of new material into an existing schema.

babbling—Repetitive patterns of meaningless vocalizations produced by infants.

childhood—The period of the lifespan covering the years between infancy and puberty.

chronological age (CA)—The age of an individual in terms of the years, months, and days since his birth.

Glossary

classical conditioning—The pairing of an unconditioned stimulus with a previously neutral stimulus.

cognitive-developmental psychology—The study of the development of the thought processes and their relation to other behavior.

conformity—The tendency to express opinions which agree with those of other people.

conservation—Recognition of the invariance of certain physical properties such as mass, quantity and weight under certain transformations such as change in shape, grouping, or location.

cross-sectional method—A method of child study which involves comparing groups of individuals of different ages.

discrimination learning—Learning to distinguish between two or more stimuli.

discrimination shift—A discrimination learning problem in which the mastery of one discrimination is followed by the learning of a new one sharing some of the same elements.

ectomorph—A thin body type characterized by a predominance of the skin and nervous system.

ego—A personality structure in Freudian theory characterized by reality-governed pursuit of satisfaction and control of id impulses.

Electra complex—A conflict brought about, according to Freud, by the preschool girl's unconscious sexual attraction to her father and envy of her mother.

endomorph—A stocky, fat body type characterized by a predominance of the abdominal organs.

experimentation—Controlled study through the manipulation of aspects of the environment.

extinction—Reducing the strength of a conditioned response. In classical conditioning: repeated exposure of the conditioned stimulus without the unconditioned stimulus. In operant conditioning: repeated failure to deliver reinforcement following the response.

frustration—The blocking or thwarting of attainment of a goal.

genetics—The study of hereditary transmission.

Gestalt theory—An approach to psychology which emphasizes principles of organization in perception, thinking, and behavior.

grammar—The rules which underlie the combination of words in meaningful language.

heredity—The biological transmission of characteristics from parent to offspring.

holophrastic utterance—A word expressing the meaning of an entire sentence.

id—A personality structure in Freudian theory characterized by the pursuit of immediate gratification of primitive needs.

imprinting—Very rapid learning which occurs during critical periods early in the life of certain animals.

incentive—A motivating condition or object. Something which reinforces.

infancy—The period from birth until about age two.

insight—A sudden solution to a problem.

intelligence quotient (IQ)—The ratio of MA divided by CA all multiplied by 100.

learning—A change in behavior resulting from experience.

longitudinal method—A method of child study which involves following the same child or group of children over a long period of time.

look-say—An approach to reading instruction which emphasizes the learning of whole words.

mediation—A process assumed to intervene between external stimuli and responses. In the Kendlers' theory: a symbolic representational response and its covert feedback cue.

mental age (MA)—A score obtained on an intelligence test which summarizes an individual's mental attainment in relation to that expected at a given age.

mesomorph—An athletic body type characterized by a predominance of muscle and bone structures.

modeling—Learning through imitation of another individual (the model).

Moro reflex—The response of the newborn infant to sudden loud sounds or loss of support. It involves throwing the arms out, drawing them back, and crying.

motor skill—A skill which requires muscular strength and coordination.

nonreversal shift—A discrimination shift in which previously neutral cues become positive.

object permanence—The notion that an object which is out of sight and hearing continues to exist.

observation—A method of child study characterized by freedom from interference by the observer.

Oedipal conflict—A conflict brought about, according to Freud, by the preschool boy's sexual attraction to his mother and envy of his father.

orthogenetic—A name given to Heinz Werner's theory of development.

paired-associate learning—Learning to associate one nonsense syllable, digit, or word with another.

perceptual learning—Modification of perception as a result of experience.

phonics—An approach to reading instruction which emphasizes the learning of individual letters.

predeterminism—The doctrine that development is prepotently controlled by hereditary factors.

presleep monologue—The soliloquies two-year-olds utter before falling asleep.

prosocial behavior—Behavior which has a favorable social impact, e.g., altruism, cooperation.

psychoanalysis—The method of treatment of mental illness based on Freudian theory.

psychosexual development—The sequence of stages in the Freudian theory of development, each having a characteristic body region as the pleasure source (oral: mouth; anal: anus; phallic & genital: sexual organs).

pupillary reflex—Reflexive constriction of the pupil when stimulated by bright light.

reinforcement—Providing a positive outcome for a behavior, or one that increases the liklihood of the behavior being repeated.

response—A well-defined segment of behavior.

reversal shift—A discrimination shift in which previously negative cues become positive.

rooting reflex—Reflexive head-turning by the newborn in the direction of stimulation of the mouth or cheek.

rote learning—Memorization through repetition.

schema—A cognitive unit coordinating related actions and perceptions.

single-link association—A stimulus-response association which does not include mediation.

sociometric—Measurement of relationships within a social group.

stage—A period during which particular behaviors differ qualitatively from those during other periods in development.

stimulus—A property of the environment which the organism is capable of reacting to.

Glossary

S-R psychology—An approach to psychology which is concerned with the formation of associations between stimuli and responses.

stranger fear—Infants' fearful reaction to unfamiliar people.

superego—A personality structure in Freudian theory which incorporates society's moral standards.

synaesthesia—A process in which stimulation of one sense modality gives rise to a secondary sensation in a different modality.

tabula rasa—A blank slate. A name given to theories which see the environment as the prepotent determiner of development.

trial—A unit into which the learning process is conveniently divided.

transfer—The influence of learning one task upon performance of subsequent tasks.

unconditioned stimulus—A stimulus which elicits a response unconditionally (i.e., without the need for classical conditioning).

weaning—The process of training an infant to drink from a cup.

Index

accelerating parents, 227
accommodation, (see Piaget, Jean)
achievements of first year, 27
Achilles, E.M., recognition & recall, 92
acuity of vision, 64
adjustment to nursery school, 123-124
adult conversation, 154
adultomorphism, 35
African children walking, 27
aggression, 13, 134-138, 208, 230
aggressive modeling, 134-138
Alcott, Bronson, 11
Aldrich, deafness in infants, 39
alternate uses task, 178
Altus, ordinal position of child, 148-149
anal fixation, 42
anal stage, 42
anger in infants & children, 105-106
anticipatory symbolism, 152
acquisition of motor skills, 28-29
art in children, 121-122
Asch, Solomon, conformity, 196
assimilation, (see Piaget, Jean)
athletic prowess, (see motor skills)
attachment, 89-91
attention getting stimuli, 63-64
attention in memory, 93
autobiography of Piaget, 22
Azin & Holz, punishment, 206-207

babbling in infants, 30
baby diary, (see also Candida, Piaget), 11, 47-48
baby talk, 31
Bandura & Huston, observational learning, 46
Bandura & Walters, punishment, 208
Bandura, Ross & Ross, aggressive modeling, 135
behavior modification, 38, 40

Berenda, Ruth, conformity, 196-197
Berlyne, D.E., problem solving, 246
Binet, Alfred, intelligence tests, 175-177
biological maturation, 28-29
Birch, insight in problem solving, 165-166
Bisett & Rieber, incentives, 169
Bishop, Carol, reading, 213
Blonsky & Buseman, only child, 150
Boring, (see autobiography of Piaget)
Bower, T.G.R., depth vision, 59
Bowlby, John, attachment, 90
Brackbill & Jack, incentives, 169
brain development, 194
Braine, Martin
  Learning grammar, 76
  pivot grammar, 68
Bridges, Katharine, emotions at birth, 104-105
Brown & Bellugi-Klima, expansion, 77-78
Brown, D.G., child's sex role development, 17
Brown, Roger,
  cognitive development, 34
  early behavior theory, 33
  language development, 107
  naming objects, 67-68
  telegraphic speech, 75-76
Bruner, Olver & Greenfield, Oliver,
  enactive representation, 80-81, 109
  ikonic representation, 80, 109
  symbolic representation, 80
Bryan, peer modeling, 126
Buhler, C.,
  memory in infants, 91-92, 95
  only child, 150
Burtt, Harold, relearning, 93

California Test of Mental Maturity, 177

Index

Candida,
 acuity of vision, 64
 addition, 193
 adjustment to nursery school, 123-124
 adult conversation, 154
 adult-oriented dependency, 227
 aggression, 135
 athletic prowess, 247
 attachment, 90
 attention getting stimuli, 63
 being read to, 231
 body build, 228-229
 brain development, 194
 chain complexes, 34
 cognitive developmental theory, 47
 competition, 197
 concept of don't, 106-107, 108
 concept formation, 33
 conformity, 197
 conservation, 191-192
 creativity in speech, 179-181
 deferred imitation of words, 23
 development of conscience, 53
 distinctive feature concept, 31
 drawing, 120-121
 drawings of people, 174
 emotional dependency, 226
 emotional development, 102-103, 105-106
 exercise play, 151
 expansion, 78
 facial grimaces, 16, 21
 fear, 210-211
 Freud's anaclitic theory, 47
 Freud's stage theory, 44
 frustration-aggression, 137
 fusion of thought with speech, 109
 games of construction, 153
 holophrastic speech, 55, 75-76
 imagination, 140
 imitation in learning, 75-76
 informational reward, 168
 inhibition of inappropriate behavior, 245
 instrumental dependency, 226
 intellectual achievements, 190
 involuntary memory, 95
 language development, 29-33
 learning set, 162
 left and right concept, 194
 material incentive, 169
 memory, 92-95
 motor development, 249
 motor representation, 79-80
 naming objects, 68
 negativism, 88-89
 only child, 149-150
 past tense, use of, 108-109
 peer modeling, 126-127
 peer-oriented dependency, 227
 perceptual learning, 66-67
 pivot grammar, 68
 popularity, 228
 pre-sleep monolog, 142
 problem solving, 164, 166-167, 168, 245-247
 punishment, 206-208
 reading, 212
 recognizing pictures, 58
 reflective tempo, 244-245
 rehearsal, 94
 riddles, 244
 ritual, 139
 rote counting, 192
 schema, 22
 self-assertion, 210, 229
 sense of smell, 65
 social interaction, 196
 social interchange, 82
 social learning theory, 47
 sociometric popularity, 247
 stage fright, 210
 stranger fear, 21
 symbolic play, 151-152, 163
 television, 321
 telegraphic speech, 75-76
 temper tantrum, 37-38
 toilet training, 44
 transfer, 160
 verbal coding, 93-94
Campbell & Yarrow, popularity, 228
Carmichael, Hogan & Walter, verbal vs. visual imagery in adulthood, 80
Carpenter, Aileen, skills in children, 248-249
cause-effect relationships, 13
Cazden, Courtney, expansion, 78
chain complexes, 34
Chamberlain & Chamberlain, extensions in word meanings, 32
Charlesworth & Hartup, reinforcement, 124-125
child-centered families, 227
children's drawing, 120-122
child's sex role development, 17
Chomsky, language is inherent theory, 79
Chukovsky, Kornei, creativity in speech, 179-181
Clark, B.S., peer modeling, 125
classical conditioning
 in child development, 38-40
 Pavlov, with dogs, 38
classificatory riddle, 243-244
codification of rules stage, 139

272

Index

cognitive development, 21, 79
  in riddles, 243-245
cognitive development theory, 46-47
Comanche baby talk, 31
communication through pictures, 120-123
compensation, 152
competition, 196-198
concept formation, 33
concepts, 35
conditioning, 40
conformity, 196-197
conscience in children, 51-55
consequences of frustration, 137-138
conservation, 190-192, 195-196
consonants in infants, 29-30
Constanzo & Shaw, conformity, 197
constructing a series, 194
contentives, 76
contiguity, 38
cooperation stage, 139
creativity in speech, 179-181
creativity test, 178-181
Croake, J.W., fear, 212
cross-sectional method, 18
crying in infants, 29
curiosity, 246

Darwin, Charles, 11
Davitz, J.R., aggression-frustration, 138
deafness in infants, 39
deferred imitation of words, 23
De Laguna, Grace, holophrastic grammar, 56
Dembo & Lewin, frustration-aggression, 137
de Medici, Marie, 16
Dennis, Wayne, aquisition of motor skills,
  among Hopi Indians, 28
  in orphanages, 29
  with twin girls, 28-29
Dennis, Wayne, and Marsena, infant smiling, 19
dependency, 226-228
depth vision, 59
development of conscience, 44
development of language, (see language)
development of sex role, 44-45
developmental psychology, 13, 242
diary, (see also, Candida, Piaget), 12, 13, 16
Dickens, Charles, 63
differential tendency, 46
Dinitz, Dynes & Clarke, preference for male offspring, 17
discovery method, 246

discrimination shift, 161-162
distinctive feature concept, 31
doctrine of recapitulation, 153
Dollard, Doob, Miller, Mowrer & Sears, frustration-aggression, 137
dominance, 210
drainage hypothesis, 230
drawing, children's, 120-122
drawings in intelligence tests, 174-175
Draw-A-Man test, 174-175
Dryden, 178

early behavior theory, 33
ectomorph, 229
ego, 41
egocentric speech, 110, 139-142
egocentric stage, 139-142
egocentrism, 139-142
eldest child, 148-149
Electra conflict, 45
Ellis, Havelock, eminent first-borns, 148
eminent first-borns, 148
emotional dependency, 226-227
emotional similarity, 34
emotions at birth, 104-105
emotions in infants, 103-107
enactive representation, 80-81
endomorph, 229
Erikson, Erik, motor skills, 247-248
Eron, television, 230
Eron, Walter, Toigo & Lefkowitz, punishment, 208
error factors, 163
Ervin, Susan,
  pivot grammar, 77
  past tense, 108-109
Estes, William K., punishment in rats, 206
European children walking, 27
exercise play, (see play)
expansion, 77-78
external speech, 110
extensions in word meanings, 32
extinction, (see operant extinction)

facial grimaces, 16, 21
facilitation, (see positive transfer)
failed realism, 121
fear, 208-212
fear in newborn, 103
Ferguson,
  foreign baby talk, 31
  reinforcement, 125
Feshbach, television, 230
fetus
  conditioning, 38

Index

heart rate, 20
finding hidden objects, 56-57
first words, 31
Flavell, Beach & Chinsky, verbal labeling & rehearsal, 94-95
foreign baby talk, 31
Forer,
  study of eldest child, 148-149
  study of only child, 150
fortuitous realism, 121
free association, 40-41
Freedman, J.L., punishment, 207
Freud, Sigmund, 13, 248
  anal fixation, 42
  anal stage, 42
  autobiography, 41
  development of conscience, 44
  development of sex role, 44-45
  ego, 41,42
  Electra conflict, 45
  free association, 40-41
  id, 41-42
  identification
    anaclitic, 45
    defensive, 45
  infantile sexuality, 41
  latency stage, 42
  Oedipal conflict, 42, 45-46
  permissive training, 43
  phallic stage, 42
  psychoanalysis, 40-41
  stage theory, 44
  superego, 41-42
  symbolic play, 153-154
  toilet training, 40, 42, 44, 248
  weaning, 42
frustration-aggression, 137-138, 208
functors, 76
Furth, Hans, thought in deaf children, 81
fusion of thought with speech, 109

Galton, Sir Francis, eminent first-borns, 148
games of construction, 153
games with rules, 153
Gardener, Allen & Beatrice, recognition of pictures in chimps, 59
Geber & Dean, African children walking, 27
Geneva Museum, (see Piaget, Jean)
Gestalt psychology,
  mental growth, 33
  theory of thinking, 164-165
Gibson, Eleanor, perceptual learning, 66-67
Goodenough, Florence,
  anger in children, 105-106
  art in children, 122
  development of conscience, 53

intelligence tests, 174-175, 181
graphic language, 122
Greenberg, P.J., competition, 197
Groos, Karl, play, 153
Guilford, J.P., intelligence test, 177-178
Guilford & Worcester, only child, 150
Gutteridge, Mary, motor skills, 248

Hall, G. Stanley,
  doctrine of recapitulation, 153
  only child, 150
Harlow, Harry,
  attachment in monkeys, 91
  interactions of monkeys to one another, 82-83
  learning set in monkeys, 162-163
Hartup, reinforcement, 123-125
Hartup & Coates, reinforcement, 126
Heathers, Glen, emotional dependency, 226-227
Heilman, Arthur, reading, 212-213
Helmreich & Collins, study of eldest child, 149
Henry IV, 16
Héroard, Dr. Jean, oldest published baby diary, 16
Hicks, D.J., aggressive modeling, 135
Himmelweit, Oppenheim & Vince, television, 229-230
Hindley, Filliozat, Klackenberg, Nicolet-Meister & Sand, walking in infants, 27
Hochbert & Brooks, recognizing pictures, 58-59, 121
Hoffman, Martin, punishment, 207-208
holophrastic grammar, 56
holophrastic speech, 55-56, 75-76
Hopi Indians, (see Dennis, Wayne)
Horowitz, incentives, 168
Hudson, recognition of pictures in African adults, 59
humor, 242-244
Hunt & Synnerdahl, conformity, 197
hypotheses, 163

id, 41-42
Idelberger, concept formation, 33
identification, 45-46
ikonic representation, 80-81
imaginary play, (see play)
imitation, 22-23
impulsive tempo, 244
incentives in learning, 168-169
infant,
  cheerfulness, 19
  emotional development, 103-107
  memory, 91
  motor development, 20
  patterns of interaction, 82

response to other infants, 82
  sexuality, 41
  smiling, 19
informational incentives, 168-169
inhibition of inappropriate behavior, 245
inner speech, 110
insight, 164-167
instances task, 178
instrumental dependency, 226
intellectual development, 22
intellectual realism, 121
intelligence tests, 174-178, 190
intentional distortion, 232
interaction of monkeys to one another, 82-83
interference, (see negative transfer)
I.Q. tests, (see intelligence tests)

Jack, L.M., self-assertion, 210
Jakobson, Roman,
  distinctive feature concept, 31
  presleep monolog, 142
James, William, 63
Jeffrey & Samuels, reading, 213-214
Jensen, sense of taste in infants, 65
Jersild,
  consequences of frustration, 136-137
  fear, 211-212
jokes, (see humor)
Jones, study of eldest child, 149

Kagan, Jerome,
  attention getting stimuli, 64
  infant's cheerfulness, 18-19
  middle class mothers more affectionate to infant girls, 17
  reflex smile, 19
  social smiling, 19-20
Kagan & Kogan, impulsivity, 244-245
Katz, Gestalt theory, 164-165
Kelleher, reversal shift, 161
Kellogg, Rhoda, art in children, 121-122
Kenderline, humor, 243
Kendler & D'Amato, reversal shift, 161-162
Kendler, Howard & Tracy,
  discrimination shift, 161
  mediational learning, 162
  problem solving, 167-168
  reversal shift, 161, 190
  single-link learning, 162
Kendler, Kendler & Wells, reversal shift, 161
Klima, Edward & Ursula, development of language, 107-108
Koch, Helen, study of eldest child, 149

Koffka, Gestalt theory, 164
Kohlberg, cognitive development theory, 46
Kohler, Wolfgang, problem solving in chimpanzees, 164-165
Kraus & Sendak, defining words in terms of actions, 34
Kuhlmann-Anderson Intelligence Tests, 177

language development, 29-30, 47-48, 107-108
language is inherent theory, 79
latency stage, 40
law of effect, 206
learning,
  mediational, 162
  punishment in, 205-207
  single link, 162
learning grammar, 76
learning set, 162
  in monkeys, 162-163
learning social behavior, 124-127
Lenneberg,
  motor development & language, 29
  pivot grammar, 77
Leuba, C., competitiveness, 197
Levinson & Reese & Levine, learning set, 163
Lewis,
  concept formation, 33, 35
  emotional similarity, 34
  extension of word meanings, 32
  infants adoption of adult classification system, 35
Lewis & Brooks-Gunn, infants response to other infants, 82
lies, 231-233
Lipsitt, Engen & Kaye, sense of smell, 65
Long & Welch, counting test, 192-193
longitudinal method, 18
long-term memory, 92-93
look-say method, 212-214
Lorenz, Konrad, attachment in birds, 90
Lorge-Thorndike Intelligence Tests, 177
Lousa & Brophy, study of eldest child, 149
Luquet, G.H., children's drawing, 120-122
Luria, A.R., external speech, 110

male favoritism, 17
Marathi baby talk, 31
marble playing, (see Piaget, Jean)
Matching Familiar Figures Test, 244
material incentives, 168-169

Index

maturation, 28
Maudry & Nikula, patterns of interaction in infants, 82-83
McCandless & Marshall, dependency, 228
McGraw, Myrtle, skills, 249-250
McNeil, phonological development in children, 31
McNeill, telegraphic speech, 76
mediational learning, 162
memory in infants & children, 91-95
mental age tests, 174-178
mental development, 189-196
Merrill, Barbara, frustration-aggression, 137
mescalin, 180
mesomorph, 229
Messer, attention in memory, 93
Miller & Estes, incentives, 169
Miller, George, presleep monologs, 142
Mischel, Walter,
  observational learning in sex role, 46
  social learning theory, 46
modeling, 123-127, 134-138
modeling theory, 230
  aggressive modeling, 134-138
modification of speech to young children, 154-155
monkeys,
  attachment, 91
  interaction to one another, 82-83
  learning set, 162-163
moral behavior, (see Piaget, Jean)
Moro reflex, 65
Moss, mothers imitating girl's vocalization more, 16
motor & individual stage, (see Piaget, Jean)
motor development, 29
motor skills, 246-250
Murray, Frank, conservation, 195-196

naming of objects, 67-68
naughty words, 232
negative attention, 226
negative transfer, 160-161
negatives in children, 106-108
negativism in preschoolers, 88-90
Nelson, Carskaddon & Bonvillian, expansion, 78
Nelson, Reid & Travers, punishment, 207
nonreversal shift, 161-162
normative survey, 27
numerical aptitude, 193
nursery school, adjustment, 123-124

objective similarity, 34

observational learning, 46
Oedipal conflict, 42, 45-46
Oetzel, R.M.,
  aggression in boys vs. girls, 136-137
  dependency, 227-228
only child, 149-150
operant conditioning, 39
operant extinction, 39-40
oral stage, 41-42
ordinal position of child, 148
orthogenesis, 180
othogenetic theory of perception, 213
Otis-Lennon Mental Ability Tests, 177
overgeneralization in speech, 108-109

paired-associate learning method, 161
Papousek, problem solving, 245-246
Parke & Walters, punishment, 207
Parten, Mildred, social interaction in children, 83
past tense in children, 107-109
patterns of interaction in infants, 82-83
Patterson, Lettman & Bricker, reinforcement in aggression, 135
Pavlov, Ivan, 38-39
peer modeling, (see modeling)
perception, 192
perceptual learning, 66-67
permissive training, 43
Peterson, preference for male offspring, 17
phallic stage, 42
phonics, 212-214
phonological development, 31
Piaget, Gerard, finding hidden objects, 57
Piaget, Jacqueline,
  adult conversation, 154
  anticipatory symbolism in play, 152
  at ten months, 23
  changeability of concepts, 34
  compensation in play, 152
  finding hidden objects, 57-58
  observational learning, 46
  one year four months, 23
  recognizing pictures, 59
  symbolic play, 151, 154
  temper tantrums, 46
  thirteen months, extensions in word meanings, 32
Piaget, Jean,
  accommodation, 22, 69
  anticipatory symbolism, (see Piaget, Jean, play)
  assimilation, 22, 69

Index

autobiography, 22
changeability of children's concepts, 34
children at five months, 22, 23
children at seven months, 23
children at ten months, 23
classical conditioning, 39
codification of rules stage, 139
cognitive development, 21, 79
cognitive operation of classification, 243-244
compensation, (see Piaget, Jean, play)
conservation, 190-192, 195
constructing a series, 194
cooperation stage, 139
deferred imitation of words, 23
diary, 12, 14
egocentric stage, 139-142
extensions in meaning, 32
finding hidden objects, 57
games, (see Piaget, Jean, play)
games of construction, (see Piaget, Jean, play)
games with rules, (see Piaget, Jean, play)
Geneva Museum, 21
imagination, 141
imitation, 22-23
intellectual development, 22
intelligence, 177
language & thinking, 81
left and right concept, 194
lying, 232-233
mental development, 189-195
moral behavior, 138-140
motor & individual stage, 137
motor representation, 79-80
observational learning, 46
play, 22, 150-155
punishment, 209
recognizing pictures, 59
schema, 22
schema of intuitive qualitative correspondence, 22
sucking schema, 22
symbolic play, (see Piaget, Jean, play)
temper tantrums, 46
theory of development, 22-23
theory of play, 69
theory of speech, 81
thought, 194-195
Piaget, Laurent,
concept formation, 33
experiments on object permanence, 69
play, symbolic & construction, 153
Piaget, Lucienne,
at seven months, 23

classical conditioning, 39
marble playing & ritual, 138-139
motor representation, 79
play, 69
reality in pictures, 59
symbolic play, 151
Pick, Anne, testing theories of perception, 66-67
pivot grammar, 68-69, 75-77
play, 22, 149-155
pleasure principle, 41
plural of nouns, 109
popularity, 228-230
positive transfer, 160-162
preference for male offspring, 17
preriddle, 244
presleep monologs, 142
problem solving, 160-169, 245-247
Progressive Matrices Test, 176-177
prototypes, (see perceptual learning)
pseudo-lies, 231-232
psychoanalysis, 40-41
psychosexual stages, 41
punishment, 205-210
in rats, 206
pupillary reflex, 65

Raven, J.C., intelligence test, 176-177
reading, 212-214
recall, 92
recognition, 92
recognizing pictures, 58-59
Reese,
learning set, 163
self-esteem & popularity, 247
Reese & Lipsitt, reading 213
reflective cognitive tempo, 244
reflex smile, 19-20
regression, 137
rehearsal, 93-94
reinforcement, 124-126
in aggression, 135-136
in punishment, 206
relearning, 93
reversal shift, 161-162
Reynolds, Martha M., negativism in preschoolers, 89-90
Richards & Nelson, infant motor development, 20
riddles, 243-245
ritual, 138-139
Robbins, accuracy of infant diary, 12
Rorschach ink blots, 213
Rosenhan, incentives, 168-169
Rosenow & Whyte, eldest child, 149
rote counting, 192
rules, development & use of, 139-140
Rutherford & Mussen, modeling in children, 127

Index

Sameroff, classical conditioning, 39
Schaeffer & Emerson, attachment, 90
Schaffer, H.R., (see stranger fear)
schema, (see Piaget, Jean)
Schramm, Lyle & Parker, television, 230-231
Schwarz & Wynn, adjustment to nursery school, 123-124
Sears, attachment, 91
Sears, Maccoby & Levin,
  development of conscience, 54
  punishment, 208
  toilet training, 43-44
Sears, Robert, study of conscience, 53-55
self-assertion, 210
self-esteem & popularity, 247
senses in infants, 65-66
sensitivity of smell, 66
sex role development, 17, 44-47
Sheldon, W.H., 229
Shelley, 79, 81
Sherif, Muzafer & Carolyn, competition, 197-198
Sherman, Mandel, infants emotional reactions, 104
Shirley, Mary, walking in infants, 27-28
short-term memory, 92
similarities task, 178
Simon, Theophile, (see Binet)
single-link learning, 162
skills, (see motor skills)
Skinner, B.F., social behavior, 123
Skinner box,
  operant conditioning with rats, 39
  operant extinction in rats, 39-40
  punishment in rats, 206
smiling in infants, 19-20
Snow, Catherine, adults talking to children, 154-155
social contact, 196-197
social incentives, 168-169
social interaction in children, 83
social learning theory, 45-47
social play, (see play)
social smile, 19-20
socially isolated child, 228
socially rejected child, 228
sociometric, 228
Sontag, Lester, fetal heart rate, 20
Spanish baby talk, 31
speech, 154-155
Spelt, classical conditioning, 38
Spiker, Charles,
  transfer, 160-161
  verbal coding & rehearsal, 94
Spitz, Rene, (see stranger fear)
stability of traits in infants, 18
Staffieri, J.R., body build, 229-230

stage fright, 211
stages in art, 122
stage theory, Freud, 44
Stanford-Binet test, 176-177
Starkweather, conformity, 197
Starr, A.S., short-term memory, 92
Stein, Aletha, television, 230
Stern, objective similarity, 34
Stern, William, (see also Lewis),
  lies, 231
  naming objects, 109
Stevenson, Harold, learning set, 163
Stevenson, Weir & Zigler, incentives, 169
Stott, concept formation, 33
stranger fear, 20-21, 211
submission, 210
Suchman, discovery method, 246
sucking schema, (see Piaget, Jean)
superego, 41
Sutton-Smith, Brian, riddles, 243-244
swearing, 232
symbolic play, (see play)
symbolic representation, 80
synaesthesia, 180
synthetic incapacity, 121
Syrian baby talk, 31

Taine, Hyppolyte, daughter's language development, 47-48
telegraphic speech, 75-76
television, 229-231
temper tantrums, 37-38, 40
templates, (see perceptual learning)
Terman, Lewis, Stanford-Binet test, 176-177
Terrell & Kennedy, incentives, 168
Terrell, Durkin & Weisley, incentives, 169
testing theories of perception, 66-67
Thomas, Chess, Birch, Hertzig & Korn, traits for rating infants, 18
Thorndike, Edward L., punishment, 205-206
thought, 194-195
thought in deaf children, 81
time-sampling, 12-13
Titkin & Hartup, reinforcement, 125
toilet training, 40-44
Toman, Walter, only child, 150
traits for rating infants, 18
transfer, 160-161
two-year-old negativism, 88-90

Uddenberg, Almgren & Nilsson, adjustment to child of opposite sex than hoped for, 17

velar consonants, 31
verbal coding, 93-94

verbal labeling, 94
verbal vs. visual imagery in adulthood, 80
visual realism, 121
voluntary & involuntary memory, 94-95
vowels in infants, 29-30
Vygotsky,
    chain complexes, 34-35
    concepts, 35
    egocentric speech, 110-111, 120, 142
    extensions in word meanings, 32
    external, egocentric & inner speech, 110-111, 190, 195
    motor imagery, 80
    speech & thought, 109-110, 111
    study of concepts in children, 34

Walker,
    body build, 229
    creativity test, 179
walking in infants, 27
Wallach & Kogan, creativity test, 178-179
Wallach, Michael, creativity test, 178
Walters, Pearce & Dahms, time-sampling study of development, 13
Watson & Morgan, origin of emotions, 104

Watson & Raynor, fear in newborn, 103
Watson, John B.,
    anger, concept of don't, 106-107
    emotional development, 103-104
weaning, 42
Weir, Ruth, presleep monolog, 142
Werner, Heinz,
    creativity in speech, 179-180
    reading, 213
Weschler Intelligence Scale for Children, 176
White, Burton, smiling in infants, 19
White, Sheldon, learning & cognition, 190, 194
Whiting & Child, attachment, 91
Williams, C.D.,
    observational learning, 46
    operant extinction in temper tantrums, 40
WISC, 176
Wohlwill, J.F., numerical aptitude, 193

Zamet, 16
Zaporozhets & Elkonin,
    memory experiments, 92
    sensitivity of smell, 66
    voluntary & involuntary memory, 94-95
Zigler, Levine & Gould, humor, 242-243